Additional Praise for
Grow Globally: Opportunities for Your Middle-Market Company around the World

"Mona Pearl has offered a road map for middle market companies seeking to take their businesses global. She provides concrete guidance typically available only at a cost most middle market business owners do not want to incur. I thoroughly recommend this as a "must read".
—Frederic D. Floberg, Managing Director,
The Chicago Corporation

"Mona Pearl offers insights on global strategy of value to everyone . . . from the beginning international business student to the seasoned veteran. Topics range from due diligence and demand forecasting to cross-cultural negotiations and issues affecting future global business success. The end-of-chapter Pearls of Wisdom provides readers with an excellent summary of key learning points."
—Les Dlabay, Professor of Business, Lake Forest College;
Author of International Business, 4th ed.

"For any executive whose organization has entered or *aspires* to be part of the global arena, *Grow Globally* is a must-read. It is an in-depth, comprehensive, A-to-Z discussion of all the elements to be considered when taking a business global. While experienced C-Suite and Corporate Development leaders understand the need for strategy and risk assessment, *Grow Globally* goes beyond the lip service of 'buzz words.' Mona Pearl with her vast 'on the ground' experience provides practical, detailed, and insightful approaches to creating successful global business outcomes. She is a highly regarded member of AM&AA, who exemplifies the spirit of collaboration that is so well-articulated in her new book."
—Michael R. Nall, Founder, Alliance of M & A Advisors

Grow Globally

Grow Globally

Opportunities for Your Middle-Market Company Around the World

Mona Pearl

WILEY

John Wiley & Sons, Inc.

Published by John Wiley & Sons, Inc., Hoboken, New Jersey.
Published simultaneously in Canada.

For general information on our other products and services or for technical support, please
contact our Customer Care Department within the United States at (800) 762-2974,
outside the United States at (317) 572-3993 or fax (317) 572-4002.

Wiley also publishes its books in a variety of electronic formats. Some content that appears
in print may not be available in electronic books. For more information about Wiley
products, visit our web site at www.wiley.com.

Library of Congress Cataloging-in-Publication Data:

Pearl, Mona, 1964–
    Grow globally : opportunities for your middle-market company around the
world / Mona Pearl.
        p. cm.
    Includes bibliographical references and index.
    ISBN 978-1-118-03015-8; ISBN 978-1-118-12894-7 (ebk);
    ISBN 978-1-118-12895-4 (ebk); ISBN 978-1-118-12896-1 (ebk)
        1. Small business—Management.   2. International business enterprises—
Management.   3. Globalization—Economic aspects.   I. Title.
    HD62.7.P43 2011
    658'.049—dc22   2011016576

Printed in the United States of America

10 9 8 7 6 5 4 3 2 1

This book is dedicated to the fellow warriors and explorers, men and women, the brave and curious, the dreamers and the executioners who see the globe as their playground, and fearlessly venture to navigate the oceans of the business world.

Contents

Foreword

It's easy for executives to look out from their desks and only see their own private little domain. Dealing with the day-to-day pressures they encounter can shrink their vision to a keyhole—intensely focused but largely ignorant of the bigger picture.

Having that keyhole focus today is counterproductive at best and catastrophic at worst. The realities of the global economy make it absolutely unforgivable for midmarket executives to keep their vision restricted to what goes on within the four walls of the office. Both opportunity and opposition can be found outside in the world beyond. The only difference is that, although you have to go outside to look for the former, the latter will track you down no matter what you do.

Opening up your eyes to see the bigger picture of the global marketplace is one of the most important steps leaders in the 21st century can do to help their businesses succeed. Unfortunately, it is also one of the easiest and most devastating actions they can fail to take. For those who spent their whole life looking at the world through a keyhole, throwing the door wide open can be overwhelming. There's so much to take in that it is easy to miss opportunities that could be right in front of your nose.

Grow Globally is an effort to help middle-market executives open the door to the global marketplace and establish their presence without losing their way. Being in the position they're in, these high-level corporate professionals don't have the luxury of sitting back and taking it all in before making a move. They're competing against much larger and savvier competitors who have the resources to gather information quickly and strike with precision. Middle-market companies need guidance to craft a global strategy that will work right the first time, and that's exactly what Mona Pearl has given them with this book.

Stop peeking through the keyhole, open the door, and step outside.

Christopher Petersen
Special Projects Editor, *Management Today* magazine

Preface

This book is written for Boards of Directors, C-suite, and corporate development leaders of organizations who aspire to be global leaders. However, *Grow Globally* is not intended to be a textbook but a book that triggers your thinking about proven effective approaches and strategies to use when entering new regions of the world or expanding your base in the international arena. For those who are already global players, this book will help refine your skills, adjust your mind-set, reaffirm your focus, and, in some cases, retest your strategy and modify your direction. For those embarking on their first global adventure, this book will help create a framework that enables you to see, identify, respond, think, plan, and operate. In the end, it is about building your skills, gaining access to essential tools, and learning how to think about ways to capitalize on global opportunities. *Grow Globally* will help you identify what questions you need to ask, how to evaluate information, assemble the right team, develop a leadership position, and stay focused on success.

This book was motivated by my personal experience as an international strategic development expert. Frustratingly, I have witnessed otherwise successful organizations from around the world making similar mistakes when seeking to expand internationally. Mistakes that obviously arise from a lack of familiarity with world markets and very limited "hands-on" experience. While I applaud their initiative, business leaders must understand that growing globally is not simply an extension of what works domestically. Rather, competing across borders is a much more complex, competitive, and dynamic environment with unique economic markets and realities. As such, companies must deal with a host of unfamiliar and challenging strategic issues such as different rules of engagement, emerging as well as declining regions, new business models, and complex negotiations. *Grow Globally* helps readers identify and examine key aspects of developing a successful strategic plan by breaking down the steps into manageable pieces such as market readiness, developing a global competitive advantage, strategic alliances and growth models, competition, negotiations, future trends, and emerging markets.

In addition to my practical and hands-on international experience, I speak six languages and have lived abroad. I have also acquired firsthand business know-how by building and operating several global companies. As such, I understand the practical aspects of running a global organization and have experience with product licensing, manufacturing, supply chain, distribution, culture, negotiations, and other key issues that arise when running an international company. In other words, I have been in your shoes, in the "global trenches," and dealt with many of the same issues you have or will face as you cross the threshold into the global arena.

Ideally, *Grow Globally* will help take the mystery out of entering or expanding into new international markets. After reading the book, you will understand how to develop a strategy that will help you choose a foreign market to sell your product or service, and you will learn what factors are important, from income, urbanization, and language to culture and purchasing patterns. You will also learn how to:

- Develop strong and lasting relationships across borders
- Overcome cultural differences
- Offer a customized value proposition in each market and win sales
- Develop a competitive advantage and beat the competition
- Design and execute the best strategies and tactics to enter each country/market

- Take advantage of the most effective international and sustainable growth models
- Implement the most suitable strategies for your company that will leverage and sustain global presence
- Manage risk and diversify your sales and marketing portfolio globally

In addition, please visit www.monapearl.com/books/grow-globally-by-mona-pearl for an array of valuable information to use alongside this book, including assessment tools, checklists, and examples to further your understanding of the theory and practice of growing your business globally.

Grow Globally provides you with the expertise to plan and implement cost effective and sustainable global growth plans that improve your company's bottom line and help you realize seamless and flawless international operations, so you can focus on what you do best. So let's get started now!

Acknowledgments

"Never give up your dreams. Follow the signs."
                                        —*Paolo Coelho*

Writing a book is a very lonely, solitary, and introverted process. It takes time, energy, endurance, and focus. Most important, though, is to have the stimulation and encouragement of people close to you. I have been blessed in that way. There are some very special people who had a profound impact on me and created the signs along my way in life. As a result, they changed my soul, ignited my imagination, molded my direction, and helped shape my present and outline my future. Without their inspiration and continuous encouragement, I would not have been able to accomplish my passion and realize my dream. So here's a sincere and hearty thank you to the people I have always looked up to.

Avi Aroch (Managing Director and COO of UMI Ltd.): Throughout the many years, we've spent many hours discussing global business issues as well as leadership, success, spirituality, and what it takes to have the drive to accomplish our goals. Our friendship has survived the test of time, distance, culture, and borders. Thank you for the sharing, confiding, and planning we did together throughout the many years.

Prof. Shlomo Avineri (Hebrew University): You opened my eyes and introduced me to comparative thinking, viewing the world through a panoramic lens, the world of writing, speaking, and publishing. You are a renowned world thinker, educator, and role model for intellectual curiosity, situational analysis, and the questioning and understanding of the underlying forces of events, their role and significance in the geo-politics, history, and world order.

Mikey (Michael Reis of the European Language Center): A loyal friend for over 20 years. You exposed me to the way U.S. business is conducted and from you I learned what not to do, which is an impor-tant lesson by itself. I value your simple common sense and your sharp understanding of human nature, which have provided me with a global perspective and keen insights that were so indispensible to me in writ-ing this book.

Joel Willard (of many ventures): On his deathbed, he held my hand and told me that "nothing is impossible" and that I could do everything I set my mind to. I will always appreciate his encouragement and be grateful for teaching me to pursue my dreams and live them, and not to fear fail-ure, but simply get up and try again; that the sky is the limit and to always reach for the stars. They are usually closer than we imagine.

Alan Weiss (Summit Consulting): How many times did you ask me, "What's your point?" or say "Get to the point. Don't let people waste your time, focus, and, most of all, know what you want. Stop finding excuses for not doing something, and don't be average. Don't be afraid to be controversial. It's not about perfection, it is about success." Thank you for your sage advice and for opening my eyes to a profession and a lifestyle that I didn't imagine existed. In my heart, I know I wouldn't have succeeded without your constant judgment, constructive criticism, and admonition to "stop worrying." You are my professional mentor and through your constant feedback, you raised my bar. You role-modeled what it means to live by the highest standards, achieve great success, constantly innovate and reinvent, and to simply thrive to be the best.

Suley (Suleyman Sozeri, Turkish Economic Attaché to the Midwest): How I value your genuine hospitality and the hours of dis-cussing international affairs, global trends, and international opportunities in your office over Turkish coffee or tea. You are a man with a wealth of knowledge, drive, and ambition, who is eager to share and help. We have developed a special friendship, and I am touched by your belief that I am going to leave a legacy by writing this book.

Carlos Gutierrez (former Secretary of Commerce and CEO of Kellogg): You are the real driving force behind this book. You validated for me that everything in life comes with a price, and that there is no beauty without vulnerability. You role-modeled what hard work, dedication, and the pursuit of dreams can look like, and you are a prime example of a person who has truly achieved the American dream. I am eternally grateful.

Clients: Thank you for your trust and the opportunities to work together. We established mutual respect and learned from each other. Even though it was difficult for some of you to open up and share your organizations' dilemmas, issues, and challenges, it is a sign of great leadership when top executives roll up their sleeves, face their impediments to success, and use newly acquired knowledge and information to change direction and plan for a better future. Thanks for the opportunities to be the co-pilot and together navigate to achieving success.

Family: Spread over three continents, with roots in two other continents, we are a truly global family. I am blessed to have such a loving family who had the confidence in me, even during the times that I had self-doubt. Truly, there is nothing like the love and support that comes from family. My parents and my one and only brother have always encouraged me, stood by my side, and made so many things possible by being who they are. I love you from the bottom of my heart.

Grow Globally

Introduction

Growing Globally

What You Need to Know to Get in the Game

"If you want something you've never had before, you've got to do something you've never done before."

—*Drina Reed*

Going global is similar to embarking on a new adventure, a bold mission, and you are the commander. As such, it's important to learn not just from the successes of others but also from the failures of others. For example, consider the *Titanic*'s tragic encounter with an iceberg on the Northern Atlantic waters in 1912. On a clear night, in a calm sea, under the command of a seasoned captain, disaster struck. Even after warnings of iceberg sightings, disaster struck! However, damage to the ship wasn't caused by the iceberg's tip, which rose visibly above the water's surface. Rather, the fatal damage was caused by the massive section of iceberg, hidden from view, beneath the surface of the water.

This great tragedy serves as a vivid illustration of the dangers that lurk beneath the surface for businesses embarking on global expansion. While every business prepares elaborately for perceptible issues, few businesses take the initiative to develop an awareness and sensitivity to all that lies below, hidden from view, and waiting to cause chaos. It's the same today as it was in 1912. People don't know what they don't know. Worse yet, no one can plan for something that has never been anticipated.

What's under the surface in international business? A lot! The culture, social norms, values, customs, reasoning, thinking patterns, decision making, negotiations, and body language are just a few of the minefields businesses encounter as they attempt to navigate the global marketplace. While the legal system, tax issues, and the political situation all seem visible, in many regions they are not always as they appear. For example, in some countries the lack of transparency functions just like an added tax. And the implications of these unknown "taxes" are not easy to calculate. How can you deal with these issues? How can you evaluate a global market? Plan a product launch? What should you know? Where do you start? Right here.

An Example of Looking for Success, but Finding Trouble

Setting out to conquer a new market with promising growth potential, a very successful transportation company took confidence in its strategic plan. The target market was Eastern Europe, and the strategy was simple. Hire a "native" country manager in each one of the three targeted countries with the greatest potential—Poland, the Czech Republic, and Hungary. This plan would allow for a centrally managed expansion that is locally driven. Each in-country CEO would be paid by and report to headquarters. In return, each would be expected to hire and train the people necessary to align his country-specific business plans with the overall corporate mission and vision. Perfect. Well, not exactly.

After a year of low sales, and losses that registered in the millions, the humbled corporate CEO searched for the root cause of the trouble. He concluded that the overall plan was good, but the wrong people were hired for the in-country manager positions. While it's easy to hang the blame on the newly hired native managers, the fact is that no global expansion fails for just one reason—even if that reason is a lack of local talent. A well-conceived expansion strategy should include the communication, training, and guidance necessary so that the right talent can be identified and developed. After many conversations with the corporate CEO, the real causes of disaster became clear.

First, the plan short-circuited many steps in a comprehensive market-readiness assessment. While the target markets were growing and offered much potential, little was done to identify, understand, and relate to the actual consumers. Who was the target audience? Was it the younger generation, the aging professionals, or the affluent? These questions, and many others like them, were never raised, answered, or even considered. Naturally, the plan failed to properly segment the markets in each of the three countries. The lack of an identified target audience made it impossible to create a persuasive sales pitch and communicate with future consumers. Also, without identifying a target audience, key decisions that deal with the competition, marketing, and pricing were made in a vacuum with no basis in facts or circumstances.

Another mistake was going into any new market without leveraging a clear "local" competitive advantage. Because this business had competed very successfully against other well-known brands in other countries, it assumed that local competition in Eastern Europe would not pose any threat. It also assumed that native country managers would perform well if paid well and wouldn't require any corporate training. However, Eastern European managers, many of whom may have spent their formative years under communist regime, have different perceptions of "work" and different notions of loyalty. In the end, the desire for quick profits coupled with overconfidence and oversimplification of the expansion process created an environment ripe for trouble—and trouble it found. While it's time consuming and costly to prepare a comprehensive expansion plan, it's a lot less costly than undoing an international blunder.

Successful Expansion: Taking the Road Less Traveled

In his poem "The Road Not Taken," Robert Frost writes about how taking the road less traveled has the potential of making a dramatic difference in one's experiences. The global marketplace is literally a vast network of untraveled roads, and the "difference" can be unparalleled growth for your business if the approach for bringing a product or service to market is carefully executed with commitment, purpose, and direction.

Taking the road less traveled requires a significant investment of upfront resources to choose the right market(s) and target them correctly. "Be prepared" is not only a well-conceived Boy Scout motto but sound advice for companies considering global expansion. The move is intricate and starts with understanding cultural habits and perceptions in order to accurately forecast sales, interpret trends, and evaluate the existing competition and the potential for new rivals. It also involves understanding the region's overall economy and how to best position your product/service in the present and for the future as well. While tedious and time consuming, the questions involved in this kind of upfront investment in analysis is key to a successful expansion.

Asking Key Questions

Taking the road less traveled requires effective strategic planning with a *long-term* strategy deployed with careful thought and introspection based on answers to such questions as:

- *Where to go and why.* With 200-plus countries to consider, where in the world should you start (i.e., where in the world are your next customers)? Also, if you choose one country over another, why is that the right destination? Knowing the "where" and "why" makes it much easier to develop an effective strategy for the "how."
- *With whom.* Will you go it alone, with partners, or follow a client?
- *With what and how to decide.* Will you continue with the same domestic product, make modifications, or develop a new product/service to maximize appeal in the new market/region? Do you look at your product and choose a destination? Or, do you look at global market trends and modify your product?
- *What are the other considerations?* It's important to think about culture, consumption habits and potential, transportation costs, distribution issues, calculating demand, competition, and legal issues, among many other things.
- *And finally, what are the goals?* How will you measure both the potential and overall success of your expansion?

The Importance of Finding Traction

After expansion is considered, enacted, and under way, success in the global marketplace occurs when an organization brings unsurpassed value to a targeted market. As such, it is vital to understand the concept of value from the perspective of the targeted marketplace. After all, "value" is an exceedingly relative term. With absolute certainty, a company must be equipped to understand what each target market wants and needs and have the required skills to validate the approach. Only then can the company begin to evaluate both the options and the feasibility of aligning its expansion strategy with the needs and desires of any particular region or market and gain traction in that marketplace.

To visualize traction, consider the daily occurrence at ski resorts around the world. As the last skier races down the mountainside and the lifts have stopped carrying passengers up the hill, a ski resort begins preparation for the following day. Snow groomers, designed for *traction,* make their way in what appears to be an effortless journey up the slopes, smoothing and molding the mountain. The same tenacity and endurance are necessary to succeed in a new marketplace, especially those markets on the road less traveled. Like the snow groomer that works hard to defy gravity and tame nature, introducing a product or service requires the ability to navigate obstacles and overcome challenges. Ultimately, traction will be the deciding factor between success and failure.

In terms of business, traction is the ability of an organization to pull itself forward with power, purpose, rhythm, and momentum. Traction occurs when a connection is struck with the market that allows the business to achieve its goals and surpass competitors. When a business achieves traction, it achieves efficiency. Through greater efficiency, valuable and limited resources such as time, money, and labor are more wisely invested and yield greater returns. Thus, traction creates a cycle of success as higher yields are channeled back into the key drivers of success.

Obviously, the specifics of creating traction will vary by market and by industry, but there are generic principles that every business can follow to develop traction. The key principles illustrated in the following 10 chapters include:

- Embarking on Your Global Adventure: Navigating Beyond the Borders of Your Organization and Your Home Country
- The Search for the Right Talent: A Driving Force in Going Global
- Improving Your Market Readiness through Effective Planning, Action, and Commitment
- Gaining Competitive Advantage: A Little Difference Makes *All* the Difference
- Sound International Negotiations: Unlocking the Secrets of Success across Borders
- Corporate Partnerships: A Match Made in Heaven . . . or Hell?
- Corporate Business Models: Growing Your Business from Within

- Focusing on Success
- Looking into the Future: New Players, New Rules, New Game
- Growth and Discovery

Learning and Mastering the "Dance"

Ultimately, a successful global expansion is dependent on an organization's ability to view the world in a new way. After all, the global economic tsunami of this century is reshaping the world's economy, creating new players, new rules, and new challenges. In response, U.S. businesses must view the future through a new filter focused on global opportunities with a willingness to learn new ways of conducting business. It's like learning to dance, which, for many of us, requires professional instruction and an expert. You also need to practice regularly, especially if you want to "dance with the stars"—or even be the star—and succeed in this global economy.

While the ultimate goal of any dance is pleasure, every dance is different. Moving to different rhythms and learning new numbers is challenging. For example, if you only know the merengue, performing a tango will require a significant effort. You may not even recognize tango music when it's playing over the sound system!

After some general instruction in the basic principles of a dance, you then have to choose a partner, a venue, and a specific dance step. If the dance is a tango, then you would select a partner skilled in tango at a venue that provides the right music. In this example, you have the specific understanding of the situation—i.e., it may be the tango in a certain venue—but it may still include a few steps and nuances you didn't anticipate (what kind of tango?). Alternatively, if your interest is line dancing, the partners and the venue will be completely different. Neither is right or wrong, just different . . . and the same principles apply to international business.

If you are embarking on your first global expansion effort, you will have to learn new rhythms, new rules, and new steps, different from the ones you have employed domestically. But after your first experience, you will be better equipped to make sound choices about who, what, where, and when to engage abroad.

To stretch our metaphor, too often, U.S. businesspeople race to the nearest "dance floor," cling to the first available "dance partner," and start "dancing" before they understand the "music" or the "rhythm." If the topics were only dancing, the worst result might be embarrassment, but when the subject is business, missteps on the dance floor, especially when the "dance floor" is global, could be disastrous. Instead, slow down.

Albert Einstein once said, "In the middle of every great difficulty lies opportunity." In today's increasingly complex and competitive global environment, time and skill are needed to evaluate options, manage risks, and execute a winning strategy. It's important to remember that, should an organization fail to grow successfully on its first attempt in this day and age, it may not get another chance. Yet when approached with careful deliberation, cross-border expansion can be a fruitful and rewarding strategy for any business. Instead of gazing with fear at the process, participants should remember to focus with excitement at the opportunities and, most important, plan for success.

■ ■ ■

Every chapter of this book is designed to provide the insight necessary to navigate each phase of a global expansion process. Regardless of the country of origin, and regardless of what international market is being explored, similar steps apply.

While many examples in this book refer to U.S. businesses, that is merely a function of the disparity in international experience. Understandably, U.S. businesses have less international experience when compared to their foreign counterparts who have relied on foreign business to supplement much smaller domestic markets.

Along with practical steps, you will find encouragement to look at the world in a new way with a new mind-set that focuses on possibilities, not fear. For a quick summary of key points, each chapter concludes with a list of Pearls of Wisdom.

Chapter 1

Embarking on Your Global Adventure

Navigating beyond the Borders of Your Organization and Your Home Country

"The wave of the future is coming and there is no fighting it."
—*Anne Morrow Lindbergh*

North American Tool is a small manufacturer with 100 employees operating from two plants located in Illinois and Michigan. Seeking growth, its CEO made the decision to expand operations into the global marketplace. The decision was formed in unison with other members of the United States Cutting Tool Institute, a trade association. It started with a tooling show in Italy where U.S. companies were invited to gauge foreign interest in their products. North American Tool left the trade show with 800 sales leads and more than enough motivation to go global, but how?

Ultimately, the company formed a joint venture with three other U.S. companies and opened manufacturing and sales operations in the United Kingdom. Today, this company does business in 56 countries. When asked about the biggest internal challenge, Bernie Bowersock, North American Tool senior vice president, responded with one word: commitment. Once the commitment was made, however, many logistical challenges presented themselves: payment terms, shipping costs, brokerage fees, VAT and GST taxes, product terminology, product pricing, currency issues, and time zone differences for supplying quotes.

These problems were resolved through education and tapping into the appropriate resources for assistance. The biggest external challenge was following up on sales leads. This required visiting various markets, learning new cultures, and trying to find local representation. As North American Tool has developed more international expertise, each new launch has become easier and more successful.

Today's Economy Is Truly Global

The world has transformed from a collection of regional or national economies into a truly global economy through advances in technology, communication, the opening of new markets, trade agreements, lower tariffs, and improved transportation. By 2020, a whopping 95 percent of the world's consumer base will reside outside United States boundaries.

This transformation offers unprecedented opportunity for U.S. businesses to expand sales and partnerships into new world markets. Except for one thing: the vast divide that separates this rapidly expanding global economy from the average American business person: experience. It's a fact: Most U.S. business people have a net deficit of worldwide market experience and initiative when compared to business people in other parts of the world.

That said, U.S. businesses remain the international benchmark for productivity, quality, and innovation; however, the gap is rapidly closing. That's because new entrants to the global marketplace already possess the fundamental skills necessary to succeed in today's global economy: skills that are still foreign to many U.S. businesses. In contrast to America's inward-looking focus, other countries possess an inherent global approach and established tradition of connecting with the international marketplace. This is especially true for smaller countries that historically relied on global growth and expansion for survival.

"We've had the luxury in the United States to sometimes say we want to engage or that we do not want to engage. We're still the big kind of indispensable nation," commented Deere & Company Chairman and CEO Robert Lane.[1] While this coveted status is generally considered a strongpoint for the United States, it has contributed to a great weakness in terms of embracing the new world order. Many smaller countries have learned to start thinking globally well before they launch their business locally. On the other hand, U.S. businesses continue to wait until they achieve success at home before pursuing global markets. Mistakenly, this approach relegates the global marketplace to an afterthought that often leads to failure abroad. No longer can U.S. businesses afford to sit on the international sidelines and watch.

Brazil, Russia, India, China (the BRIC countries), Central Europe, and other smaller countries are making great strides in adapting, perfecting, and in some cases surpassing the treasured U.S. model of innovation in their economic institutions and traditions while competing for limited international talent needed to succeed. These nations are also investing significant resources into higher education—emphasizing mathematics, science, and engineering. They are building state-of-the-art infrastructures to compete effectively both today and into the future.

Likewise, to ensure our future, U.S. companies must begin to explore opportunities in the vibrant and growing global marketplace and to learn how to navigate the business world beyond our borders. Business plans must be created that discard the old strategies of cost-cutting and downsizing and instead embrace new methods and new solutions designed for today's new world order by integrating global strategies, tactics, and human capital. Savvy business leaders know that globalization is no longer a choice. It is a necessity. It is reality.

Getting in the Game

The opportunities for global expansion are infinite, and the potential for exponential growth is alluring; however, attaining success demands a well-conceived global expansion plan that is grounded in accomplishing specific corporate goals through the careful formulation of business development strategies. Regardless of size or ownership structure, companies that take a proactive, strategic approach to evaluating and understanding both risks and costs will stay one step ahead of the competition and reap the benefits of a successful globalization initiative. It's a matter of developing the right strategy to win local markets and their consumer base by asking the right questions at the right time to the right people.

A company in the hospitality industry made the decision to expand internationally. With no tangible evidence of research, the company chose Latin America and Mexico as its target markets. With that decision made, the company launched into compiling a list of issues to tackle from each division (finance, sales, marketing, etc.). The questions compiled included queries such as "Should we open a local bank account?" "What accounting system should we use?" "Does this culture respond better to mobile messaging?" While these questions may represent relevant inquires at some point in the expansion process, attempting to answer them before investing in the development of an effective strategy almost always derails the entire process. The issues raised were more about the "how" as opposed to the "why" and "where." It's putting the cart before the horse.

Any decision to go global must start with developing a long-term action plan that aligns corporate vision, mission, and activities and leverages corporate strengths while identifying opportunities in desirable and compatible markets. It's about strategy, not tactics. Realistically, before any tactical questions can be answered, it's necessary to thoroughly examine individual markets and get the expertise necessary to understand the people and their culture. Unfortunately, due to a lack of international experience, U.S. business executives gravitate toward what they are most comfortable with: tactics—actions in a vacuum without a well-conceived conceptual framework. In the case of the hospitality company, the lack of strategic direction led to a market choice based on bad assumptions. Latin America is not a homogeneous country and Venezuela, for example, has little to no similarity with Mexico. Latin America is a conglomeration of vastly different countries, each with diverse markets that offer unique opportunities that must be understood at a local level before any tactical issues can be properly addressed.

This lack of strategic focus is a major contributor to the high failure rates of U.S. companies in the global marketplace. In fact, when KPMG's Global Enterprise Institute surveyed U.S. middle-market companies in late 2007, it found that 58 percent of all businesses surveyed planned to increase their global presence over the next five years, and one-third planned to maintain their current global presence.[2] Interestingly, in the same survey, fewer than half of all respondents said their expansion efforts over the past two years had been successful; therefore, 50 percent were unsuccessful! With failure rates like these, what must be done differently to improve chances for future success in the global marketplace? And the new global economic normal will not make success any easier to achieve. If anything, the current crisis may make the United States even more vulnerable to globalization.

Your Greatest Challenge May Be Mind-Set

As world leaders in innovation, it is important for U.S. businesses to look at the world from a fresh angle with a new perspective. "A global mind-set is the opposite of economic isolationism. We are part of the globe, and should stop looking inward, but look out," commented Carlos Gutierrez, former Secretary of Commerce. It's time for U.S. businesses to take the next step internationally through the development of a winning expansion strategy—a rational approach that eliminates surprises and gets it right the first time. After all, there is no challenge too great for a country that has proven itself over and over again. For example, Intel, the largest high-tech venture capital company in the world, historically made 90 percent of its investments in the United States and very little in China. The company now makes half of its investments in the United States and half in China and India. Intel Chairman of the Board, Dr. Craig R. Barrett, has commented:

> Sometimes when we talk about China we focus our thoughts on low cost manufacturing. Do not think that China is not innovative. Do not think that they don't have creative ideas. Do not think they're not entrepreneurial. They are and they're copying the best that we have and that is creating universities that look like ours and then an investment environment that is just like ours to create globally competitive startup companies.

Global expansion is the antidote for shrinking domestic markets. It offers unparalleled opportunity for growth, increased sales, diversified markets, and increased profit. Unfortunately, many U.S. businesses gaze with trepidation at the process and surrender to fear before making an earnest effort. The main problem is mind-set. But this problem also contributes to a lack of experience, talent, and confidence when navigating the global world.

Penetrating and developing an international market requires an entrepreneurial philosophy and drive—the same kind of philosophy and drive behind every successful startup business. Following that logic, America—the birthplace of the modern entrepreneurial spirit—should perform well in the global business. Also, with its multi-cultural diversity, theoretically is should improve its chances for global success. Yet American businesses fail at a rate of three to four times the rate of other countries in their ability to expand globally. Even worse, the majority of U.S. businesses never make an attempt. Of all the obstacles to success abroad, the greatest hurdle is simply mind-set. Our entrepreneurial drive, vision, and expertise just don't compensate for our lack of global perspective, drive, and success.

Fueled by our rugged individualistic and isolationist heritage, it's no surprise that collaboration across international borders requires a significant level of reconditioning. The United States must move beyond the "us-against-them" approach and recognize that a prosperous world translates to more business for U.S. companies—a win-win situation for all. This attitude is necessary for the United States to maintain its long-standing and valued leadership in the world. Fortunately, with a large dose of commitment, mind-set can be corrected, and this challenge can be overcome. How quickly depends on how serious American companies are about joining the global marketplace. As proven in previous decades, when American business embraces challenge, it finds success.

While it is tempting for U.S. businesses of all sizes to focus and dwell on the many overwhelming issues of the day, such as weak economic growth at home, an uncertain credit crisis, a shrinking pool of skill and talent, and increased foreign competition, the fact remains, these issues are not within the control of corporate management. Instead, corporate leadership must take one large step back and look into the global marketplace to discover new opportunities and new avenues to generate future growth. While larger corporations have more resources to invest in exploiting these new opportunities, smaller companies are more agile and can more readily adapt to change. In order to determine if your organization needs a mind-set adjustment, let me raise the following questions:

1. Do you realize that your business is already competing globally with international businesses at your doorstep?
2. Have you tried to access consumers outside the United States? Remember, they will soon represent 95 percent of the world's consumers!

3. Have you identified one market outside the United States that would desire your product or service?
4. Are you willing to collaborate with businesspeople from another country?
5. Can you look at global opportunities without being paralyzed and distracted by uncertainty and fear?
6. Are you aware of what it may require of your company, in terms of resources, to go global?

These questions and many others must be addressed honestly and openly in the context of strategic planning sessions for the executive leadership team to assess the willingness and commitment to exploring global opportunities.

Ten Steps in Planning Your Global Expansion

Going global begins with leaders who think proactively, sense and foresee emerging trends, and act upon them without fear. Next, it requires a product development strategy that is carefully planned all the way through distribution and delivery of the product. Each step in the process, from design to delivery, needs to be made in the context of the target market's local interest and culture, not that of the United States. For example, in many countries the delivery infrastructure Americans are accustomed to (UPS, FedEx, or the U.S. Postal Service) for every town and city may not exist: Products may be delivered strapped to the backs of bicyclists. Therefore, make no assumptions, *think locally,* and utilize every available local resource. To get started, consider the following steps, which will be explored in more depth throughout this book:

1. *Make a commitment.* Entering the global marketplace requires a tremendous dedication of resources, capital, time, and leadership. It has to become a priority.
2. *Assemble your team.* Avoid costly mistakes by starting with the right team of experts. Seek assistance from known experts in international business development, trade associations for contacts, attorneys for your protection, accountants to help you assess your

financial aspects, marketing for promotion activities, and global growth experts to help you identify, assess, and implement your strategy. Tap into their wealth of experience, talent, and information because few American companies have the in-house skills necessary to launch a global strategy.

3. *Leverage a competitive advantage.* Discover core competencies that can be developed into sustainable competitive advantages and identify unique attributes that can differentiate your product/service from the competition. For example, how could your current product/ service be modified to meet a need or create a need in a target market?

4. *Perform a thorough market readiness assessment.* Do your homework! Perform the research necessary to identify target markets and learn to think locally, or acquire this expertise, if needed. A detailed assessment will get your expansion right the first time around and avoid costly financial and opportunity losses.

5. *Calculate risk and look at risk analysis as an opportunity.* Never use risk as an excuse to shun the global marketplace. Learn to identify risk, calculate risk, and plan accordingly.

6. *Choose the right partners.* You don't have to go it alone. Greater success can be accomplished by collaborating with local businesses through innovation, mergers and acquisitions (M&A) or business clusters, and many other forms that suit your needs, plans, and global trends.

7. *Investigate the options and models for global expansion.* The opportunities to grow a business abroad are unlimited. Choose the model that is right for your goals and objectives.

8. *Establish realistic goals—everything takes longer than expected.* Do not underestimate the time and expense of launching products into the global marketplace. Also, be prepared both financially and emotionally for business to take much longer than you anticipate. Set measurable goals for establishing relationships, networks, and channels of distribution, but plan for delays in the process.

9. *Know the culture.* Consider language, negotiation styles, gender issues, and local business practices. Remember, there is no "one way" to do business. Adopt appropriate polices and strategies to

cope with different cultures. These sensitivities can make or break a deal.

10. *Stay focused and be fast, flexible, innovative, motivated and enjoy the adventure!*

In the end, your thoughts on these steps will navigate your business through the labyrinth of decisions that must be made in order to expand globally and do it well the first time. These steps will also maximize the success of any global venture by building a virtual link connecting your company's unique mission, vision, values, goals, and objectives with well-suited opportunities in the global marketplace. But you must embrace your thoughts on these steps and allow them to mimic a homing device always pointing to the "right" destination and ensuring a safe arrival, on-time and within budget.

Determining the "Right" Opportunity

Even though a preponderance of evidence and research suggests that cross-border engagement is a critical path for U.S. businesses, going global for the sake of going global is a recipe for failure. Instead, it is important to seek out the "right" opportunity by allowing overall corporate goals and objectives to guide the decision-making process. By pursuing global opportunities that correlate directly with your company's overall strategic plan, your entrance into the global marketplace will reflect a long-term commitment that is more likely to generate value and future success. But you need to ask the right questions and seek the right advice in order to get on the right track to success. If you don't know what you don't know (and you don't), it may be difficult to move in the right direction without surrounding yourself with experts who have hands-on experience in the global arena.

A few common goals for going global include expanding customer base, lowering manufacturing costs, and creating a competitive advantage in the marketplace. Although these common goals are shared by many businesses, accomplishing these goals may require very different strategies for each individual business. While pursuing identical goals, each business needs to identify the unique global expansion opportunity for its product(s) or service(s). This process requires both an internal and external assessment.

Internally, companies have to consider their strengths, weaknesses, motivations, and resources—both financial and human. Externally, the analyses should include a panoramic view of all reasonably viable markets with an in-depth understanding of their local culture, the competition, standard of living, infrastructure, business practices, legal environment, and political stability. At some critical point in this assessment process, an advantageous alignment should be revealed that pairs up a business's goals and objectives with unique qualities and opportunities for one or two global markets.

Where in the World Should You Go?

You know you should make a move, and you think your product or service could perform well in a foreign market, but how do you decide where you should target your efforts and what efforts are necessary? From the G-7, to the BRIC, to the Next 11 (N-11), the search is ongoing for markets that promise growth and new opportunities for businesses around the globe. To that end, Goldman Sachs and others have conducted extensive analyses of market conditions in countries far off the traditional radar screen. However, what companies need to pay close attention to when selecting a new target market isn't just one country's market performance over another. Rather, the right target market has everything to do with aligning your company's unique product/services, goals, vision, and global strategy with the most suitable country and then region.

What factors are important when choosing a target market? Everything from income, urbanization, language, culture, purchasing power, regional/local trends, and many more considerations. As such, this process involves taking the abundance of available data from a growing number of market possibilities and filtering that information to identify the best possible target market for your particular business. At a minimum, the value of this process comes from a changed mind-set and a willingness to scan the world for opportunities beyond those traditionally considered—beyond the G-7, beyond the BRIC, and even beyond the N-11 when appropriate. It's about exploring all the possibilities and planning for tomorrow's success today.

The N-11 and Beyond

Goldman Sachs introduced the concept of N-11 (Next 11) in late 2005. The goal was to identify emerging markets with the future potential of the BRIC countries. The BRIC countries were originally identified by Goldman Sachs in 2003 as the four fastest-growing developing economies in the world. Today, these markets are both well-known and well-exploited by business people worldwide. Despite the recent global economic downturn, each BRIC country has posted consistent economic growth since 2001. In 2010, for example, economic growth registered 4.8 percent, 4.9 percent, 7.3 percent, and 10.2 percent for Brazil, Russia, India, and China, respectively, and these BRIC markets are looking for growth in 2011 to be 4.5 percent for Brazil, 4.2 percent for Russia, 7.6 percent for India, and 9.3 percent for China.[3]

To illustrate the collective success of these BRIC countries, consider the fact that they now contribute 45 percent of total world growth compared to 20 percent from the G-7, and 11 percent from the N-11. Downstream, this success is shared with every business that embraced opportunities early, assessed the risk, did the strategic planning, and took action, yesterday. It's time for U.S. businesspeople to open their eyes and look at the world through a new lens and see what opportunities must be explored today to ensure success tomorrow.

These N-11 economies represent the next big growth stories or the markets "worth keeping an eye on." Specifically, the N-11 includes Bangladesh, Egypt, Indonesia, Iran, South Korea, Mexico, Nigeria, Pakistan, Philippines, Turkey, and Vietnam. While these markets are culturally, geographically, and economically diverse, each one is positioned for success by population size, resource-wealth, and sub-regional dominance. For example, each N-11 country has a large population coupled with high population growth rates that far exceed those of more developed economies. Between 1980 and 2008, population growth was highest in Pakistan at 110.8 percent and lowest in South Korea at 28.4 percent. Large populations indicate greater consumer market potential while high growth rates mean that this market will expand rapidly and provide more potential customers.

Is a growing population an important market trait for every business? Of course not. Population growth is only critical for businesses looking to establish that market as a consumer base. Alternatively, many businesses expand globally to access skilled labor, more economical manufacturing, proximity to other (future) markets, improved distribution channels, or myriad other reasons. Not to mention that the recent unrest in the Middle East may change the balance, time frame, and the way we should plan for doing business with these countries. Again, the right market for any global expansion has more to do with matching the goals and vision of one organization with the unique characteristics of one (or more) potential market(s).

Looking back 20 years, the options were far fewer, which made the decision process much simpler. Today, the choices are seemingly endless and the information overwhelming. The key is to ask the right questions, focus on actionable data, interpret the data as it may apply to your company, make an informed decision, and then align your expansion strategy to leverage your organization's strengths and create a long-term competitive advantage. While the regions represented by the N-11 have a long way to go before challenging the overall economies of the BRIC nations, they do represent a good starting point for any expansion analysis being conducted today.

Future Prospects

Since the initial report by Goldman Sachs, the Philippines and Indonesia have performed better than most of the N-11 economies. Bangladesh, Egypt (until very recently), South Korea, Turkey, Nigeria, and Vietnam have performed in line with original projections. Meanwhile, Iran, Pakistan, and Mexico have largely disappointed the analysts. The differing levels of performance have everything to do with country-specific factors. For example, Mexico's struggles are indicative of their dependency on the U.S. economy, which experienced decelerating growth in 2007. By contrast, Vietnam's growth was fueled by an increase in tourism and a diverse export market.

Across the board, the N-11 experienced sharper contractions during the economic crisis; however, they've since posted stronger rebounds as well. Interestingly, seven of the N-11 (Bangladesh, Egypt, Indonesia, Iran, Nigeria, Philippines, and Vietnam) contributed more to world growth from 2007 to 2008 than collectively from 2000 to 2006.

Nevertheless, these countries face extraordinary challenges and a difficult economic environment that could prevent them from following the BRIC growth path. Consider infrastructure. From roads, telecommunications, and transportation to legal policies, accounting rules, and government regulations, these countries are very early in the development phase. Another important factor for success is human capital. Many of these countries lack the skills necessary to reach their potential.

Ultimately, the success of any N-11 country will depend on more than just population, population growth, and access to natural resources. It will require the international business community to identify potential and pursue opportunity. That means finding ways to *grow with* these economies. Established economies must believe in the potential, invest in their progress, and participate in the development of these emerging economies. Success will also require stable governments that are pro-business, open to trade, and willing to invest in education.

Although today may not be the day for all companies to begin conducting business with Nigeria, Vietnam, Bangladesh, or any other N-11, today is the day to put these countries on the strategic radar screen. Investigate the strengths and weaknesses of these emerging economies and understand how they might synchronize with your long-term strategic goals. Start building relationships. Alternatively, ask how you might modify long-term goals to take advantage of these opportunities. The N-11 dream can become a reality for those businesses willing to begin today, think strategically, do the homework, and be patient.

Balancing Risk and Reward

As you consider where to go, the spotlight of a global expansion program should stay focused on opportunities for growth, increasing profit, enlarging market share, and gaining further competitive advantage. It's

important to complete a detailed risk analysis assessment. Ed Morris of
Clifton Gunderson LLP explains:[4]

> The analysis should answer the questions: What is the ROI
> (return on the investment) for international expansion and
> will that ROI be sufficient to reward the company for the
> associated risks? For example, if a company invests $1,000,000
> in plant and equipment domestically and receives a return
> of $200,000 in additional profits; but could have invested
> $1,000,000 in a foreign country and received $250,000 in
> additional profits that additional $50,000 reward is prob-
> ably not worth the additional risks associated with global
> expansion. On the other hand, if the global expansion gener-
> ated $400,000 of additional profits it is probably worth the
> additional risks.

Specifically, a thorough risk assessment is composed of the following components:

- *Operational risks — transportation, distribution, supply chain, information
  technology, and personnel.* Each of these operational functions can
  look different and offer unique challenges from one market to the
  next. In the Middle East, for example, businesses must consider
  longer customs waiting periods and political instability that affect
  insurance rates and delivery times.
- *Financial risks — taxation, transfer pricing, repatriation of profits, foreign
  exchange, credit, and cash flow.* All too often, firms in the process of
  international expansion find themselves with little working capital to meet daily operating needs and capitalize on opportunities
  internationally. There are firms that will assist with the most basic
  benefit of increasing working capital, with their extensive global
  experience that can navigate the challenges of cross-border business transactions.
- *Strategic risks — local competition and cultural differences.* The role of
  local brand loyalty cannot be underplayed in many foreign markets.
  Also, culturally, many international consumers are very consumed
  and easily impressed about social status and the allure of using certain brands of cars, clothing, telephones, and accessories. For this

reason, collaboration with established local businesses is often an advantageous market-entry strategy.

- *Legal risks—contracting, regulatory, compliance.* In addition to political instability, some foreign markets experience a significant amount of legal instability. Regulations, local or national, can change overnight, requiring immediate action. Lately, there were quite a few companies in that region that their ownership agreements and licenses were voided by the new governments, and there was practically nothing they could do about it.

Again, the purpose of a risk assessment is to understand the market's specific risks, not to provide justification for rejecting a global initiative. For example, consider a U.S. business that wants to increase its presence in Western Europe. In this case, the risk assessment must include the likelihood of strikes and work slow-downs. While Italy's *lo sciopero* (planned strikes) can bring transportation to a halt during the summer season and disrupt any business, Italy may still be a good market choice. But the decision must be based on a calculated risk and acceptance of that risk.

Focus the risk assessment process by examining key areas that have caused businesses the most difficulty. In a study conducted by Grant Thornton,[5] respondents were asked to list the three biggest barriers they experienced in cross-border transactions. The five most commonly mentioned areas of difficulty were:

- *Cultural issues (39 percent).* Spend time getting to know local customs and practices.
- *Regulatory environment (35 percent).* Be prepared for unexpected legal and/or regulatory changes and understand the provisions of the Foreign Corrupt Practices Act (FCPA).
- *Legal environment (35 percent).* Make no assumptions based on geography. Every legal system is really very different.
- *Intellectual property protection (31 percent).* The ability to protect intellectual property varies greatly from country to country.
- *Due diligence (27 percent).* Do your homework with an emphasis on getting actionable data and utilize experts to assist in relating market information to specific business issues.

The Opacity Index: A Tool to Measure Risk

One tool that can assist businesses in evaluating potential risks in various countries is the Opacity Index[6] created by the Milken Institute. The Milken Institute is an independent economic think tank whose mission is to improve the lives and economic conditions of diverse populations in the United States and around the world by helping business and public policy leaders identify and implement innovative ideas for creating broad-based prosperity. Drawing on a decade of research, the Milken Institute has created a tool that offers businesses new ways to anticipate, analyze, and manage hidden global business risks.

The Opacity Index is a measure of five components identified by the acronym CLEAR:

C—Corruption
L—Legal system inadequacies
E—Economic enforcement policies
A—Accounting standards and corporate governance
R—Regulation

It is a broad measure of the effectiveness of a country's economic and financial institutions as well as overall risk. To place the tool into perspective, the 48 countries covered in the index account for 65 percent of the earth's land mass, 77 percent of the world's population (in 2007), 94 percent of 2007 world GDP, 93 percent of world financial assets, and 99 percent of world equity trading volume.

Higher opacity scores represent a more opaque business environment. For example, the most recent Opacity Index for the year 2007– 2008 (available at www.milkeninstitute.org/pdf/2008OpacityIndex) ranks the top three countries (i.e., lowest opacity scores) as Finland, Hong Kong, and Singapore. The bottom three countries (i.e., highest opacity scores) are Venezuela, Lebanon, and Nigeria. In countries with high opacity scores, the effect is like another tax—a tax that is not easily calculated.

The understanding of how one country compares to another along these five dimensions is a useful tool for businesses that wish to expand globally. Essentially, it measures "the lack of clear, accurate formal, clear-cut practices in the broad arena where business, finance and government meets." The index also allows countries to monitor improvements and progress towards eliminating fraud and corruption.

Knowing the Costs

In addition to patience, planning, and preparation, global expansion requires a substantial investment in financial and human capital. The consequence of underestimating either of these can be disastrous. Instead, it is important to perform extensive research and interpret it accurately. Ideally, this research should eliminate surprises and aid businesses in anticipating potential problems and ensuring that they are equipped with both the money and talent to succeed. In the study conducted by Grant Thornton, 56 percent of all respondents noted that meeting objectives took longer than expected. In other words, meeting objectives required more financial resources than expected.

Once an opportunity is identified and the risk analysis is complete, it is critical to perform a thorough analysis of all costs. For example:

- *Opportunity cost.* What is the cost of not expanding globally? It could be higher materials costs, loss of competitive advantage, or shrinking customer base. Alternatively, what is the opportunity cost of going global? It may require eliminating existing domestic operations or terminating a domestic product line.
- *Human capital.* Employing the right talent (abroad and at home) to support the expansion and get things done is essential to success. Can existing employees support the needed infrastructure and deliver? Do they need training? Will new positions need to be created? Remember, employees abroad will represent the business and have the potential to build or destroy the corporate reputation.
- *Transportation and distribution.* This can represent a significant portion of total overhead expense and requires a cost benefit analysis to determine what level of control is acceptable and for what price. More control will always cost more, and additional money is not always an option.
- *Supply chain and global sourcing.* U.S. companies have never had so many choices when it comes to global purchasing opportunities. The decision to manufacture or outsource, and the overall coordination

of a globally dispersed supply chain are key strategic areas that require consideration and expertise.

- *Taxes, insurance, and other costs.* On a local and national level these "other" operating costs must be clearly identified and budgeted.

Both the risk assessment and the cost analysis require global expertise and knowledge that many U.S. businesses do not possess. Consequently, it may be necessary to rely on global expansion experts who can oversee and coordinate each component of the global expansion plan, within the appropriate context and, therefore, like in a puzzle, get all the parts to fit. Gaining an expert's perspective on globalization can eliminate both surprises and costly mistakes.

Staying One Step Ahead

Long-term success requires a strategic focus based on a long-term commitment. For example, if an organization's long-term goal is to penetrate Eastern Europe and the Middle East, establishing a presence in Turkey may be an ideal first step. It is well-positioned geographically since it is located on two continents (Europe and Asia), and it is relatively inexpensive to conduct business. Plus, Turkey offers political stability and gets along with neighboring countries. By establishing relationships in Turkey first, future advances toward Eastern Europe and the Middle East can be accomplished without having to reestablish a local presence.

Another strategy is to identify and act on future trends. For example, consider the burgeoning middle class in China and India. Imagine each one with a middle class equal to the entire population of the United States! A recent survey by the American Chamber of Commerce in China reports that 80 percent of respondents cited a desire to serve customers in China and elsewhere in Asia as their reason for having a presence in China. Only 16 percent indicated they were in China to export products back to the United States. Any U.S. business already on the ground in China with years of experience conducting business in that region is ahead of this trend and uniquely positioned to leverage their existing business relationships.

Pearls of Wisdom

Henry Ford once said, "No one can guarantee the future. The best we can do is size up the chances, calculate the risks involved, estimate our ability to deal with them and make our plans with confidence." Here is a list of key points to keep in mind from this chapter when embarking on your global adventure:

- Going global is no longer a choice. It is mandatory for a business to survive and thrive. Organizations and their members need to adopt a global mind-set.
- Ninety-five percent of the world's consumers will reside outside the United States by the year 2020. Developing a well-conceived expansion plan grounded in solid goals through sound business strategy is key.
- The global marketplace is an antidote for shrinking domestic markets.
- Today, U.S. businesses fail at a disproportionate rate when attempting expansions abroad. Understand that high failure rates abroad illustrate a lack of planning, *not* a lack of worthwhile opportunities.
- There are 10 key steps to utilize in order to separate success from failure.
- Goals and objectives must be the overall drivers of global decisions. Learn to identify the right international opportunity for your organizations. Don't just follow the competition.
- Structure drives process. Process drives strategy. Actionable strategy drives successful execution.
- There are many emerging economies to consider and put on the radar screen. Try to stay one step ahead by tuning in to future trends.
- It's important to integrate the calculated risks into your strategic operations. Investigate available resources to familiarize yourself with emerging markets: The Opacity Index, Ease of Doing Business Index, and other strategies are useful to this end.
- It's critical to identify all associated costs to eliminate potential surprises. Your analysis should consider opportunity costs, human capital, transportation and distribution, supply chain, taxes, insurance, and other significant costs that may have to do with not embarking on the opportunities.

No question about it, the decision to go global is an important step for companies to make if they want to survive, strive, and thrive. But once the decision is made, no action can be completed and executed without having the right people in place—at headquarters, as well as in the countries or regions being targeted.

Talent acquisition, retention, development, and management are critical to the success of global expansion initiatives, and we discuss these things in detail in Chapter 2.

Chapter 2

The Search for the Right Talent

A Driving Force in Going Global

"Never doubt that a small group of thoughtful, committed people can change the world. Indeed. It is the only thing that ever has."

—*Margaret Mead*

Sitting down recently with the head of a leading Spanish bank, Wharton management professor Mauro Guillén asked the CEO if he foresaw any bottlenecks in the bank's rapid growth around the world. "Managerial talent," Guillén recalls the CEO replying immediately. Although the bank was able to move easily into Latin America, Europe, and other markets that presented low cultural barriers, it had to bypass opportunities in Asia because of a lack of leadership talent, said Guillén, who is also director of the Wharton School's Lauder Institute. This decision to bypass opportunities in Asia, however, came at a cost—a cost other businesses in similar situations refuse to bear.

Alternatively, other companies get creative, reevaluate, and prioritize the skill set required. Consider a technology company from the West Coast with annual sales of $10 billion also looking to expand into Asia. This high-tech company identified a deficit of board-level talent to direct the expansion. The organization lacked board members with both native and proven global experience. When the search was initiated, the defined requirements were for a person from Singapore with Chinese market experience and high-tech industry experience. But this combination of skills was not found in any one person.

Upon further analysis, the search committee agreed that the most important criteria was someone who "lived and breathed" the target market's business environment. The revised criteria led them to a CEO from one of the largest travel industry companies who brought tremendous leadership experience. What he lacked in specific industry experience, he compensated for with the knowledge of Asian markets, an ability to develop and implement corporate strategy, and lead a business into new markets. By redefining the necessary experience and casting a larger net, this organization was rewarded with tremendous success as it entered the Asian marketplace.

Instilling a Global Mind-Set

Historically, the United States has been the leader in world economy. As we enter the second decade of the 21st century, that position has changed. We're not even second or third! According to the 2010–2011 Global Competitiveness Report, the United States ranks *fourth*, behind Switzerland, Sweden, and Singapore.[1]

To regain our standing as the most competitive economy in the world, we need to refocus and tap into what has traditionally been our strength: our talent for creativity, vision, and rapid innovation. That means using our intellectual capital and human resources to create new products and services or to adapt existing products and services for the global marketplace. Meeting this challenge requires the right leadership and the right talent. "Talent is number one in any strategic execution," says Lou Kacyn, a Chicago-based partner at executive search firm Egon Zehnder International. Only by identifying, attracting, training, and retaining the right mix of globally minded individuals and strategically positioning them throughout the organization will companies be able to ensure their future prosperity.

In the fall of 2010, U.S. Commerce Secretary Gary Locke underscored the pressing need for an internationally minded American workforce when he wrote in the U.S. International Trade in Goods and Services Report, "We are fast approaching the time when 95 percent of the world's consumers will live outside the borders of the United States." This fact defines the new world order. However, tapping into these emerging markets with growing consumer demand requires a skill set that many U.S. business leaders fail to possess. A skill set that is built upon a global mind-set rather than a U.S.-centric perspective of the world.

The term "mind-set" is especially important when it comes to the ability to succeed in the global economy. Mind-set is defined as a fixed mental attitude formed by experience, education, and prejudice. It is a predisposition to see the world in a particular way that creates boundaries based on expectations and provides explanations (right or wrong) for why things are the way they are. It is a cultural filter that allows some people to observe certain things, including opportunities that others never see.

Success abroad starts with leaders who can develop and instill a global mind-set throughout an entire organization accept the uncertainties of how business is conducted worldwide and guide a diverse workforce in previously unexplored directions. In an economy where, historically, so much was so predictable and replicable, U.S. leadership has to develop a new set of skills, which is a given in most other countries around the world, but relatively new and uncomfortable for corporate America. As Nitin Nohria of Harvard Business School confirmed through years of study and analyses, the CEO accounts for up to 40 percent of a company's performance and is potentially worth billions of dollars in terms of market capitalization. So it's important to get this position right.

What Is True Global Leadership?

Fueled by a heritage of rugged individualism and isolationist polices, the American ability to innovate is unparalleled. But collaboration across borders poses significant challenges. Given the sheer size of the U.S. market, most American business people have elected to forgo global expansion and, therefore, lack the experience necessary to lead their organizations into the world marketplace. The global marketplace is at our doorstep, and like it or not, we are all competing globally, intentionally, or otherwise. Just consider the extent of foreign inbound investment and foreign acquisitions of both U.S. businesses and landmarks. In response, we must move beyond our "us-against-them" mentality and recognize that a prosperous world translates into more business for U.S. companies—a potential win-win situation for all.

Global leaders are able to scan for opportunities, think proactively, sense and foresee emerging trends, and act upon them. They know what questions to ask, what to look for, and how to investigate the available information as well as search for the missing pieces, and they do so without fear or hesitation. Remember the iceberg theory? As captains on the journey abroad, global leaders must have the awareness to anticipate danger, both seen and unseen, so that the organization is always prepared to deal with whatever challenges emerge. This is done through compiling information and also being aware of what one doesn't know and preparing for the "unknown unknowns." In this new world order, simply having the right product and the right technology will not suffice. Rather, it is the caliber of the leadership and the ability to innovate and collaborate that will make the difference between success and failure.

It starts with global-minded leaders equipped with the skills to:

- Manage uncertainty and fear while constantly adapting to the changing global environment. These leaders realize that unpredictability is the only constant in a fast-paced, changing world. As the Greek philosopher Heraclitus (c.535 B.C.–475 B.C.) is attributed with saying, "The only constant is change."
- Integrate a global strategy into the overall corporate strategy and change thinking patterns from a single domestic focus to a broader global focus. Global growth cannot succeed when treated as an isolated incident. It has to be tied in, integrated, and given the right amount of attention and commitment. Your global strategy has to be aligned with your company's vision, mission, and resources and cannot succeed in a vacuum or without the proper attention.
- Attract and combine diverse cultures into a unified corporate workforce as well as your board of directors by investing in people, embracing their diversity and leveraging their differences. Tapping into diverse talent, cross industry expertise, and cross-cultural mind-sets can only strengthen the company, but has to be managed and directed to create and follow the globally enhanced corporate culture.
- Collaborate with partners around the world by successfully managing global teams and alliances. It is not about who is in control. It is about clearly defining the rules of engagements, and working together to get results and achieve success.
- Understand the long-term value of balancing profit and competition with sustainability and collaboration opposed to focusing solely on short-term issues, such as quarterly shareholder value.

A global economy requires leaders who have cross-cultural knowledge gained through hands-on experience. Individuals who appreciate, understand, respect, and have personal experience interacting with people from different cultures and nations are the most valuable assets for companies conducting business internationally. Not only are these individuals better team players but they also find it easier to embrace change and transfer both ideas and business processes from one culture to another. These attributes lead to greater innovation and greater competitiveness. Since a country's language expresses and represents its culture, being well-versed in several languages gives a person insight into the deeper values and fundamentals of a country and, hence, the way a nation conducts business. Still, cultural fluency is one of the most valuable skills and in most cases its benefits surpass language fluency.

For example, while assisting a U.S. client in Spain through the final steps of a business transaction, a U.S. negotiating team was increasingly discouraged and ready to leave the country. While the Spaniards were wonderful hosts, two and a half days of being shown around town, meeting the company's president and his family, and eating lavish meals at his home represented too much time "wasted" without a concrete word about the future of the deal. The U.S. team was eager to talk terms and misinterpreted these events as distractions. Understanding the culture, the language and the need for relationship-building before deal-making, I advised the team to be patient. Just before dinner on the third night, an agreement was reached on the terms and conditions, and the deal was sealed. Leaving early in frustration would have been a very costly mistake. But it takes experience and time to develop a comfort level for doing business across borders. Unfortunately, global experience is a rare commodity in the United States, and businesses are running out of time to develop it internally.

The Value of Cross-Industry Experience

Outside the United States, executives at every level have been developing international experience for decades and are well equipped for the new world order. In many countries, especially those with limited consumer markets, engaging internationally has always been a requirement for survival. In the United States, however, going global has been more of an option, not a necessity—until now. For that reason, companies at every level will find it very difficult, if not impossible, to locate U.S. leaders with global experience. As such, it may be necessary to cast a larger net in the search for global talent rather than pass on global opportunities. Similar to our above story, it may be necessary to revaluate the leadership experience needed and understand the nature of transferable skills.

When searching, consider attributes that can substitute for cross-cultural experience. For example, seek candidates with cross-industry experience. In many ways, the skills necessary to successfully switch industries mirror the skills necessary to cross borders. After all, leaders who possess cross-industry knowledge are naturally more open-minded and more flexible. In addition, they are likely to embrace solutions from outside their normal comfort zone. These leaders tend to be the most innovative when it comes to transferring technologies, tools, and processes from one industry to the next. Because these leaders go a step beyond looking outside the proverbial box, their companies tend to be more innovative and more competitive. Entrepreneurs who regularly switch industries often create new companies and even new industries by taking one industry's products, tools, technologies, or services to a new level. With some targeted training, this same skill set will enable leaders to maximize the opportunities being presented in today's global markets and create a new pool of talent.

In fact, some of the best business leaders today are those who have crossed industry boundaries. Their varied experience has given them a broader perspective and the fresh thinking necessary to go beyond the traditional approaches to competitive challenges and corporate product, marketing, and demand fulfillment strategies. Lou Kacyn from Egon Zehnder International comments:

> Perhaps one of the most well known examples of a leader who has successfully crossed industries more than once is Louis Gerstner, Jr., first the CEO of American Express, then CEO of RJR Nabisco, and then Chairman and CEO of IBM where he was not only successful, but achieved cult status.

Gerstner is responsible for keeping IBM together by repositioning its corporate strategy rather than splitting the company apart as others had suggested at the time. His historic turnaround of the company from the brink of bankruptcy and mainframe obscurity back into the forefront of the technology business is chronicled in his book *Who Says*

Elephants Can't Dance (Harper Business 2002). In his introduction to that book, he states that when he was first approached to lead IBM, he could not conceive of running the company given his lack of technical background. However, he changed his mind when members of the search committee made a passionate appeal that the board was not looking for a technologist but rather a broad-based leader and change agent.

When a leader comes from outside the industry, he or she brings a fresh outlook and no baggage. That's why at one point Steve Jobs of Apple picked John Sculley who was president of Pepsi-Cola to be the CEO of Apple, a job that he performed from 1983–1993. (Sculley's adventures upon switching industries are chronicled in his memoir *Odyssey: Pepsi to Apple* [Harpercollins 1987].)

There is much emphasis today on the requirement that leaders, especially global leaders, be flexible and adaptable. What better way to acquire and practice those skills than by switching industries? It takes a flexible individual to grasp and control knowledge from a variety of industries and apply intelligence gained in one for the benefit of another. Likewise, these same skills are the foundation for taking U.S. innovations from our consumer markets to those of emerging markets. But keep in mind that these skills need to be on your executive team, board of directors, as well as on your local team. In each step of the way, the knowledge, experience, and the ability to make sustainable long-term strategic decisions have to be in place.

Today, there are tools and technologies that are easily adaptable from one industry to another and from one global market to another with only slight modification. Why reinvent the wheel when a cutting-edge solution to a problem or need for greater efficiency is only a minor modification away? Why not change the lens the company is looking through, transform a concept, and thus create and innovate a new solution? Look at Starbucks and its transformation of the concept of having a cup of coffee. The company created a whole new experience for coffee enthusiasts in the United States at a time when it didn't seem like there was much room for innovation in the field.

In another case, a portfolio management company transferred a customer relationship management process from the airline industry. It established the equivalent of airline frequent-flyer clubs and VIP lounges in order to gain market segmentation, reach and serve its clients, as well as grow its client base and cross-sell new services to existing clients. Depending on their investment balances, clients are assigned to virtual clubs and treated differently. For instance, the various club levels earn different rates of interest, pay different interest rates for loans, and are charged different fees for services. At first glance, these two industries appear to have nothing in common, but closer examination revealed an opportunity and the opportunities could continue into the global market.

A Note on Specialization

Cross-industry experience is about businesspeople having universal skills. But many business professionals—whether leaders, human resource managers, or consultants—still believe success is most easily accomplished through specialization. While this may be accurate for technical experts such as engineers, accountants, or medical professionals, it is a false assumption at the corporate executive level. The truth is, specialization in a particular industry is unnecessary and may even contribute to a lack of creativity and innovation as it pertains to the C-suite and other top management levels. More important, global leaders must have universal skills such as choosing and nurturing the right people, overseeing and growing a business, and especially *how to manage change*.

It's also critical for global leaders to have the ability to develop goals and strategies by identifying customer needs and wants while building the virtual road map that integrates the two. The intimate knowledge of how to manufacture those ensuing products, of course, is best left to engineers and other technical experts. The fact is: Leaders whose experience is limited to a single industry's strategies, processes, techniques, and tools cannot deliver what the global marketplace demands of companies today—nothing short of extraordinary and sustained creativity and innovation.

The Essential Core Competencies of a Global-Minded Team

While flexibility and adaptability are desirable attributes for global leaders, you should also look for people who have demonstrated ability in the following core competencies across industries (or at least in different divisions of the same company):

- Strategic planning followed by successful execution
- Changes in management that leads to growth (not just making change for the sake of change)
- Creativity and innovation demonstrated by new products or modified products that gain an organization access to new markets
- Business acumen and financial knowledge
- Customer focus, both internal and external
- People skills, such as conflict management, relationship building, coaching, and the ability to motivate
- Global skills and a multi-national mind-set

In addition, look for leaders who fit the profile of "Level Five" leaders—a term described in Jim Collins's book *Good to Great* (Harper Business, 2001). Every good-to-great company in his book had Level Five leadership during the pivotal transition years. "Level Five" refers to the top of a five-level hierarchy of executives capabilities. These are leaders who:

- Embody a mix of personal humility and professional will
- Are ambitious for the company, not only themselves
- Set up their successors for even greater success into the future
- Are modest, self-effacing, and understated
- Are fanatical drivers, infected with an incurable need to produce sustained results
- Display diligence, but more as plow horse than show horse
- Attribute success to factors other than themselves
- Take full responsibility when things go wrong
- Possess the right chemistry with existing management and embody a natural entrepreneurial spirit

Once the top leadership is in place, the next challenge is identifying, developing, attracting, and retaining globally minded talent throughout the entire organization—both at home and abroad. And that is becoming a formidable challenge.

Finding the Right Talent

Gary Hamel, who was named by the *Wall Street Journal* as "the most influential business thinker in the world"[2] in 2008, argues that the power of organizations is shifting from the center to the edges as we move from a knowledge economy to a creative economy. According to Hamel and other leading scholars, organizational success is increasingly being determined by talented individuals at the edges of the organization. Often these individuals work in non-hierarchical and cross-functional teams that form around key projects or strategic opportunities. They partner with other organizations (competitors, suppliers, and customers) to drive innovation and create new sources of value. But the demand for these talented individuals with global experience far outnumbers the available supply.

Worldwide, there is a shortage of talent from skilled labor and management to top executives and board members. This promises to be a major obstacle for organizations seeking to go global. In fact, several companies report the only thing limiting growth abroad is the lack of people—engineers, sales staff, marketing—who are bilingual, globally oriented, and willing to live abroad. With emerging markets around the world, the United States is now forced to compete for the talent it once took for granted. As Louis J. Kacyn in Egon Zehnder's board practice (which assesses and recruits top-level management resources for clients), says:

> We are frequently asked to find non US board members for US boards. For most Fortune 500 companies, over 30% of their revenues come outside of the US, and in many cases, considerably more. And yet, less than 15% have a non-US member on the board. In addition, the rate of growth from non US revenues is twice the rate of domestic. It becomes clear that having more non-US experience on the Board is a sound practice.[3]

Businesses in India, for example, expect to recruit in one year the number of skilled workers they traditionally hired during a ten-year period. In 2003, China had only eight companies on the Fortune Global 500; in 2010, they have 29.[4] All the international students who used to come to the United States for higher education and stay now have many more options, including those closer to home. The result is a virtual wave of intellectual emigration from the United States at a critical point in time where expertise and diversity are needed more than ever. To make matters worse, these well-educated people leave our country and cleverly adapt our methods, products, and services to

Talent

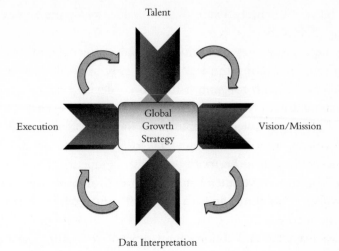

Execution   Global Growth Strategy   Vision/Mission

Data Interpretation

Figure 2.1 "All Organizations Are Perfectly Designed to Get the Results They Get." —Arthur Jones

meet their country's needs. As you can see in Figure 2.1, talent is a crucial component of a successful global growth strategy.

Having the right people on your team is critical to defining, planning, and executing your global strategy. In each stage you need people that know global business and can make the right decisions.

However, when you combine intellectual emigration with the advancing age of senior executives, the result may be an unprecedented shortage of talent and skills. In a 2007 survey[5] conducted by Egon Zehnder International and Harvard Business School, participants from 50 international organizations said they expected the number of executives in the 35- to 45-year-old age bracket to fall by 30 percent over the next six years. Many firms are sensibly trying to address this growing shortfall in their home markets by sourcing their future talent needs from countries like China and India. In fact, companies plan to increase the percentage of their senior executives from markets outside their home market by 32 percent over the next six years. This transition, however, will not be easy. Despite more favorable demographics in developing economies, the high potentials in these markets will be increasingly difficult to attract and retain in the future. These individuals tend to be savvy, acutely aware of their value, and quite aggressive in managing their careers.

The best companies in China and India already understand the importance of recruiting the right talent early and aggressively. They are collaborating with top universities to co-develop degree programs that are aligned with their specific business needs and even establishing on-premise private college campuses. In the face of these radical initiatives, western multinationals seeking to attract talent in developing economies will need to be more proactive, competitive, and prepared to make long-term investments in the future. Moreover, western companies will have to think and act very differently when recruiting in their home markets.

Today, many up-and-coming businesspeople recognize the value of international experience and the opportunities for career advancement that such experience will offer them throughout their careers. They understand the power of the global economy and want to participate defining their company's role in a worldwide expansion. Many of the individuals possess personal characteristics such as drive, energy, and curiosity that compel them to explore new ideas, cultures, and vocational challenges. They are eager to learn and take risks to gain professional and personal growth. But identifying these individuals, attracting them, training them, and retaining them pose many challenges. Here are some of the major obstacles:

- While the number of executives willing to work abroad is growing, the pool of genuine international talent remains quite small. Only a very small percentage of highly talented executives have worked in three or more countries for 18 months or longer. Further, during times of severe economic downturn, executives in secure positions—even highly qualified for international work—demonstrate far less willingness to relocate abroad.

- Geographical differences (both real and perceived) work against a "perfect market" for international talent. In a perfect international talent market, the flow of executives back and forth among countries would be steady and proportional. But this is not the case. Regardless of opportunities, some countries are magnets for international talent, while others are not. For example, European executives are eager to work in the United States because of the size and power of its market. Many European executives are also willing to work in China or India. By contrast, many Americans are less willing to work in Europe, and it is even more difficult to recruit for positions in China and India.

- Money and professional opportunity are no longer sufficient inducements.
- Many executives, despite appearances and desire, are not well-suited for working abroad. Because international experience is increasingly seen as a wise career move, more and more executives are likely to seek it, even though they may not be appropriate for it. They may believe that they are ready and they may insist that they want to do it. But unless they genuinely possess the personal characteristics and professional competencies required for working in an unfamiliar environment, they and their employers are likely to soon regret their association.

These challenges are further compounded by assessing the competencies of candidates, determining their fit with the company's culture, and reaching an agreement on compensation. For these reasons, acquiring international talent can challenge even the highly adept HR departments of successful global companies. Hiring the wrong people for positions, and having them perform poorly or depart abruptly, will leave a trail of unfulfilled business objectives, missed opportunities, and wasted financial resources. The cost to a company can be anywhere from $250,000 to $1 million on wasted training and executing another round of recruitment for the position. But those costs pale in comparison with the larger business costs of thwarted global strategy.

Attracting and Retaining Future Talent

Hiring global talent is more important and more difficult than ever before. In general, every firm faces two broad options: hiring local talent or importing talent from the home market. There is no right or wrong choice. However, these options must be carefully analyzed in the context of strategic goals with a full understanding of the pros and cons of either option. For example, consider what happens in China and other parts of Asia. Too often global companies will assume a person with Chinese origins is the best-bet for a position in China. After all, they can understand and speak the language. However, many Chinese have never lived in China and the advantages of knowing the language can't be so quickly overcome by a lack of other skills. Ultimately, whether the talent is hired locally or imported from home, it's the retention and development of that talent that matters most. To that end, firms must provide targeted training based on each person's strengths and weaknesses. Organizations must also invest in future talent earlier and more deeply.

They also need to be more rigorous, more disciplined, and more aware of what motivates this new generation of potential talent before making important personnel decisions.

In addition, companies need to know what they are looking for, the value they put on these positions and be specific and diligent in the set of skills they need to utilize in the future in order to execute their strategy. This can be done through targeted training or a thorough search for talent. In both cases, this is not to be taken lightly. For example, the X and Y generation are different from their predecessors. They are loyal to their careers, not to companies. Moreover, they choose positions based on meaning, purpose, and relationships, rather than organizational power and status. Those organizations with management structures and processes that reflect these needs and aspirations will attract and retain the best talent. This generation of talent is also characterized by a volunteer mentality. Its members will only bring their creativity and passion to work if that work, and the work environment, is intrinsically satisfying and stimulating. Gary Hamel calls it the "gift economy." Creativity cannot be commanded; it can only be released. In other words, successful companies will have to merit this gift to attract talent in the future.

In a panel organized by Egon Zehnder International with over 100 top executives from the United States, Germany, the United Kingdom, and France, only half of the executives believed that they were actually successful at identifying high potentials in their organizations. In many large companies, important people decisions are relegated to individuals untrained in proper assessment methodologies and lacking a clear definition of what the position requires. Thus, judgments are clouded by personal biases or political agendas. And the fallout can be disastrous as companies run the risk of promoting the wrong people into key roles or losing their best people as a result of bad hiring decisions. In other cases, hiring the wrong person can have life-long consequence because firing a person in some countries is not an option. Don't leave the identifying and hiring of international talent to HR. This may be a task managed among and split with the executive team, board of directors, or all of the above. The same personality and skill tests, scores, and expectations may not work for global talent, and recruiting as well as retaining may need a new approach that in most cases, the HR department is not equipped with or qualified to handle.

Creating an environment that nurtures talent is the key to recruiting and retaining the right people. Successful firms identify top performers early using systematic, rigorous assessment programs. These companies offer their best staff a wide range of learning opportunities, as well as an equitable and well-structured reward system. In China, money is important. Consequently, many top multinationals use higher, performance-driven compensation packages to attract talent. The top multinationals also give their Chinese senior management much media exposure. Capable Chinese executives enjoy receiving credit for their achievements in public, so this is a key strategy for keeping them on board.

Despite the strongly stated desire of many companies to attract international talent, candidates are often treated as national hires rather than people being asked to accept tremendous challenges in unfamiliar parts of the world. All too often, executives are hired and left to sink or swim. While working abroad is fraught with many challenges, companies that provide strong organizational training and support can help ease the transition.

Reducing Culture Shock

Culture shock is a very costly experience that can be avoided if people are properly trained and prepped. The recruitment and selection of expatriates requires an understanding of the unique demands placed upon those in international roles. Expatriate managers and employees are faced with numerous cross-cultural challenges, including language, customs, different work ethics, homesickness, family and spousal adjustment, and varied standards of living. Unfortunately, U.S. firms continue to use domestic criteria for the recruitment and selection for international jobs in spite of the multitude of obstacles expatriates face during international assignments. This shortsightedness often results in culture shock, which is a very expensive and misunderstood aspect of international business.

In short, it refers to the sudden realization that "I am unprepared for exposure to this alien environment." The experience often consists of three distinct phases. The first phase of excitement and enamoration refers to the period of time when differences between the old and new culture are seen in a romantic light and considered wonderful. For example, people who move to a new country might, at first, love the new foods, the pace of life, the cultural habits, the architecture, and other differences. Then, after a few days, weeks, or months, they hit the reality check phase, where the enjoyment of these differences is overridden by a longing for home. Some people will long for food the way it is prepared in their native country, the pace of life may seem too fast or slow, or they may find the local people's habits annoying or unpleasant, or simply miss their friends and "the familiar." Finally, they emerge into the acceptance phase. After a few days, weeks, or months, most people grow accustomed to the cultural differences, they develop new routines, and the new culture becomes the norm. Many expatriates face similar stages when returning home, which may require a different type of training that is most neglected.

Some people find it impossible to deal with culture shock. They give up trying to assimilate and return to their home countries. Research indicates that expatriate failure rates among U.S. companies due to culture shock range from 10 to 20 percent.

Many expatriates experience their first taste of culture shock on the job. To minimize shock, cultural induction courses should be offered to all overseas staff and should be conducted by qualified cultural trainers. Over several days, these programs emphasize the importance of an open-minded attitude in the foreign workplace. They also teach managers how to avoid putting up cultural barriers the first day on the job. Management styles are a constant source of stress and cultural discord among expatriates and their hosts. For instance, in American business settings, goals and objectives must be reached by the quickest and most efficient route, and the single-minded pursuit of profit is invariably the motivating force. In contrast, the French are suspicious of profit. They are much more driven by the notion of perfection and tend to think in terms of concepts.

Differences in management styles can also lead to lost productivity. For example, in Indonesia, China, Japan, and Latin America, subordinates expect to be given clear instructions and directed forcefully; otherwise they will sit back and do nothing. Managers in the United States, on the other hand, expect staff to take the initiative. Business methods such as brainstorming and teamwork, which may be carried out through a variety of management styles, are an integral part of the American management philosophy; however, these methods are appalling to Italians, Portuguese, and other cultures.

For a nation that has contributed so much to the world business culture and the free market system, American businesspeople are culturally challenged. As a result, we often create needless obstacles, many times due to a lack of knowledge of foreign social customs and languages. This ignorance can lead to international blunders and misunderstandings, which in turn waste time and money.

Learning about Other Cultures through Applied Training

Whether U.S.-based companies purposefully go global as part of their corporate strategy or suddenly awaken to the fact that they have a global workforce through M&A activity, they need a process for determining what training programs are needed and who should be trained. That means implementing an applied program of education, training, and personal development that enables one to learn and master the nuances of other cultures, leading to understanding and the ability to deal successfully with prospective business partners in many lands.

Successful adjustment to the many complex demands of an unfamiliar culture is a significant achievement and requires thorough preparation. Managers need effective training in the language and customs of their destination abroad. They need a regimen that helps them develop the skills needed to communicate effectively and to function purposefully in an otherwise alien environment. Such a regimen, referred to as cross-cultural or intercultural training, is best carried out prior to the departure of managers and before they are assigned to an overseas location. In addition to training managers, senior executives must also be trained to ensure that future business deals are not jeopardized.

It's important for any training to be centered on the individuals in terms of what they need to know and how to best present the knowledge and skills to be learned. What sets global training apart from other programs of corporate training is an increased focus on the background and culture of the host country.

Global training can be divided into three steps:

1. Developing and refining an awareness of existing cultural differences.
2. Increasing specific knowledge and understanding of a host country's culture and how their values may influence the training process.
3. Assessing, redesigning, and customizing training content based on the previous two steps.

The content in the training must incorporate cultural knowledge, openness, and empathy. It also has to focus on adaptive problem-solving skills for both managers and employees. These skills encompass a flexibility that enables redefining strategies and reinventing structures within the global organization. Remember, global awareness is not the exclusive domain of managers on expatriate assignments. A common company language at home is necessary for the discussion of international business opportunities. Therefore, training should not be limited to top-level or international marketing personnel, but should extend to those who design and manufacture products sold abroad.

U.S.-based companies eager to increase their competitiveness usually concentrate training on areas they consider to be areas of weakness. However, for most executives working worldwide, the fundamental reason for insufficient global training is that headquarters does not always believe such training is necessary. In terms of American companies, they tend to make false assumptions that the American way of business is the norm, both in the United States and abroad, and that a manager who is successful in New York or Los Angeles will also be successful in Tokyo, Shanghai, or Moscow. By contrast, companies in

Japan and the U.K. see global experience as integral to the employees' management development and advancement within the organization. Accordingly, in other countries, if managers want to reach top-level executive positions, they must have international experience. As such, companies in other countries are more discriminating in selecting their global managers.

If the cost of providing the requisite cross-cultural training for all employees seems steep, revisit your cost benefit analysis. The direct costs of lost opportunities are higher than ever before and must be factored into the analysis. These direct costs include not only the loss of business and failed ventures in the targeted country but also loss of reputation for the U.S. company. U.S. firms lose over $4 billion a year on failed foreign assignments and initiatives. These losses could be eliminated or reduced dramatically through proper cross-cultural training. Successful business interactions that result in profitable deals, manager productivity, cost-effective expatriation, and a smooth transition to the prospective country or region are the main benefits of investing in pre-departure cross-cultural training for the managers involved.

Growing Your Talent from Home

While finding inquisitive personalities and shaping corporate culture may seem like nebulous tasks, companies often have the most control when they take the time to build their leadership pipeline—when they construct a series of experiences to rapidly develop the firm's next leaders.

Royal Dutch Shell, based in The Hague, offers a successful model of leadership development, according to Michael Useem, a Wharton professor of management who works with Shell executives through the Shell/Wharton Group Business Leadership Program. Like many companies, Shell rotates high-potential managers through positions in various aspects of the enterprise, including overseas postings, so that "by time they hit 40 and want to enter senior management, they have in their mind's eye what it looks like to be in an oil field in Nigeria when the call comes that there's been an explosion and the local mayor wants to shut the operation down," says Useem.[6]

Moving among multiyear foreign assignments is "very much a part of Shell culture," adds Mathilde de Boer, who consults on leadership development for Shell Learning, a part of Royal Dutch Shell. Although employees are sometimes reluctant to constantly uproot, "with dual-career couples, it's more and more of a challenge," she notes. Of course, a willingness to travel and live overseas is a bottom-line requisite for advancement. "When you make a choice to develop yourself into a senior leadership role, you will be faced with a job that will be located somewhere else."[7]

The benefits of overseas experience are visible when executives get together for more formal leadership training, says de Boer: "You can see it in the way they learn. Because they have experienced so many different situations, they can quickly grasp new ways of doing things. They have had a mirror held up to their leadership styles."

Diversifying one's leadership style may be essential to running a large multinational, according to Wharton management professor Mauro Guillén:

> Your managers in different parts of the world may need different kinds of support. In Germany, for example, the CEO of a subsidiary will deal with a board comprised half of shareholders and half of workers. That's a very different set up. If you are the CEO of an American or Japanese firm in Germany, then you have to pick a leader who is comfortable with the situation, and then empower that person in a very different way than you might empower your top executive in, say, Brazil.[8]

But talk of developing long-term leadership capacity may seem irrelevant to high-growth multinationals that need international talent immediately. As Michael Useem found out from asking a group of Indian executives how they rated Indian leadership talent compared to U.S. and European talent:

> The essence of their answer was that it is good, but they primarily have people who have worked only domestically, in India. By contrast, they saw that in European firms, nearly everybody in middle to senior management had worked outside of their home countries.

Guillén agrees that European companies lead the way in giving executives international experience and notes that such rotations are less frequent in United States and Japanese companies. When companies find themselves squeezed for internationally experienced talent, they may face the choice of either losing an opportunity or making do with what they have. Notes Useem: "Sometimes you might find yourself saying, 'You're just going to have to figure it out when you get there.'"

Pearls of Wisdom

If U.S.-based companies are to flourish, their perspective needs to be global—not only in driving toward higher profits but in their operating principles Only then will they find a greater understanding of their foreign counterparts, which, through mutual interdependence, can then lead to higher profits. To attain a global perspective, many American businesspeople need to adapt their current operating principles to a more encompassing, more cosmopolitan viewpoint of business. Much remains to be done in both corporate and entrepreneurial America for this worldwide perspective to take hold, and much is at stake. The very success of the economy in the United States tomorrow depends on the ability of today's business leaders to change thinking patterns by developing a global mindset and strategies that bridge the widening gap of opportunities domestically and abroad. With the right leadership, and the right people in the right places, U.S. businesses can look at the global market and see opportunities, not obstacles.

With 95 percent of the world's consumers residing outside U.S. borders by 2020, it is clear that the future of the U.S. economy depends upon embracing a global strategy.[9] The ultimate success of global initiatives is, however, linked to effective global leadership. Businesses must attract and/or develop leaders with the skills necessary to succeed abroad. How does your leadership measure up? Does your organization think proactively and foresee emerging trends? Does it embrace corporate diversity? Does it balance profit and competition with sustainability and collaboration? It will need to be answering these questions by implementing sound strategies in order to succeed in the coming years.

Here is a list of key points to keep in mind from this chapter:

- Global business is essential for the economic future of companies, especially those in the United States.
- Effective global leadership is the key to an organization's long-term success.
- We face a shortage of globally oriented talent: leaders, managers, board members, etc.
- While cross-cultural experience is ideal, cross-industry experience and entrepreneurial prowess are good substitutes.
- Culture shock is an expensive yet avoidable mistake.
- Cultural training must be both individualized and corporate-wide.

Once the right people are in place and properly trained, it's time to inspect your organization and take a look at its culture as well as the external conditions that comprise its predispositions so you can evaluate and modify its market readiness.

Chapter 3

Improving Your Market Readiness through Effective Planning, Action, and Commitment

"When I started out in business, I spent a great deal of time researching every detail that might be pertinent to the deal I was interested in making. I still do the same today. People often comment on how quickly I operate, but the reason I can move quickly is that I've done the background work first, which no one usually sees. I prepare myself thoroughly, and then when it is time to move ahead, I am ready to sprint."

—*Donald Trump*

Recently, a successful U.S. company in the precision machine tool industry decided to expand into the global marketplace and selected Switzerland as its first international venture. Next, the company hired a local agent and assumed that sales would start flowing. The company's leaders understood it would take time to establish business in the new market and proceeded with patience. But after a year of no sales, they started asking questions: Is it poor representation by the local agent? Is it a marketing issue or a product issue?

In reality, the lack of success went even deeper. It was an irreparable problem that occurred the minute they chose Switzerland as the target market. Here's why . . .

Switzerland is the biggest competitor to the U.S. precision tool industry. Under no circumstances could any U.S. tool manufacturer successfully compete on Swiss turf—not on quality, not on price, and not on any other competitive advantage. The Swiss are very loyal to domestic brands and associate quality and perfection with Swiss-manufactured products. Bottom line, the company wasted its limited resources including time and money, damaged its international reputation, and was forced to return to step one in its attempt to enter the global marketplace. This blunder could easily have been avoided with a little due diligence.

What's at Stake in the Decision to Go Global?

In the not too distant future, U.S.-based companies will be placed into one of two categories: those that skilfully enter into the global marketplace and those that sheepishly retreat. A wait-and-see mind-set is nothing short of organizational suicide. On the other hand, a reaction-ary, ill-conceived global expansion is no improvement. That too spells disaster. What's needed, then, when faced with these two choices?

So far, we've discussed the importance of a mind-set overhaul fueled with 100 percent commitment. Now it's time to do some homework and conduct a market readiness assessment. None of this should be any surprise for entrepreneurs who have launched successful domestic busi-nesses. However, as Bill Gates reminds us, "success is a lousy teacher; it seduces smart people into thinking they can't lose." Consequently, many "smart" businesspeople approach global expansion as just that, an expansion of their existing business. This approach short-circuits the fundamental key to success aboard—a well-constructed strategy built from a solid foundation.

Consider Egypt's ancient pyramids. Mystery abounds in our under-standing of how these pyramids were once constructed. But one thing is certain: These pyramids, still standing after thousands of years, were built after meticulous planning. The crowning peaks were not con-structed until the placement of every stone at the base was calculated and carefully positioned. This is an important lesson for businesses that are planning global expansion. Too often, U.S. businesspeople want to start with the peak, leaping into foreign markets without first lay-ing the proper foundation and building the necessary relationships. Recklessly, they follow competitors, cheap labor, or abundant resources without truly understanding the target market. While these factors are important considerations, they are but pieces in the context of a much larger and more intricate puzzle.

Laying the proper foundation for global expansion requires accurate and actionable information that is interpreted and applied correctly. Interestingly, 95 percent of failures result from inaccurate or unreli-able information. Unlike decades past, the challenge is no longer a lack of information—it's too much information. Today, the real knack for dealing with information is sifting through the overwhelming abundance of it and harvesting what is applicable and significant to a unique set of circumstances. It requires knowing exactly what infor-mation is necessary, where to find it, and how to apply that informa-tion to a specific set of circumstances.

First Things First: Doing the Due Diligence

Occasionally, there are global business success stories that result from intuition, a sixth sense for good opportunities, luck, or any combination of these factors. However, most successes result from a brilliant strategy based on accurate information that is interpreted and applied flawlessly to a new market. Success depends on each execution and implementation step and how those steps are carried out in an ever-changing world. While many theories and strategies look great on paper, it's the ability to foresee change and adapt quickly that separates the failures from the successes. It starts with asking the right questions in order to collect reliable information to support decisions and move an organization forward. Next, it requires knowing where to search for that information, how to interpret it, and, finally, how to apply it in a proper and creative context—before it becomes obsolete.

International companies operate in an environment shaped by cultural, political, legal, economic, trade, monetary, governmental, and institutional forces. These forces are constantly evolving and shaping the environment for international business. As a result, what is relevant today could quite possibly be irrelevant by tomorrow, especially in some regions of the world. Still, the decisions we make today are really for tomorrow and understanding tomorrow is, therefore, essential to success. For example, which global markets will be emerging? A decade ago this question was easy to answer. Today, with the BRIC (Brazil, Russia, India, and China), the Next-11 (top 11 emerging new economies), and so many other up-and-coming regions around the globe, choosing the right market is much more complicated. So, without a crystal ball, how does a company determine where in the world to go? What information is required to make the right choices? What tools are available to help target the right global markets? Whom can you rely on to help make sure the correct decision is reached? What is the cost of not getting the information?

All these questions and more are answered accurately when analyzed against a backdrop of thorough due diligence. But understanding exactly what business intelligence is needed and how it will be evaluated is complex. Before proceeding, be sure to address these issues carefully and take action to:

- Identify your goals and objectives, and formulate a strategy to achieve them.
- Define the exact information you need to support your decision-making process.
- Prioritize what data are needed at the outset and what information can wait.
- Create a timeline with activities and an action plan for implementation.
- Understand the costs of getting the necessary data and weigh them against the costs of not obtaining this information.
- Define any budgetary constraints and how the future expansion will stay within those means.
- Develop a contingency plan and make sure you are prepared for other options—there is never only one way of doing things.
- Consider third parties such as research agencies with access to information to assist and closely manage the information points selected until they produce the agreed-upon deliverables.
- Analyze, validate, and integrate the output with your strategic corporate process.

Because the quantity of available information is overwhelming, it's critical to stay focused on actionable data.

Only Actionable Research
Leads to Action

Actionable insights come from actionable data, and actionable data come from asking the right questions and listening objectively. In general, performing actionable research has four critical steps:

1. Defining clear objectives
2. Designing the right questions
3. Utilizing the appropriate data-gathering methodology
4. Conducting research with the future in mind

It starts by asking the critical question: "What do we want to accomplish?" This is essentially asking yourself "What are the goals and objectives of my company?" The answers, of course, lead to subsequent questions that must be answered in order to proceed. The most actionable insights come from open-ended questions that give participants an opportunity to express opinions, views, and perceptions. Of course, it is experience that helps people know what questions to ask, and experts in the field can lead you in the right direction. Ignorance of a target market's culture, its belief system, and its values will prevent a person from knowing what important questions to ask. In addition to experience, asking the right questions requires clear objectives and a well-understood mission. Once the objective(s) are clearly identified, the questions flow naturally and will produce more actionable results.

For example, a company that is contemplating a new product for a new market may seek answers to the following questions:

- Who are the potential customers (demographics, income, marital status, employment, age, etc.)?
- What are their needs and motivations for purchase?
- Who makes the purchasing decision? Is loyalty to national brands an issue? (Remember the Swiss example from earlier in this chapter?)
- What features and options do they expect?
- What quality is expected?
- How much are customers willing to pay?
- Will customers want several versions with different features in different price ranges?
- How will potential consumers learn about the product?
- How often will they purchase it and when?

Such questions should be asked not only of senior management but also employees across the organization. It's critical to get feedback from any employee with close customer contact. In business-to-business research, seek input from current and former customers, vendors, and suppliers. Former customers can help identify potential problems that may be magnified when going across borders. If the goal is to expand into a second global market, make sure you fully understand how the product and your organization are viewed in the existing region. Identify what you do well so you can capitalize on this information, replicate it, and use it as your competitive advantage. On the other hand, if there are things not being done well, this can also be very useful information. This is what we call knowledge with a purpose—knowledge that can assess and help reduce a company's risks and exploit new opportunities more effectively.

For research to be valuable, it must consider the future by understanding trends and being flexible. Keep in mind that certain markets operate contrary to what you would expect, and they change rapidly. The decisions we make today, however, are really made for tomorrow. So always plan with tomorrow in mind. Ask the right questions, connect the dots, and really seek to understand so that the search for information answers specific questions. Then locate the actionable data that can guide decisions specific to those goals and objectives—what does the data suggest for your company, your resources, your vision, and your products? Still, market research can be very complicated and may require the assistance of experts who can translate the information into a successful strategy, execute critical decisions, and customize it to achieve specific corporate goals and plans. Remember, the purpose of the data is to provide a proper foundation for growth and to support an information-driven, evidence-based, decision-making process. That way, planning for expansion is based on knowledge, not just hopes and desires.

Getting Ready for a Market: The Six Pillar Foundation

While this process may seem tedious and cumbersome, it is far better (and more cost-effective!) than it is to go through it now, than the process of undoing costly mistakes later. To simplify the process, let's break market readiness analysis into six action steps. These may occur simultaneously or in a different sequence depending on the unique circumstances of your organization and target market. They are not necessarily in chronological order. Also, keep in mind that the process for assessing your product potential cannot be limited. Always assess into the future by reviewing your company as it is today against what it will look like in the future. This assessment is an integral part of growing in today's world/market economy and will continue to be in the future. See Figure 3.1.

Action Step 1: Internal Assessment

Before trying to proceed, onward and outward, dive deeply inward. Conduct an honest self-assessment with close examination of organizational

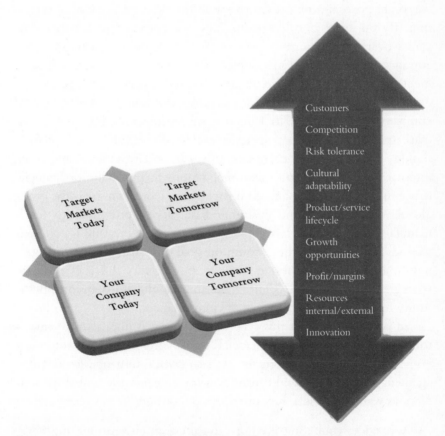

Figure 3.1   Is Growing Globally in Your Cards? A Strategic Approach
Copyright © 2010. All rights reserved to Mona Pearl, BeyondAStrategy, Inc.

commitment, budgetary constraints, human capital, international expertise, tolerance for risk, and global objectives. Take an inventory and figure out what you have; what you need; when, why, and how much it is going to cost. If the cost is prohibitive, assess the risk and know the cost of not getting the information. Also, reevaluate the company's current operations and organizational structure, mission, vision, and values to determine whether going global is really a desirable option. Even though a preponderance of evidence suggests that cross-border engagement is critical for the future success of U.S.-based businesses, expanding globally for the sake of going global is a recipe for disaster. It's far more important to seek out the right opportunity by allowing overall corporate goals and objectives to guide the decision for global expansion. By pursuing global opportunities that correlate with your company's overall strategic plan, economic reality, and world trends, your entrance into the global marketplace will reflect a long-term commitment that is more likely to generate value and sustain future success.

The overall objective of this internal assessment is to evaluate your company's preparedness to launch a successful entry into the global marketplace and sustain that activity. The end result of this analysis should include a list of corporate strengths and weaknesses regarding international business and recommendations for resolving deficiencies that could hinder achieving company goals. Common goals for going global include expanding customer base, access/proximity to lower manufacturing costs or less expensive services, or creating a competitive advantage. While these common goals are shared by many businesses, accomplishing these goals may require very different planning strategies. The goal is to identify the unique global expansion opportunity for your firm's unique set of circumstances.

In order to conduct this type of analysis, it is important to inventory and gather relevant financial information, tangible resources, relevant skills, and competencies. It's also critical to gauge senior management commitment and motivation for entering the global marketplace as well as skill sets. Key questions to consider in this phase are:

- What does your company hope to gain from international business?
- Is international business expansion consistent with other company goals?

- How will the international component of operations be integrated into the overall operation?
- What demands on resources (such as management, personnel, finance, production, and marketing capacity) will be put on companies that operate in the global marketplace?
- How will these added demands be met?

Today's decentralization and technological advances have leveled the global playing field, allowing plenty of room for both small and middle-market entrants. In fact, the agility of small to middle-market corporations challenges their less nimble, larger competitors in the race for international market share. In the dynamic global marketplace, corporate size is not an indicator of success. It is in the planning, flexibility, and execution through which the smallest companies can still achieve exponential growth and gain access to amazing opportunities.

Action Step 2: Product Assessment

Another inward inspection should focus on the suitability of existing products and services for foreign markets. Does your company's current product or products appeal to any particular global region? Or has a need been identified that could be met through innovation and adaptation of an existing product(s)? Each product must be scrutinized based on the social norms of the markets under consideration, not just for functionality. Analyze a product's appropriateness for a specific market and remember to consider packaging, branding, pricing, and after-sales servicing. In terms of suitability, a bike designed for U.S. or European roads will not suffice in most emerging countries given the different climate and terrain. If the product is an appliance, average home size in the target market must be considered. Appliances such as refrigerators and stoves designed for U.S. homes will not appeal to those in Japan, where the average home size is significantly smaller, or in Africa where electricity is scarce. If modifications are necessary, how much will these changes cost measured against ROI and market potential? Some products will never meet the needs, desires, and customs of certain world markets. Never assume a product that performs well in, say, the United States will catch on in other markets, or that success in China will translate to success in Latin America.

When choosing a product to adapt, consider products that cater to a universal need, like health care, energy, environmental compliance, etc. Alternatively, look for a product or service that address a need not well served in a particular foreign market, like investment management or home mortgages. Another option is to look for a new or emergent need abroad. For example, natural disasters like earthquakes and tsunamis create an urgent need for portable housing. Diseases such as AIDS and malaria in Africa create a need for pharmaceuticals, medical supplies, and special apparatus like mosquito nets.

The overall objective of this step is to conduct a systematic assessment of a product or service's suitability for international customers, assess where in the world your next customer base is and calculate the degree of fit between the product or service and these future customers' needs. The outcome of this assessment should include a list of factors that may hinder a product's market potential in each target market. It should also include recommendations for product adaptations that may be required for an initial market entry.

To assess the suitability of a product for a particular market, consider the following issues:

- Target customer characteristics such as culture, loyalty, and needs
- Government regulations like environmental issues
- Expectations of intermediaries like distributors
- Characteristics of the competitors' offerings

Action Step 3: Validate Potential Markets

With over 200 countries to examine for global expansion opportunities and a number of "hot" markets and emerging economies that have unprecedented promise, the first questions to answer are: Where will your product or service find its highest demand? Where will the next customer base come from? Do you know your current customer base? How can this information help you define and refine your value proposition across borders?

Finding the answer to these questions requires a leadership team to step back and take a panoramic view of all potential markets. Then investigate the most promising markets with a more detailed and focused emphasis on important criteria such as infrastructure, standard of living, economic/political stability, and general attitude toward foreign investment. Make use of available information that is relevant to your business to help guide the decision-making process regarding which markets will yield the greatest demand and warrant further consideration.

Embrace this process as a cultural learning experience and understand that billions of consumers are waiting for products designed by people who understand the way they live. In terms of U.S.-based companies, the goal should not be to change the way other countries' consumers live and force American ideals into their way of life. Strategies like that have lead to many failures. Rather, the goal is to offer products and services that meet consumers of different regions around the world exactly where they are today and where they will most likely be tomorrow.

Consider China. The fact that China has billions of people may look promising to a manufacturer of widgets. However, population size means nothing if that population cannot afford your product. Even if segments of the population could afford it, what would they be willing to pay for it? Is the product designed to fit their needs and desires? In a best-case scenario, let's assume a segment of the population wants the product, can afford the product, and will pay for the product. Now, is there a distribution channel for the product to reach the people? Choosing the right target market is complex and the questions that must be answered will not be answered correctly until the consumer and the marketplace are fully understood.

The overall objective of this step is to scan the global marketplace and reduce the number of countries that warrant in-depth investigation as potential target markets. It is also designed to help your company look and analyze opportunities that were not thought of beforehand, and may provide better avenues for growth. It also helps laser focus on your offering and realize the value proposition you bring to the market(s). Ideally, the playing field will be reduced to five or six of the highest-potential country markets. The criteria that must be examined includes market size, growth rate, market intensity (buying power in terms of income level), consumption capacity (size and growth rate of the country's middle class), the country's receptivity to imports, infrastructure for doing business, economic freedom, and political risk. The catch is that these factors must be understood not only in terms of today but also in terms of future trends. More specifically, it's important to exercise caution and understand the following:

1. *Cultural similarity with the target market.* Some businesses target countries that appear "physically" similar in terms of language and culture. Remember the iceberg example from earlier in the book? On the surface, some countries and regions appear very similar when in fact they are worlds apart in terms of how they use a product, how they perceive value, loyalty to domestic brands, and other issues. Don't assume people who speak the same language, salute the same flag, and look similar will mirror each other's buying habits and interest in your product.

2. *Understand the industry locally.* Understand the value from the perspective of the buyer, and some industries are so steeped in tradition that value looks very different from a U.S. viewpoint. For example, look at agriculture. Countries where farmers earn a good income and own abundant land may still reject technologically advanced farming equipment geared toward increasing efficiency. Unlike the U.S. mind-set, it's not all about making more money and improving efficiency. There are other considerations besides financial that weigh more heavily in the decision-making process. For example, in some countries, for myriad reasons, there is insufficient demand for increased production. In situations like this, even the best product at the right price with extensive post-sale service will not be enough to penetrate that market.

3. *Targeting a region (not just one country) may make more sense.* From a long-term planning perspective, it often makes sense to target a region with the most promise rather than a specific country: The European Union, Latin America, the Middle East, Northern Africa, or Asia. The next step would be to plan a logical sequence of markets within that region to exploit. This establishes a more cohesive long-term strategy that maximizes the investment of resources.

   Choosing the "best" country within that region to begin the expansion effort would look at criteria such as cost and availability of commercial infrastructure, tax rates and wages, access to high-level skills, and capital markets. Risk factors that must be calculated include regulatory, financial, political, and cultural barriers and the legal environment for intellectual-property protection. But once a business is on the ground in one country, it will be easier to chart a course for further expansion in the region.

Consider an American company whose cosmetic products appeal to the African American population. The initial panoramic view of all potential markets may point to several regions for equal consideration— Latin and South America, the Middle East, or areas in Africa. While each of these regions would make sense, thorough due diligence will reveal the actionable data necessary to make the best selection. Data that, when interpreted correctly, will answer strategic questions, allow for the formulation of various simulations and the comparison of those simulations as different scenarios are presented. Some fundamental questions that require actionable data include:

- What is the existing competitive landscape for my product/service? Loyalty to national brands is a monumental obstacle in some markets and in other markets consumers are just slow to switch brands.
- What is the buying power in the market, or markets, and what are the trends?
- Should the market entry plan incorporate the full line of potential products?
- If not, which product mix should be considered? What price points?
- What options are available for a potential joint venture with a local company? Or, would M&A be the better alternative to penetrate these markets?
- Should you enter the market as a direct sale? Or maybe manufacture locally?
- What is the optimal distribution channel, and is it economically feasible?

Understand, however, that unlike North America, other regions of the world are not homogeneous populations of people. For example, each Latin American country is unique in terms of language, culture, tradition, government, legal system, and business etiquette. While many countries share certain commonalties such as a relaxed approach toward time and the need for relationship building before deal making, there are important differences among different regions in the same country. Sometimes these differences may appear subtle to an outsider, but awareness of the nuances is critical to success.

A common stumbling block for U.S.-based businesses going abroad has to do with understating the local competitive environment and domestic brand loyalty. Even if your product is better and cheaper, it may not be the product of choice. Remember how reluctant Americans were to buying "Japanese" cars years ago, and today U.S. consumers are equally sensitive about buying products made in China. In fact, today many American consumers are willing to pay more for less functionality if the product was made in the United States.

In general, it's critical to evaluate target markets on three broad dimensions:

- *Financial structure.* Consider cost of labor, infrastructure costs (for electricity and telecom systems), distance from other markets, distance to the customer, tax and transfer issues, and other regulatory costs.
- *People skills and availability.* Evaluate the supplier's experience and skills, labor force availability, education and linguistic proficiency, and employee attrition rates.
- *Business environment.* Assess economic and political aspects of the country, commercial infrastructure, cultural adaptability, ethics, and security of intellectual property.

There are several resources to utilize when comparing region against regional and country against country. One important resource to consult is the Ease of Doing Business Index (EODB). The EODB index provides a quantitative measure of regulations for starting a business, dealing with construction permits, employing workers, registering property, getting credit, protecting investors, paying taxes, trading across borders, enforcing contracts, and closing business. A fundamental premise of EODB is that economic activity requires rules—rules that establish and clarify property rights, reduce the costs of resolving disputes, increase the predictability of economic interactions, and provide contractual partners with core protections against abuse. With one glance, EODB makes it possible to evaluate and compare every possible country in the world in a consistent manner.[1]

Another resource is called the Opacity Index. This index measures five components that expose "negative social capital"—that is, corruption, legal system inadequacies, economic enforcement policies, accounting standards and corporate governance, and regulation. A high score on this index indicates higher levels of opacity, which translates to a hidden tax.[2] It's also important to quantify the availability of government incentives such as availability of tax holidays, subsidized training costs, grants, or low-interest loans. These factors should be carefully weighed when looking at the appeal of one potential location over another. Of course, there are many more indexes available;[3] however, the real value comes when the data is interpreted correctly and then applied appropriately in terms of achieving goals. The right application of this information should be used to answer specific questions such as: Is this market a good fit for your company? And how do you incorporate it into your overall strategic plan?

Action Step 4: Estimate/Forecast Market Demand

Up to this point the analysis has focused more on the "soft" issues of going global. Now it's time to crunch the numbers. After identifying the global markets with greatest potential, calculate market demand by estimating the size of industry-wide sales within each target country. The outcome should be at least a two- or three-year forecast of industry sales for each target market. The official term is "industry market potential," which is different from "company sales potential." Industry market potential looks at the likely sales that can be expected by all firms in a particular industry during a specific time period. Company sales potential is simply the share of industry sales your firm expects during a specific period. Businesses should forecast sales at least three years into the future for both industry market potential and company sales potential.

There are additional indicators of industry market potential, and they include the following:

- Market size, growth rate, trends in the specific industry, or innovative ways to introduce a product/service to different market niches

- Tariff and nontariff trade barriers to enter the market
- Standards and regulations that affect the industry and consumer usage
- Availability and sophistication of local distribution channels
- Unique customer requirements and preferences

Ultimately, the demand for a specific product will vary greatly from one region to another for myriad different reasons. The demand for certain products will differ significantly due to climate, culture, beliefs, and traditions. For example, the demand for cameras correlates with the average number of sunny days in a typical year. The demand for laboratory equipment varies with the local governments' position and ability to fund healthcare expenditures as well as educational and research institutions. For HVAC equipment, demand varies depending on the number of institutional buyers, such as restaurants and hotels, as well as the infrastructure of the country to support such products.

Some practical methods for estimating industry market potential are as follows:

1. *Consider simple trend analyses.* This approach represents a deeper understanding of the potential market(s), not only in the present but how will current economic, cultural, geopolitical, and other indicators affect future potential and create demand.
2. *Monitor key industry-specific indicators.* Is the industry expanding, contracting, innovating, or looking for new products? Also, look at the top-side measures like GDP and labor. For example, Caterpillar (the world's leading manufacturer of construction and mining equipment, diesel and natural gas engines, industrial gas turbines, and diesel electric locomotives) examines all announced construction projects, building permits, growth rate of households, and infrastructure development when evaluating foreign markets.
3. *Keep an eye on key competitors.* Do not limit the field of competition to businesses selling exactly what you offer. Look at perceived competition that accounts for interchangeable products and services. For example, if Caterpillar is considering Chile as a potential market, it first investigates the current involvement in Chile of its number-one competitor, the Japanese firm Komatsu. But the real issue is to be able to interpret these findings and identify all

potential competitors and how these competitors will affect the go-to-market strategy.

4. *Follow key customers.* Automotive suppliers can anticipate where their services will be needed next by monitoring the international expansion of their customers such as Honda or Mercedes-Benz.

5. *Tap into supplier networks.* Firms can gain valuable leads from current suppliers by inquiring with them about competitor activities.

6. *Attend international trade fairs.* Industry trade fairs and exhibitions are excellent venues for obtaining valuable market information.

7. *Look at best market reports for insights and trend.* Identify the top 10 country markets for specific industry sectors.

8. *Read and study country commercial guides.* Analyze economic and commercial environments of countries.

Action Step 5: Search for Partners

Local business partners contribute greatly to the success of any global expansion effort. These partners may include distributors, suppliers, joint ventures, investors, financiers, cultural experts, international trade experts, intellectual property lawyers, government officials, accountants, logistics specialists, customs brokers, or others. For many reasons, choosing the right partners is absolutely critical. For example, a U.S.-based commercial real estate company in Latin America had its properties confiscated by the local government, prohibiting them from taking any capital out of the country. These situations are not unusual in many emerging markets. How they play out, however, varies greatly depending on the circumstances. Trusted local advisors can help mitigate the damages or avoid such problems entirely.

After the right targets and partners are selected, learning to work collaboratively with these partners is the next key to success. First, repeat after me, "There are other ways of doing business that work equally well as those practices of the United States." Too often, American businesspeople frustrate themselves and their foreign business partners by insisting that things be done according to U.S. customs. While issues that relate to Sarbanes-Oxley legislation and other U.S. laws must be complied with, there is no requirement that business proceedings be carried out according to U.S. customs. Instead, use these opportunities to learn how business is conducted in your target market. Open your mind to new ways of conducting business and learn to respect local practices. Not everything can be resolved with legal action, and even if you win, you cannot always enforce the law.

Oftentimes this mind-set adjustment is best accomplished with an understanding of that region's religion, political system, and history. In order to work well with a business person for South East Asia, for example, you must develop an in-depth appreciation of East Asian philosophies and the personal and business traits deriving from their ancient belief system. Rest assured that they would do the same regarding your culture in order to better understand you. These shifts in mind-set offer new ways of thinking about old problems that can result in better solutions. At a minimum, openness to new ways of conducting business will improve understanding, dispel preconceptions, promote greater awareness of the foreign business environment, and foster closer, more cooperative relationships.

The objective of this step is to decide on the type of foreign business partner needed, clarify partner qualifications, and plan a mode of entry. The outcome should be an understanding of the most suitable types of foreign business partners, a list of attributes desired of these foreign business partners, and a determination of value-added activities foreign business partner can contribute. Manufacturing and marketing expertise in the industry, commitment to the international venture, access to distribution channels in the market, financial strength, quality of staff, technical expertise, and infrastructure and facilities are just some of the important criteria to seek out.

In addition, when partnering with a foreign company, some basic qualifications to consider must include the following:

- The company should be financially sound and resourceful.
- It should have competent management, as well as qualified technical and sales staff.
- It should be willing and able to invest in and grow the business.
- It should have strong industry knowledge and increase your access to distribution channels and end-users.
- It should be well-known in the marketplace and well-connected with local government.
- It should have a good reputation and the ability to execute strategies, as well as be committed and loyal.

This all may sound easy and seem like common sense, but these features and how they translate in a different cultural, financial, and political environment are crucial. These types of questions are not always as transparent to American businesspeople as to others in the world, and these factors need to be "translated" when looking to partner with a local business reality.

Action Step 6: Diversification, Market Potential, and Reality

Again, company-specific sales potential is an estimate of the share of annual industry sales that the firm expects to generate in a particular target market during a given time period. In this step, the objective is to estimate with the highest degree of certainty possible the likely share of total industry sales your company can achieve. It's important to formulate this analysis for every possible target market and for each possible mode of entry: import/export, M&A, franchise, joint venture, etc. The formulation should forecast results for a three- to five-year time period. Also, be aware of what can go wrong and always have a contingency plan.

The criteria necessary to formulate the estimated sales potential require highly refined information about the target markets that is retrieved from a reliable source. The old adage "garbage in, garbage out" should be a constant reminder of how important it is to verify information and make sure it's both accurate and timely. The end result should be a projection of your firm's revenues and expenses for three to five years into the future from the international business activities. Such projections are challenging enough in domestic activities taking place in a relatively stable economic environment like the United States or Canada. When going abroad, especially into emerging economies, these estimates are further complicated by evolving government regulations and costs of doing business that can fluctuate greatly over the course of just one year.

At a minimum, it's important to explore, understand, and quantify the effect of these factors:

- *Partner capabilities.* The competencies and resources of foreign partners will determine how quickly the firm can enter and generate sales in the target market. This is why developing the right relationships is so important.

- *Access to distribution channels.* The ability to establish superior channel intermediaries and distribution infrastructure will impact sales potential.
- *Intensity of the competitive environment.* Local or third-country competitors are likely to intensify their own marketing efforts when confronted by new entrants. Also, know whether your competition is well connected politically and how this may play into your plans. Such leverage could greatly increase the difficulty you will experience when penetrating a new market.
- *Human and financial resources.* Such resources are a major factor in determining the proficiency and speed with which success can be achieved.
- *Execution timetable.* What is the right strategy for your company as well as for the target market? What would be the most effective tactics for a smooth roll-up? How do you determine your best chances for success? Gradual entry gives the firm time to develop and leverage appropriate resources and strategies, but may yield some advantages to competitors in getting established in the market. Rapid entry may allow the firm to surpass competitors and obtain first-mover advantages, but it can tax the firm's resources and capabilities.
- *Risk tolerance vs. risk aversion of the management team/board of directors and other stakeholders.* Management's understanding as well as its tolerance for risk and a company's ability to meet the financial strain of going global will impact decisions and results.
- *Reputation.* A firm can succeed faster in the market if target customers are already familiar with its brand name and reputation, or you choose a partner that can complement your product/service with its reputation.

Some practical approaches to estimating company sales potential can include surveying customers, suppliers, vendors, or even engaging in a "mystery shopping" study by a third party. The firm can survey a sample of customers and distributors to identify the size of a potential market. Also, firms can engage in trade audits. Managers visit retail outlets and question channel members about relative price levels of competitors' offerings and perceptions of competitor strength. The trade audit can indicate opportunities for new modes of distribution, identify types of alternative outlets, and provide insights into relative competitive strength.

To conduct a competitor assessment, your firm can benchmark itself against principal competitor(s) in the market and estimate the amount of sales it can realistically attract away from these local competitors. Which rival firms will have to be outperformed? Don't let size scare you. Even in regions of the world dominated by large firms, research can reveal market segments that are underserved or ignored altogether by large dominant firms. In fact, the larger the company is, the less nimble it is to react to a smaller firm's entering the local marketplace. Another option is to seek estimates from local partners such as distributors, franchisees, or licensees already experienced in the market. Some companies may choose to engage in limited efforts to "test the waters" of a foreign market. If designed, managed, and executed properly, these test markets can help gauge long-term sales potential while also allowing you to gain a better understanding of the market.

This method of analogy also allows to draw on known statistics from one country to gain insights into the same phenomenon for a similar country. For example, knowing the total consumption of citrus drinks in India then, assuming that citrus drink consumption patterns do not vary much in the neighboring Pakistan, a rough estimate of Pakistan's consumption can be made with an adjustment for the difference in population. Or if your experience is that 100 bottles of antibiotics are sold in a country with 10 physicians per 1,000 people, then it can be extrapolated that the same ratio (100 bottles per 10 physicians for every 1,000 people) will apply in a similar country.

From Findings to Execution

Market assessment is just one part of a much larger strategy that serves as a basis for decision making. It begins with determining research goals and extends to the interpretation of findings and, finally, the execution of the right actions. When selecting a research firm, recognize that some firms specialize in particular industries, which can be an advantage. On the other hand, specialization can limit their

perspective and hamper creativity. While market research firms are positioned to assist with research design and administration, they are not
qualified to make strategic inference.

Due diligence is just one small piece of an intricate puzzle.
Strategic planning and decision making require a management-level
view coupled with a panoramic view of the operations and global
markets. Experts in the field of international strategies and business
development have the experience and perspective necessary to reveal
innovative solutions. They can help companies with the entire strategic process, from goal-setting and research design to interpretation of
results and execution of actions. A blending of strategy and research,
vision and practice, and ideas and execution is the best way to avoid
the common mistakes made in market research. In the end, it is the
strategic application of the research conducted that will make the difference between success and failure.

Successful businesses strive to know every insight possible about
their target markets. The most successful companies rely extensively on
market assessments and have learned to use the information derived to
make strategic decisions and execute those decisions flawlessly. Market
assessments have become increasingly important with the emergence
of so many new markets from the staple economies of Canada and
Mexico to the BRIC countries to the Next-11 emerging economies.
Making the right market choice starts with a well-constructed market
readiness assessment. No shortcuts, no assumptions, and no excuses.
It is always better to invest in planning than to live with the consequences of failure.

Pearls of Wisdom

Whether the goal is domestic expansion or international expansion,
the recipe for success is identical: decisions based on accurate, reliable,
and relevant information that are interpreted correctly and applied
flawlessly with consideration of the goals, vision, and mission of your
organization. From an international perspective, the real challenges
are interpreting information and applying it correctly because, many
times, businesspeople not yet engaged in the global marketplace do not

understand its context. Every country, every region, and every market is unique. It just takes an investment of time to gain the requisite experience.

In the long run, the time invested in performing a market readiness assessment will save your company from negative consequences of an international deal gone awry.

Here is a list of key points to keep in mind from this chapter:

- The foundation for a successful expansion is built on proper due diligence and a well-constructed market assessment. Actionable insights come from actionable data and actionable data is a result of knowing what you are looking for and asking the right questions.
- Understanding any market takes time, but the assessment time is an investment that will pay dividends. Does your product/service have the potential to appeal to a foreign market? Which ones? Why? How? What region of the world is a good fit for your product and company's goals?
- The market readiness assessment starts with an honest self-assessment of your organization, and it may require fine-tuning and adjustment or change management to handle new initiatives.
- Evaluate, side-by-side, multiple scenarios of possible target markets and modes of market entry as well as the potential demands to justify the costs of expansion.
- Choose the right international partners to help expedite your market entry success in other countries as well as to make it sustainable in your long-term success and not only as a touch-and-go approach.

And feel free to refer to these easily accessible resources for even more information:

- Department of Commerce
- U.S. Commercial Service—Export Assistance Centers
- Trade development offices of foreign governments
- Export-Import Bank of the United States—financing
- General Internet searches
- TradeNet.com
- International expansion experts

After assessing your company's capabilities, identifying the gaps that exist, and determining what resources need to be added, it's time to develop your competitive advantage. Chapter 4 focuses on what you can do to create products and services in a manner that allows you to truly connect with new customers and outperform your competitors.

Chapter 4

Gaining Competitive Advantage

A Little Difference Makes All the Difference

"The most meaningful way to differentiate your company from your competitors, the best way to put distance between you and the crowd is to do an outstanding job with information. How you gather, manage and use information will determine whether you win or lose."

—*Bill Gates*

E ven before the term sustainability was a way of life, the Centroflora Group, a manufacturer of botanical and fruit extracts, was on the scene. Since 1957, it has built its organization on cutting-edge ideas and innovative principles that challenge existing industry processes. This has given Centroflora an impenetrable competitive advantage.

Its vision has been to develop the best sustainable biodiversity products through science and technology by developing partnerships and promoting a better world to employees, clients, suppliers, shareholders, and local communities. To that end, Centroflora introduced new concepts such as a corporate code of conduct, social and environmental responsibility, human appreciation, and collaborative participation.

One program created by Centroflora Group integrates end consumers with the rural communities and small farmers. The program operates at a worldwide level, reaching thousands of consumers who purchase nontoxic and effective natural products, where production is safe for the environment, delivering a better quality of life to all. "The goal of our program is to develop a quality and reliable supply network while promoting sustainable agricultural and harvesting practices, improving incomes and social and economic well-being, as well as providing a model for vertical integration and transparency for our customers," explains Hans Jorg Blaich and Raquel Silveira Capaz, who are team members of the Botanical and Sustainability Department at Centroflora Group. Today, Centroflora is the leader in the production and development of standard plant extracts for the drugs, cosmetics, and food industries in South America.

Three Key Strategies: Distinguishing Your Company through Competitive Advantage

By definition, a competitive advantage refers to the manner in which a company distinguishes itself to gain market share and establish both a niche and a customer base. A competitive advantage is achieved when a business markets a product or service in a manner that allows it to truly connect with customers and outperform its competitors. Without a competitive advantage, businesses struggle to gain traction, and they often resort to selling their products or services based solely on price. This approach ultimately leads to slashing costs and other non–value-added measures.

Conversely, by identifying a particular attribute that could appeal specifically to a new market and then developing a strategic plan to promote that attribute, a company can gain a competitive advantage. Highlighting product differentiation, developing corporate recognition programs, and creating brand awareness are several methods that are tied directly to competitive advantages resulting in ongoing profitability. Fortunately, for globally minded U.S.-based businesses, competitive advantages are unlimited and waiting to be discovered.

No discussion on strategy is complete without mentioning Professor Michael Porter's pioneering work *Competitive Advantage: Creating and Sustaining Superior Performance*. In the 1980s, Porter proposed three generic strategies as uniquely different approaches for a business to achieve competitive advantage. These are cost leadership, differentiation, and focus. While each of these strategies has to be defined in terms of the industry context and the competitive forces that operate therein, each fulfills a core purpose. *Cost leadership* requires a firm to be the lowest-cost producer for a given level of quality. The *differentiation* strategy requires a product or service to have certain unique attributes that the competitors' products lack. The *focus* strategy concentrates on a narrow market segment and, within that, achieves competitive superiority through either cost leadership or differentiation. While Porter's approaches were not uniquely designed for today's global marketplace, they are timeless, borderless, and still very relevant today.

As with any generic strategy, the supportive assumptions tend to be simplistic. Cost leadership is considered to be an internally focused strategic approach where the drivers are internal process efficiencies, productivity improvements, and cost-competitiveness in product development and manufacturing. On the other hand, the differentiation strategy is viewed as being externally focused in terms of identifying what provides differentiation in the marketplace. The arguments for focus are similar; internal or external as the case may be. Porter cautions firms against the temptation to follow all three strategies simultaneously. The reality, however, is that in today's world, which is three decades more mature and more competitive than the 1980s (when Porter first propounded his landmark theories of competitive strategy), the drivers of strategy have converged.

Cost Leadership: Being the Low-Cost Provider at a Given Quality

Competing based on price is more than a strategy. It is a corporate philosophy—a philosophy that guides every decision in the effort of achieving and maintaining this competitive advantage. Being the lowest-cost provider relative to the competition requires an organization to be constantly searching for new ways to drive costs down year after year. Remember, low-cost leadership means low overall costs, not just low manufacturing or production costs. For this reason, low-cost leaders tend to have unique characteristics. They have:

- A highly cost-conscious organizational culture
- Pretty basic facilities
- Limited rewards for both employees and executives
- Focus on lean and mean
- An intensive screening of budget requests, which sometimes leads to paralysis by analysis, not to mention inability to prioritize and make a distinction between what's really important and what should be a minor issue
- Employee participation in all cost-control efforts, which creates bureaucracy, kills motivation, and diminishes any entrepreneurial spirit

Achieving low-cost leadership can be accomplished by boosting efficiency and controlling costs along the entire value chain by out-managing rivals regarding both structural cost drivers and execution cost drivers. Structural cost drivers include gaining economies of scale, discovering shared opportunities with other business units, comparing benefits of vertical integration versus outsourcing, and taking advantage of location variables. Execution cost drivers include things like increasing capacity utilization, capitalizing on timing considerations associated with first-mover advantages and disadvantages, and always considering the expense impact of strategic choices and operating decisions. Whether structural or execution in nature, the approach must be entrepreneurially creative and always one step ahead of any competitor.

Consider the following examples of methods to drive down costs along the value chain:

- Simplify product design
- Offer basic, no-frills product/service
- Reengineer core business processes
- Shift to a simpler, less capital-intensive, or more streamlined technological process
- Use direct-to-end user sales and marketing approaches
- Relocate facilities closer to suppliers or customers
- Pursue more vertical integration relative to rivals
- Focus on limited product/service to meet special needs of target segment

As the low-cost leader, you effectively create a significant barrier to entry against new competition. This strategy also offers a position of strength in terms of both supplier and buyer relationships. A low-cost-leader strategy typically works best when the product is a readily available commodity-based item and price competition among rivals is the dominant competitive force. It works especially well when there are relatively few ways to achieve product differentiation that yield actual value to the customer.

The low-cost-provider strategy is not without risk. Often, it is a temporary strategy that works only for so long and must be complemented by other creative measures to maintain a leadership position. For example, Japan was once the low-cost leader but developed into a country known for high quality. China, a long-standing low-cost leader, is being under-priced by new emerging markets and is carefully reinventing itself.

In a rapidly changing world, there is always the potential for a technical breakthrough that provides cost reduction options for rivals that negates the efficiencies you've worked so hard to gain. Once competitors discover an easy or inexpensive way to imitate low-cost methods, your advantage is at risk. Another common risk is that, over time, low-cost providers become so fixated on cost reduction that they fail to respond to market conditions such as increased buyer desires for added quality or service features, new developments in related products, or declining buyer sensitivity to price.

Differentiation: Having What Your Competitors Lack

Some companies attempt to build loyalty by differentiating their products from the competition. Successful differentiation allows a company to command a premium price, increase unit sales, and build brand loyalty. The goal is to incorporate differentiating features that cause buyers to prefer one company's product/service over a rival's and to find ways to differentiate and create value for buyers that are not easily copied. The opportunities to create differentiation are limitless and depend on the target audience, the market, and the competitive landscape. In general, businesses can create differentiation through:

- Product/service research and development
- Production process
- Distribution
- Marketing
- Customer service

When pursuing these avenues, the goal is to create specific differentiation opportunities such as new product attributes that improve product performance, new features that lower the customers' costs in using that product, or features that enhance buyer satisfaction in non-economic ways such as "satisfaction guaranteed." The approaches to differentiation are unlimited. For example, the following corporations are among those that have successfully implemented differentiation strategies in a number of areas:

- Superior service: Federal Express
- Spare parts availability: Caterpillar

- More for your money: Walmart
- Engineering design and performance: Mercedes
- Prestige: for the discriminating taste: Rolex, Mont Blanc
- Quality: at the same time as being price sensitive: Honda
- Top-of-the-line image: Escada, Chanel
- Technological leadership: 3M Corporation
- Unconditional satisfaction: L.L. Bean

When companies use a differentiation strategy, it helps buyers develop loyalty to their brand, and this loyalty acts as a barrier to entry for new rivals. This strategy also positions a business to better fend off threats of substitutes or imitations based on the customers' attachment to these unique attributes. It also mitigates the bargaining power of large buyers since other products are less attractive. To reap these rewards, however, it's important for businesses to pursue the right kind of differentiation, which means it must be difficult to imitate and offer a sustainable advantage. The most effective differentiation strategies are based on technical superiority, overall quality, product support/services, and perceived value.

Focus: Satisfying a Narrow Market through Cost Leadership and Differentiation

Before embarking on a focus strategy, it is important to understand the targeted market segment and make sure it meets certain criteria. Know your target market. First, make sure it is large enough to be profitable and offer good growth potential. Second, think twice about choosing a market that is critical to the success of a major competitor. If you still decide to pursue it, be prepared for competitive warfare. Third, make sure you have the resources and ability to serve the selected market in a superior manner. For example, some companies mistakenly believe that regions such as Latin America, Asia, or the Middle East are homogenous markets where consumers across these large regions share the same wants and desires. But, as stated previously, the fact is that each market in these large regions has different characteristics and different needs and may require a completely different strategy.

A focus strategy works best when the industry has fast-growing segments that are big enough to be profitable but small enough to remain under the radar screen of large rivals. When executed properly, a focus strategy is very defensible because meeting the specialized needs of this segment acts as a barrier to entry against new competition. Mastery of this approach demands that the business offer unparalleled focus and superior service to this market segment in order to generate the necessary customer goodwill to ward off future rivals. The risks of a focus strategy include the possibility that broad-line competitors may discover effective ways to outmatch your ability to meet the target market's needs. Or the buyers' preferences shift toward product attributes available from mass-market competitors. Another risk is that this segment may become so appealing that it attracts aggressive rivals.

Combining Strategies

The most powerful competitive approach a company can pursue is striving relentlessly to become a lower and lower-cost producer of a higher and higher-caliber product. Here, the long-term intention is to become the industry's absolute lowest-cost producer and, simultaneously, the producer of the industry's overall best product. This approach combines a strategic emphasis on low cost with a strategic emphasis on differentiation, and the result is an upscale product at a lower cost that gives customers more value for the money and creates superior value by meeting or exceeding buyer expectations on product attributes. All of this must be accomplished while beating consumer price expectations.

The goal is to be the low-cost producer of a product with good to excellent product attributes, and then use cost advantage to underprice comparable brands. In order to be successful, it is important to match competitors on key attributes and beat them on cost. This strategy creates a significant competitive advantage when the expertise to incorporate upscale product attributes is combined with the ability to produce at a lower cost than the competition. Superior research and development and innovation are the drivers to achieving success with this strategy.

Offensive Strategies

Offensive strategies are helpful in achieving a competitive advantage, while defensive strategies can protect that advantage into the future. Examples of offensive strategies include matching or exceeding a rival's strengths, capitalizing on a rival's weakness, or simultaneous initiatives on both fronts. Launching the offensive can involve underpricing, boosting advertising, or introducing new features that appeal to the rival's core customers. The best options, however, involve attacking with a better product and a lower price.

Obviously, it's always advantageous to attack competitors where they are weakest, but we can also use a strategy to attack them where they are strong but missing one component. For example, a competitor may have great customer service but poor delivery times. You can use your competitive strengths and resources to set it off balance by revealing that weakness and demonstrating your strengths. Or aggressively enter a new geographic market where rivals have no market presence. Then introduce products with different attributes and new features to better meet customer needs. Consider establishing new forms of customer support services that build brand loyalty. This approach offers first-mover advantage, which forces competitors into catch-up mode.

Some opportunities to launch a strategic offensive could include:

- Developing lower-cost product/service design
- Offering free shipping
- Making changes in production operations that lower costs or enhance differentiation
- Developing product features that deliver superior performance or lower users' costs
- Giving more responsive customer service
- Escalating your marketing efforts or pioneering new distribution channels
- Selling directly to end-users

Another option is launching a pre-emptive strike. This involves moving first to secure an advantageous position that rivals are discouraged from duplicating. Options to pre-emptive strikes include expanding capacity ahead of demand in hopes of discouraging rivals from following suit, controlling the best or cheapest sources of essential raw materials, moving to secure best geographic locations, building an image in the customers' minds that is unique and hard to copy, securing exclusive or dominant access to the best distributors, or acquiring a desirable, but struggling, competitor.

Defensive Strategies

Defensive strategies lessen the risk of being attacked and weaken the impact of any attack that does occur. The objective is to get challengers to aim attacks at other rivals while strengthening your company's present position. This is accomplished by blocking avenues that challengers can take in mounting offensive attacks and making it clear that any challenge will be met with a strong counterattack.

Some opportunities to use defensive measures could include:

- Broadening of product lines to fill gaps that your rivals may pursue
- Keeping your prices low on models that match those of your rivals
- Signing exclusive agreements with distributors or exclusive contracts with your best suppliers
- Offering free training to buyers' personnel
- Giving better credit terms to buyers
- Reducing delivery times for spare parts
- Increasing warranty coverage
- Patenting alternative technologies
- Protecting your proprietary know-how

For added effect, you could simultaneously announce your management's strong commitment to maintaining present market share while publicly committing your company to matching prices offered by rivals. Also, announce plans to construct new production capacities to meet a forecasted demand and provide advance information about new products to the marketplace. And if your company has cash reserves, you're in the perfect position to attain advantage.

Real-World Examples of Creating Competitive Advantage

In an effort to gain a competitive advantage, many companies strive to become the biggest and the best. While both represent worthwhile ambitions, neither is necessary for obtaining a true competitive advantage. Michael E. Porter from Harvard Business School states, "In an age of infinite choice, there's a better way to achieve competitive advantage. There is no best auto company, there is no best car. You're really competing to be unique."[1] Consider the following six strategies that can deliver a unique and sustainable competitive advantage.

Deploying a Regional Strategy

In a highly regionalized world, the right regional strategy can create more value than a purely global strategy or a purely local one. Regions represent just one way of aggregating across borders to achieve greater efficiencies than would be achievable with a country-by-country approach. Common forms of cross-border aggregation include products (the global product divisions at Philips), channels (Cisco, which uses channels and partners as its primary basis), customer types or global accounts (many IT services firms), functions (most major oil companies), and technologies (ABB recently, before and after trying some of the bases that were listed previously and others that weren't). Each of these bases of aggregation offers, as regions do, multiple possibilities for crafting strategies intermediate to the local and global levels. In a world that is neither truly local nor truly global, such strategies can deliver a powerful competitive advantage.

Meeting the Needs of Underserved Markets

To further illustrate Michael Porter's point, let's look at how S&C Electric gained a foothold in the global marketplace. Domestically, S&C has championed innovation by introducing unique technology that minimizes the impact of power outages. Its mission is to introduce new solutions for electric power delivery systems as the electric grid undergoes transformative change in this century by working to integrate renewable energy sources, address peak loading issues, and manage the demand aberrations of plug-in electric vehicles. To take its business global, S&C Electric decided to meet specific technological needs of underserved markets. This was accomplished by not only offering high-tech solutions, which may be popular in the United States, but also offering the "right" technology for emerging markets. For example, many countries are too poor, lacking the necessary infrastructure, or without the need for state-of-the-art technology. In addition, many customers around the world are looking for mature designs that represent the best lifecycle value for their specific needs and available infrastructure. This is innovation, creativity, and global thinking as a prescription for success.

By adapting what was leading technology in the 1970s or 1980s with newly developed applications, S&C was able to develop IT products to meet the unique needs of local businesses in emerging markets today. Such an approach, however, requires an in-depth understanding of how business is conducted in the target market. "It's important to learn, accept and work along the established lines for how business is performed in various regions/markets," comments Salvador Palafox, VP of international sales & marketing at S&C Electric. Only then is it possible to understand both a market's needs and limitations and how a corporate strategy can be aligned to capitalize on both. Most important, it requires a shift in mind-set and acceptance that business around the world is often conducted differently than it is, say, in the United States, and that difference can mean success.

Forming Strategic Alliances

Another potential opportunity for developing an effective competitive advantage comes through collaboration and the forging of strategic alliances. Strategic alliances offer a significant competitive advantage in that they are, by definition, unique to each organization.

Cedar Concepts Corporation (CCC), a midsized chemical manufacturer, currently generates 15 percent of its revenue from international sales. Linda McGill Boasmond, President of CCC, says:

Fortunately, we've been able to take advantage of new markets without stretching beyond our goals or means. We ask ourselves, who is where we want to be? How can we take advantage of going there with minimal issues? What do we make that other markets want and can easily use? What can we handle? As it happens, the answers often lay in our established relationships with customers, competitors, and CCC's diverse workforce. We form strong alliances with long-term customers that lead to opportunities in new markets.

CCC also seeks opportunities that harmonize with overall corporate strategy while addressing export issues around logistics, currency, collection, customer service, and cultural differences.

Promoting Your Corporate Mission

A third strategy for developing a competitive advantage may come from "green" initiatives. Some companies picked up early on increasingly globally aware consumers and their demand for ethical, social, and environmentally responsible corporate missions and visions. Consider The Body Shop. Once ridiculed for far-out corporate pledges to protect animals, save the planet, and engage in fair trade, this organization managed to open over 2,000 stores in 50 countries and was recently purchased by L'Oreal for over $1 billion. By recognizing the values held by its targeted audience, The Body Shop was able to develop a brilliant marketing strategy to differentiate itself in the highly competitive retail cosmetic sector.

Today, many businesses are attempting to "out-green" the competition as an effective competitive advantage. As Dov Seidman, columnist for BusinessWeek, states, "The old strategies for success—outmining, outdrilling, outconsuming, outperforming and outspending—no longer offer a sustainable competitive advantage in our hyper transparent, connected and environmentally distressed world,"[2] But to truly gain a competitive advantage through this strategy, it is important for companies to integrate green principles into their culture and create a mind-set that lives, breathes, and embodies green principles as an overall corporate strategy.

Internationally, behaving green is often a necessity. General Motors, for example, was required by the Brazilian government to build a plant in accordance with higher environmental standards and policies than those required in the United States. In addition to meeting these building standards, GM was also required to allocate approximately 180,000 square meters of land to be preserved as a natural habitat. It's a fact that many regions of the globe are now more environmentally conscious than the United States, making it important for U.S. businesses to adopt new and upgraded ways of operating in order to compete and succeed abroad.

Ultimately, the focus in developing a competitive advantage must remain on prospective customers around the globe with different life-styles and different worldviews. Businesses must also consider and com-pare the cost of developing a sustainable competitive advantage from one market to the next.

Developing New Capabilities and New Resources in a Rapidly Changing World

Leveraging new capabilities and resources starts with knowledge. Often that knowledge has to do with changes in the global marketplace and a willingness to modify internal processes in response to the changing world. For example, Zara, a major international clothing retailer and pio-neer of "fast fashion," kept much of its production in Spain and Portugal where the skills for creating high-quality fashion garments were fine-tuned. But as potential supplier firms from Morocco, India, and Turkey gained the competence to manufacture these intricately worked garments, Zara leveraged these new capabilities to add speed and flexibility to their production. Today, Zara sources from these other countries to remain competitive in the fashion industry.

Embracing a Culture of Innovation

An organization positioned to succeed must build and maintain a cul-ture oriented toward innovation in which employees buy into the cause and the mission of the organization. Ultimately, it's the people that differentiate one company from another and lead an organization on to long-term success. While investments in products and process improvements do lead to profit, major and essential innovation starts with people and how those human resources are being managed and deployed. Shaping employees into a team and transforming them into a force creates a very strong competitive advantage.

Sustaining Competitive Advantage through Core Competencies

There is no one-size-fits-all strategy that can be purchased off the shelf and easily installed, especially not internationally, as markets are so diverse and constantly changing. Rather, the exact specifications of any corporate strategy vary greatly depending on the unique circumstances of the company, product, market, and culture of the target audience. For that reason, what works well in one market may fail in another, even with the same product! To make matters worse, even the most powerful competitive advantages may not last long. But businesses with the skills to rapidly identify, innovate, and exploit new competitive advantages quickly and repeatedly will be formidable competitors both at home and abroad.

Identifying, evaluating, and executing a sustainable competitive advantage starts with an introspective assessment of your company's core competencies. Core competencies are simply one organization's strengths relative to other companies in the same industry. To filter out genuine core competencies from general strengths, ask yourself these questions:

1. Does this competency provide the potential consumer with added benefits?
2. Is this competency difficult for competitors to copy? If not, is your intellectual property protected internationally and what is your plan to gain loyalty? Remember, loyalty is much stronger in global markets.
3. Can this competency be widely leveraged to many products and markets? If yes, do you know how to gain leverage and in what markets?

The ultimate goal is to identify core competencies that yield long-term advantages and lead to sustainable competitive advantages. As a leader, remember to focus your firm's resources on what it does best and what creates competitive advantage. Unfortunately, many business leaders insist on perfecting every aspect of their operational performance, which results in working very hard, accomplishing very little, and having no measurable results. This effort is like spinning your wheels and gaining no traction.

Instead, executives should identify key corporate strengths and channel their valuable resources into areas of core competency development. As you go down this path, remember that core competencies don't have to be developed internally. You might consider acquisition of an outside firm or partnering with another firm either at home or abroad. These relationships will often provide mutual benefits *and* allow the whole to become greater than the sum of its parts.

While developing a core competency strategy may require surrendering control over certain non-key processes, it ultimately strengthens your organization and leads to greater competitive advantage. Owning your competitive advantage allows you to build it continuously, become more flexible, and eliminate speed breakers. But beware! Never outsource and always protect your core competencies. You will *never* lead in innovation or be faster to market than your competition if you depend on others for your core strengths.

Maintaining Brand Recognition

For an international company, brand recognition is a powerful core competency because it influences consumer decisions. Consequently, investing in brand development and accelerating brand awareness leads to a very significant competitive advantage that offers indisputable advantages. In terms of the global marketplace, however, localized brands deliver the best results. That's because brand recognition may vary widely across different markets within the same region and across different regions within the same country. Plus, localized brands have the advantage of taking into consideration the specifics and diversity of each target market. But this is only accomplished through information about, and an accurate understanding of, local consumer behavior.

Local brands also provide firms greater strategic flexibility from marketing and pricing to introducing new products that meet evolving needs. In contrast, firms with a global brand are forced to deliver a standardized product to satisfy the largest possible number of consumers. In many ways, local brands are just part of the trend away from pure globalization and toward a more regional approach. However, brand recognition may vary widely across different markets within a region and across different regions within a country, so how do you go about branding and still not lose your identity?

Some multinational firms have begun to recognize the virtues of local brands. Unilever, for example, has acknowledged that trust is essential to develop brands in the local and international brands food sector. For that reason, in its ice cream business, Unilever has kept the best-known local brand names, such as Miko in France, Wall's in the United Kingdom, and Agnesi in Italy. Even in the traditionally globalized cosmetic business, L'Oréal has discovered that local brands have the power to retain clients. In globalizing the U.S. Maybelline brand, L'Oréal has pursued a double-branding strategy in which Maybelline is the host brand and another name is used for the local brand. For example, the company markets Gemey-Maybelline in France and Jade-Maybelline in Germany.

Exploiting a Niche

A niche is neither a product strategy nor a marketing strategy. Rather, it's a core competency. In the past, a niche was based on developing and manufacturing products with a high level of sophistication and associated cost, which demanded premium pricing. Niche was associated with the pride of ownership and catered to a very specific and narrow segment. Niche strategy in modern times, however, needs to be a much more inclusive concept. It is no longer a strategy of identifying a narrow slot but rather the ability to retain invincibility and sustainability despite intense competition. Niche in modern times is the possession of an ability that other firms in the industry do not have.

To illustrate a modern day niche strategy, look at Apple, Inc. Apple Inc., led by Steve Jobs, has virtually rewritten the book on niche strategy, with its pioneering i-products: the iPod, iPhone, and iPad. These products are differentiated with features that multiple niche market segments appreciate and happily pay for. Cost-competitive, these products are also accessible to most people, and the various niche markets that each product occupies cover almost the entire marketplace. The introduction of i-products generated many competitors, even competitors with superior parts, yet i-products remain the market leaders with amazing invincibility. The sustainability of Apple products relates to the fact that the company leveraged its competitive advantage to offer a complete user experience with attractive ownership options and distinctive retailing formats. So far, this complete experience cannot be matched by any competitor.

Another core competency used by Apple is the ability to develop successive waves of new products like the iPad for a totally new technological and user experience. This evolution and transformation in niche positioning requires a complete end-to-end capability in terms of nimble product development, lean manufacturing, and aggressive marketing. The ability to innovate and differentiate with a low-cost global supply chain, high-end manufacturing efficiencies, and broad marketing capabilities requires a set of organizational competencies that are industry leading in each of the domains. It also requires an approach that is comprehensive, encompassing, and integrating all three generic strategies proposed by Porter at the beginning of this chapter.

A niche strategy, which by definition tends to be exclusive, may provide robust profitability but not necessarily huge revenues. As such, this strategy has some prerequisites. First of all, this strategy depends on the ability of a business to develop and manufacture a broad range of products to support that niche technology both financially and organizationally. For that reason, a niche market usually emerges as an apex built on a pyramid of a larger market base. For example, the ability of Toyota to develop clean hybrid cars (i.e., Prius) is a result of its ability to have a large and broad car manufacturing capability. On the other hand, a pure electric car manufacturer is unlikely to have either the scale or scope sufficient to support a sole, narrow niche strategy. Only with a large-scale operation is it even possible to attract the highly talented professionals who can deliver a successful niche platform.

The Swiss watch industry, especially the handcrafted watch segment, was an example of a niche-driven industrial operation where the niche was elegance, precision, and quality. However, in terms of scale and scope, the Swiss watch industry became a marginal player in the 1980s and 1990s relative to the more nimble, more efficient, and more diversified Japanese watch markers. Only after the Swiss industry integrated new research and manufacturing technologies with its traditional niche of elegance and precision did the industry, again, became a global force.

Pearls of Wisdom

As competition continues to intensify both domestically and around the globe, so does the need to identify key competitive advantages and focus on core competencies. Quality products offered at competitive prices, although important, will not guarantee long-term success. Rather, businesses must answer a critical question: "Why should customers buy my products/services as opposed to the competition, and what is my long-term plan to remain competitive and succeed in growing the business globally?" If this question cannot be answered with clarity, it is time to step back and identify a position from which your product can gain traction and be distinguished from all the other competing products.

Developing the right competitive advantage is key and will greatly improve your chances for success when launching into the global marketplace. Just remember that there is no one-size-fits-all strategy. Rather, the exact specifications of any strategy blend features from traditional models like cost leadership, differentiation, and focus to customize an approach suitable for the unique circumstances of your company, product, market, and culture of the target audience. Businesses with the skills to rapidly identify, innovate, and exploit new competitive advantages quickly and repeatedly will be formidable competitors both at home and abroad.

The key points from this chapter include:

- A competitive advantage is essential for success. What is your competitive advantage? Can it be successfully translated into global markets?
- The options for creating competitive advantages are unlimited. What strategies can you employ to leverage your competitive advantage more effectively?

- A sustainable advantage may require a blend of traditional strategies such as low cost leadership, differentiation, and focus.
- Incorporate both offensive and defensive tactics into your mix of competitive advantage strategies.
- Identifying, evaluating, and executing a sustainable competitive advantage start with an introspective assessment of the organization's core competencies.
- Develop core competencies through a review of the management, culture, and products in your organization.
- Use core competencies to exploit a market niche.

When getting close to closing the deal, don't rush. Growing your enterprise globally takes learning how to negotiate successfully in other venues, cultures, and for new customers. Companies can avert disaster by assembling the right team for their expansion, being aware of cultural differences, understanding the negotiating styles of other global businesses and potential partners, and a variety of other issues.

Chapter 5

Sound International Negotiations

*Unlocking the Secrets of Success
across Borders*

"If there is any one secret to success, it lies in the ability to get the other person's point of view and see things from his angle as well as your own."

—*Henry Ford*

Solar Turbines Incorporated, a division of Caterpillar, once learned a valuable lesson about negotiations, Russian style.

For the final phase of negotiations on a $34 million sale of industrial gas turbines and compressors for a Russian natural gas pipeline project, executives agreed to meet in a neutral location—the south of France. Up to this point, the Russians had been tough negotiators but fair and reasonable. Upon arriving in Nice, however, they became even more demanding and completely unreasonable. After several difficult and discouraging days, combined with pressure from Solar's headquarters in San Diego, the American negotiators finally diagnosed the negotiation roadblock. The Russians were enjoying the warm weather in Nice and were in no hurry to get back to Moscow!

Wisely, the American negotiators were given the okay to extend their stay, and they modified their strategy so that negotiating sessions were limited to 45 minutes in the morning followed by afternoons at the beach and on the golf course. Finally, during the fourth week, the Russians began making concessions and asking for longer meetings. After all, with four weeks spent in the beauty and warmth of the Mediterranean, they could not risk going back to Russia without a signed contract. For their patience and understanding, the Americans yielded a brilliant contract to take to back to headquarters, along with a solid foundation for creating future business opportunities.

For each international negotiation story that ends on a positive note, there are hundreds of horror stories hidden away like dirty dishes under a sink, out of sight, out of the press, and never discussed outside the organization's walls. That's why it's critical to sit up, pay attention, and learn some valuable lessons about negotiation—global style.

First, it's important to understand that negotiations are not necessarily legal matters. In fact, outside the United States, the act of negotiating and how the process proceeds is of much greater significance than any legal document the negotiations will ultimately produce. Internationally, legal documents are routinely tossed aside and never enforced. So, when assembling your negotiation team, be aware that in many situations an attorney can complicate, rather than simplify, the negotiation proceedings. Moreover, the protection offered by an attorney is nothing compared to the protection offered by a trusted global business expert with connections and the knowledge of how business is conducted in other parts of the world. Global business experts help develop key relationships, point out traps, overcome obstacles, transcend cultural differences, build a bridge of understanding and, most importantly, maintain strong relationships into the future.

Remember, the negotiating process has implications (good or bad) that extend well beyond the simple benefit of getting what you want today. While the final details of any one deal are important, it is more important to recognize that your negotiation approach establishes the groundwork and likelihood of success of any future business relationship. Whether the deal involves an M&A transaction, joint venture, a simple sale transaction, collaboration, or any other form of involvement, the negotiation strategy and expectations set the tone for that business relationship both short and long term.

For example, U.S. businesspeople approach the negotiation process with the expectation of reaching a win–win situation. However, this concept is foreign to many cultures around the world. Negotiations, in most countries, are more like a game or a sport. The ultimate goal is to achieve a position of power, respect, and control—not necessarily create a win–win scenario. So play along, but leave your attorney out of the picture until it's actually time to start signing documents. Most of all, remember that negotiations are just an opportunity to build relationships and learn the dance steps that will deliver future business deals.

In order to become an effective negotiator, negotiating parties need to understand their counterparts' negotiation styles and how culture impacts the entire negotiation process. From differing values and beliefs to long-established business customs, many challenges will surface during international business negotiations. The present and anticipated growth of international business demands a closer examination of how cross-cultural differences play out in both perceptions and methods of the negotiation process.

The Dance of International Negotiations

As we touched upon in the introduction to this book, conceptualizing the situations involved in global negotiation as a dance can be a powerful tool to help you understand the interdependent and temporal nature of the processes undertaken when expanding your business. Negotiators acquainted with the choreography of a negotiation are better able to use the metaphor of the dance as a standard to judge the quality and progress of the negotiation proceedings. A designated negotiation strategist, similar to one in hostage negotiations, can monitor the communication and convey to the primary negotiator the types of sequences being used. These include reciprocal, complementary, or structural strategies and the strategies underlying those sequences along with how much time has elapsed using those sequences and strategies. Negotiators who understand the choreography may use it to identify when a negotiation is headed in the wrong direction so they can take measures to redirect the conversation.

Unfortunately, many U.S. executives are unfamiliar with this dance and mistakenly launch directly into the detailed, technical phase of negotiations terms and conditions. Such short circuiting of the negotiating process often leads to frustration, disappointment, squandered resources, and lost opportunities for U.S. businesses. While skillful negotiation is universally recognized as paramount to long-term business success, we often fail to determine what is most important to the people with whom we are negotiating. To illustrate, consider the often-cited analogy of the orange. Two equally interested parties are locked in negotiation for one remaining orange. The most agreeable solution, and the most reasonable, is to carve the orange in half, allowing both sides a fair arrangement. Instead, the two parties engage in a process of information exchange and determine that their intended use of the orange differs greatly. One party wants only the juice while the other party wants only the rind. Consequently, both sides achieve more than a typical win–win. It gets better. Later, the two parties embark on a collaborative effort to plant an orchard that will yield future rewards and profits.

Such successful negotiations occur only when both sides understand and trust each other. Developing that understanding and trust takes time, resources, and a long-term commitment. Unfortunately, in corporate America, the activity of building trust is completely undervalued and not considered worthy of the time required. Instead, we place more emphasis on the "bottom line," and achieving short-term goals like better quarterly earnings reports. After all, there's no line item for "relationship building" on a traditional profit and loss statement or expense report, and it never pays immediate dividends. For that reason, in domestic negotiations, we agree to cut the orange in half, leave the negotiating table, and forsake valuable future opportunities that would prove mutually beneficial (like planting a joint orchard). Overseas, however, cutting the orange in half may not prove adequate for sustained success, and more effort must be invested upfront into understanding cultural differences and negotiating better outcomes. The competition is too fierce, and the stakes too high for anything less than your best effort.

Growing Globally Is a High Stakes Venture

Negotiation proceedings to enter a global marketplace can take months, sometimes years, of painstaking preparations. Stop and consider the human and financial resources already expended conducting an extensive market analysis, selecting the ideal target market, performing product modifications, and preparing the market entry strategy to position that product for success. Now is not the time to swoop in unprepared. Instead, slow down, step back, and thoroughly equip the corporate negotiating team to understand the task in hand and do its job.

As outlined in the previous chapter, this begins with an honest self-assessment and recognition that executives from other countries generally have more experience with international negotiations than their U.S. counterparts. As a nation, the United States is still wet behind the ears compared to many executives from Asia, Europe, the Middle East, and Latin America. If you've ever visited a market in China or Brazil, you know what I'm talking about. As a result of cultural influence, these countries have naturally entrenched certain skills of negotiating into their people from a very early age. It is a way of life. But U.S. executives can be quick learners, realizing the importance of this skill-set. With heightened awareness, training, and some cultural sensitivity, Americans can successfully negotiate across international boundaries with confidence. Just remember that the cumulative investment up to this point and the costly consequences of a failed negotiation are hanging in the balance. This should prompt every organization to spare no expense in preparing its negotiation team to close the deal successfully. As you can see in Figure 5.1, understanding the underlying layers of culture is a crucial component of successful negotiation.

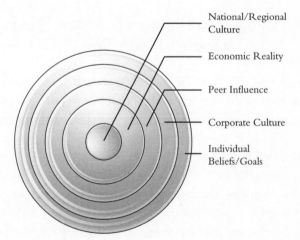

National/Regional Culture

Economic Reality

Peer Influence

Corporate Culture

Individual Beliefs/Goals

Figure 5.1   Like Peeling an Onion: Layers of Culture and Perceptions Affecting Cross-Border Decision-Making

The requisite skills to negotiate successfully in the United States do not necessarily translate to success abroad. In fact, what U.S. businesspeople see as strengths can be viewed as weaknesses on the international stage. The key for executives is to identify which skills cross over, which skills require retooling, and which skills are simply missing from the toolbox. Most important, never assume that knowledge and understanding of the business, no matter how in-depth, will compensate for lack of cultural understanding in the negotiating process. It won't. Cultural awareness is no longer a nice skill to have; it's essential for success overseas.

Accordingly, it's important to carefully select the team of negotiators that will ultimately represent and symbolize your company abroad. Depending on the business practices of the country being pursued, it may be critical to present a person with obvious authority and experience. Because some companies are represented by a multinational team, certain deals will require familiarity with more than one culture. In any case, the team of negotiators must be well-versed in and accepting of the business customs and negotiation styles of the respective participants and sensitive to all cultural differences.

Tuning in to Difference: When "Yes" Doesn't Mean "Yes"

Culture, at its basic level, is the collective mental programming of people in an environment. It refers to the conditioning of a group of people that will influence a lifetime of thought processes, behavior, and actions. Ultimately, culture is the determinant of beliefs, thoughts, perceptions, and emotions and is defined by the sum of these parts. Thus, culture is a major determinant of how negotiations will play out. It influences how groups make decisions and how groups approach, evaluate, and negotiate opportunities. Culture is the backdrop for every interaction from the seemingly obscure initial phone call to the subsequent face-to-face meetings, and all the negotiation proceedings in between.

Different cultures, languages, physical distances, communication styles, environments, ideologies, customs, traditions, and political systems are just a few of the virtual minefields negotiators will traverse during international negotiations. Many would agree that these potential minefields are, in fact, the trigger for such high failure rates for U.S. companies as they attempt to expand into international markets.

For example, while words alone speak volumes in a country like the United States, words mean close to nothing in certain countries. Rather, it's the nonverbal communication that demands close attention in many parts of the world. Unfortunately, Americans come from a low-context culture, which is a major disadvantage in the global marketplace. Our low-context culture makes it difficult to understand high-context communication. Today, this disadvantage is marginally offset by the fact that English is still globally recognized as the language of international business communication. But this may not be the case in 10 years as trends and changes in the balance of economic power, the increasing mobility of the global workforce, technology, and shifts in national policy continue. With the growth of the BRIC economies, the balance of power has changed. As a result, the economic primacy of the countries where English is a native language can no longer be taken for granted. Additionally, the number of native speakers of English is falling in absolute terms, soon to fall into fifth place behind Mandarin, Spanish, Hindi-Urdu, and Arabic.

From an ideological perspective, Western businesspeople are schooled and conditioned to rely heavily on contract terms in the event of a dispute. To the United States and other Western countries, an agreement is useless until all the terms are written, the document is signed (multiple times), dated, and initialed on every page. In contrast, Japanese and Middle East businessmen rely more heavily on oral commitments. In these countries, contracts are short and general. In some cases, written contracts are nonexistent and agreements are sealed only by word of honor. So when U.S. businesspeople show up with a lawyer to draft detailed contracts at the first meeting, their future business partners are mightily offended. Not a good first impression.

Even "time," a seemingly universal concept, can dramatically complicate international negotiation proceedings. Every region around the globe has a unique orientation to time that must be understood and planned for accordingly. Some cultures negotiate in a very fast-paced and intense manner. Others, like the Russians visiting France, may want to spend days, weeks, or months just getting to know a prospective

partner and building the necessary rapport and trust before true negotiations even begin. The U.S. mind-set that "time is money" is not universal, and is even looked at as a deficiency. In many countries, deals
are not even discussed until the second or third time prospective business partners have met socially, shared a meal, and developed a cordial
relationship. In this scenario, it's critical for U.S. businesspeople to have
the skills and freedom to spend that time earning the respect of their
potential business partners without being held to an unreasonable time-
frame established by corporate headquarters.

Some actions, including those as innocuous as sending an e-mail
or standard business letter, can have serious implications. In the Middle
East, for example, e-mail communication is never an excuse to evade
adherence to tradition. Even if it's the tenth e-mail sent regarding
the same issue, it's still important to include personal sentiments such as
"trust all is well with you" or "please send my regards to your family."
While curt, to-the-point e-mail messages are almost always accepted
in the U.S. business world, they will offend those accustomed to more
formal communications.

Body language is another important area of difference. While multiple countries may use the same gesture, they often have very different meanings. For example, the American symbol for "okay" is made
by forming a circle with the thumb and index finger. In France this
symbol means zero, but in Brazil the meaning is vulgar. The familiar V
for a victory symbol is insulting in most of Europe. So tread carefully,
be alert, and learn to read the body language of the person(s) across the
negotiations table.

In addition to all this, language, even when negotiations are conducted in English, can present a number of unanticipated issues. Although
many foreign business executives speak in English, they do not think in
English like their American counterparts. Take the simple word "yes."
When dealing with the Chinese, they are quick to offer this word without
taking adequate time to really consider the question posed. That's because
their use of "yes" does not mean "I agree" as one may assume. Instead,
"yes" can mean a number of different things. It may be offered as a sign of
respect to communicate that you were heard. It can also mean "no."

Even in English-speaking countries, words can have very different meanings. In one case, U.S. businessmen were meeting with

representatives of a South African company to talk about the ownership structure of their future company. In their discussions, the U.S. businessmen used the term "stock" in reference to shares of stock—that is, ownership. However, to the South Africans, the term "stock" is more commonly used in reference to inventory—that is, assets. Although English was spoken by both parties, this example shows how culture and language represent a mental programming that can easily lead to confusion and frustration. In this case, the resulting misunderstanding caused negotiations to come to a halt. Fortunately, the parties involved figured it out and the partnership talks ended favorably.

While culture, time, and language may seem like obvious matters, these considerations represent just the tip of the iceberg, the visible tip. Similar to an actual iceberg, what lies beneath the surface is what ultimately poses the greatest danger to the negotiations. For example, there are myriad less-known social norms, including methods of communication, chain of command, power distance, ethics, and pace of life to name just a few. Even having the right people participate in negotiations is important. To complicate matters, this can vary greatly by region.

With so much at stake, it's worth the investment of resources to prepare, train, and develop the individuals who will be conducting negotiations abroad. In many cases, this means engaging an international expert—someone familiar not only with local protocol but also business in general—someone who would know that Japanese businesspeople, for instance, present their business cards in a certain manner and expect them to be received properly. In most cases, this critical nuance would not be known by an attorney or an accountant, only an international business advisor. In the long run, having the right mix of expertise will enable you to anticipate issues and make advanced preparations, so that your side of the bargaining table will be well positioned to save money, time, and frustration.

Preparing for International Negotiations

While foreign clients, foreign suppliers, and foreign business partners obviously increase certain risks, like failed negotiations, these potential players compensate by creating enormous opportunities for developing new businesses or expanding into new markets. So never dismiss an opportunity because of risk. Instead, minimize and mitigate the risks through proper preparation.

In his book *Making Deals in Strange Places: A Beginner's Guide to International Business Negotiations*,[1] Jeswald Salacuse points out two mistaken assumptions about doing business in an international setting:

1. Corporate leaders assume that they can simply extend their successful domestic strategies to the international setting.
2. Many economic commentators assume that international business deals will happen naturally if only correct governmental policies and structures are in place.

Both of these assumptions are incorrect. Policies alone do not create business deals; companies do. Business executives need to be much better educated about international negotiating in order to make successful deals. International business negotiations are fundamentally different from domestic negotiations and require a different set of skills and knowledge. As Salacuse explains, "domestic business dealings probably have about the same relationship to international business as domestic politics do to international diplomacy."

In his work, Salacuse describes six distinctive features of international business negotiations. The first is that in international negotiations the parties must deal with the laws, policies, and political authorities of more than one nation. These laws and policies may be inconsistent, or even directly opposed. For example, in the early 1980s U.S. companies operating in Europe were caught between the American prohibition on sales to the Soviets for their Trans-Siberian pipeline and European nations' demands that these companies abide by their supply contracts. International business agreements must include measures to address these differences. Such measures typically include arbitration clauses, specification of the governing laws, and tax havens.

A second factor unique to international business is the presence of different currencies. Different currencies give rise to two problems. Since the relative value of different currencies varies over time, the actual value of the prices or payments set by contract may vary and result in unexpected losses or gains. Another problem is that each government generally seeks to control the flow of domestic and foreign currencies across its national boundaries. As such, business deals will often depend upon the willingness of governments to make currency available. Unexpected changes in such governmental currency policies can have dramatic effects on international business deals.

A third element common to international business negotiations is the participation of governmental authorities. Governments often play a much larger role in foreign business than Americans are accustomed to. The presence of extensive government bureaucracies can make international negotiation processes more rigid than is usual in the American private sector. Sovereign immunity can introduce legal complications into contracts. State-controlled businesses may have different goals from private companies. Whereas private firms are usually primarily concerned with profits, state entities may be willing to sacrifice some profitability for social or political ends such as greater employment.

Fourth, international ventures are vulnerable to sudden and drastic changes in their circumstances. Events such as war or revolution, changes in government, or currency devaluation have an impact on international businesses, which is much greater than the impact that the usual domestic changes have on national businesses. These risks require that international business negotiators have a breadth of knowledge and social insight that would not be necessary in negotiating a U.S. business arrangement. International businesses try to protect against these risks by employing political risk analysts, procuring foreign investment insurance, and by force majeure clauses that allow for contract cancellation under certain conditions.

International business negotiators also encounter very different ideologies. In particular, different countries may have very different ideas about private investment, profit, and individual rights. Effective negotiators will be aware of ideological differences. They will present their proposals in ways that are ideologically acceptable to the other party, or at least ideologically neutral.

Finally, cultural differences are an important factor in international negotiations. In addition to language differences, different cultures have differing values, perceptions, and philosophies. As a result, certain ideas may have very different connotations in different cultures. For instance, Americans and Japanese tend to have a different view of the purpose of negotiations. Americans see the goal of negotiations as to produce a binding contract that creates specific rights and obligations. Japanese see the goal of negotiations as to create a relationship between the two parties; the written contract is simply an expression of that relationship. What the Japanese see as a reasonable willingness to modify a contract to reflect changes in the parties' relationship, Americans see as a tendency to renege. American insistence on adherence to the original terms of the contract may be perceived as distrust by the Japanese.

Surmounting Conflicts

Dodging the potential landmines of any international negotiations starts with a three-step process:

1. *Learn the other side's culture.* Learn the basic components of your counterpart's culture. This knowledge is a sign of respect that will build trust and credibility. Also, awareness of culture will provide the insight necessary to choose the right strategies and tactics during the negotiation process. If time is short, try to identify principal influences that the foreign culture may have on making the deal.

2. *Don't stereotype.* Assumptions lead to distrust and barriers while potentially exposing your needs, positions, and goals. Instead of generalizing, make an effort to treat everyone as individuals. Identify the other side's values and beliefs independently of values and beliefs characteristic of the culture or group being represented by your counterpart.

3. *Find ways to bridge the culture gap.* Apart from adopting the other side's culture to adjust to the situation and environment, persuade the other side to use elements of your own culture. In some situations, it's also possible to use a combination of both cultures. Alternatively, work to create a level playing field by adopting a third culture. This can be a strong base from which to form better personal relationships. When difficulty arises in finding common ground, focus on common professional cultures to move the negotiations forward.

Negotiating is tough work. Even negotiating with a colleague, a neighbor, or family member is something few of us enjoy. Why? It's problematic! It suggests conflict and most people are uncomfortable with conflict and confrontation, especially in the United States. The way we perceive reality can be, and often is, completely different from another individual's perceptions. Just like our fingerprints, our ways of thinking, communicating, behaving, and feeling are all unique and in large part a result of our culture and environment. Accordingly, knowledge of the right foreign language is not enough to effectively conduct negotiation. Language is simply a cluster of codes used in communication that, when not shared effectively, will still present a barrier to establishing credibility and trust. One needs to follow a certain protocol in order to be successful in negotiating and having the outcomes last while developing the so much needed trust in the relationship.

Other considerations include:

- *Determining the goal.* Is it mutual satisfaction? Winning? Different cultures stress different aspects of negotiation: The goal may be a substantive outcome (Americans) or a long-lasting relationship (Japanese).
- *Following protocol.* There are as many kinds of business etiquette as there are nations in the world. Protocol factors that should be considered are dress code, number of participants, entertainment/recreation, degree of formality, gift giving, meeting and greeting.
- *Using effective communication.* Verbal and nonverbal communication are equally important. The manner used to express needs and feelings through body language and tone of voice can help us determine the way we are being perceived. Also, the use of indirect versus direct forms of information exchange needs to be used carefully. Does "it's impossible" really mean impossible, or just difficult? Ask, don't assume.
- *Assessing propensity for risk.* Negotiation always involves some level of risk. Should you trust them? Will they trust you? Certain cultures, however, are more risk averse than others, which can potentially eliminate innovative and creative solutions during negotiations.
- *Understanding view of time.* In certain cultures, time is a valuable resource that must be used wisely—that is, "time is money." Punctuality and the agenda are therefore important aspects of negotiations. If participants are late to scheduled meeting in places

like China or Japan, it is regarded as an insult. In other countries, haste is an even worse insult. That's why it is important to know the customs you are dealing with.

- *Recognizing decision-making systems.* Make sure you know who's in charge. When negotiating with a team, it's crucial to identify who the leader is and who has the authority to make a decision. The way members of the other negotiating team reach a decision will offer a hint, and it's that person whom you should focus on when presenting information.

- *Determining the appropriate form of agreement.* In most cultures, only written agreements seal a deal. The "deal" may be the contract itself or the relationship between the parties. Do you know which one would work with your counterpart?

- *Recognizing power distance.* This refers to the acceptance of authority differences between people. Cultures with low *power distance* postulate equality among people and focus more on earned status than ascribed status. Negotiators from countries like Britain, Germany, and Austria tend to be comfortable with shared authority and democratic structures. When we face a high *power distance* culture, be prepared for hierarchical structures and clear authority figures. This requires you to know who to address and who will ultimately be making the decision and signing the agreement.

- *Paying attention to personal style.* Be aware. Your individual attitude and biases establish assumptions that may lead the negotiation process towards a win–win or win–lose solution. Make a calculated decision and think about whether it's to your advantage to use a formal or informal approach to communication. In some cultures, like North America, an informal style may help to create friendly relationships and accelerate the problem-solving solution. In China, by comparison, an informal approach is proper only when the relationship is firm and sealed with trust.

Leaving Your Home Country's Legal Assumptions at the Door

In significant cross-border transactions, both parties are typically assisted by legal counsel at certain points along the journey. These advisors are invaluable because they bring both international experience and specific legal knowledge to the negotiating table. That said, it is still important for any businessperson to understand the local legal system and diligently question any underlying assumptions. Unintentionally, as Americans, we frequently carry our legal culture with us and formulate erroneous conclusions when applying our reasoning in new global markets. In other words, while sophisticated businesspeople intuitively understand that both laws and accounting rules vary in foreign countries, they often overlook the underlying implications of those differences in terms of negotiating transactions. As a result, they fail to seek expert guidance on issues that appear safe on the surface.

To illustrate, consider a basic assumption that businesspeople bring to the negotiating table: the prevailing notion of "freedom to contract." U.S. businesspeople assume that when two parties willingly agree to certain terms and conditions, those terms and conditions are enforceable. It is therefore an unpleasant surprise to U.S. representatives when they discover that certain agreements are, in fact, unenforceable—and remain unenforceable even when the other party also desires to have the agreement enforced. In most instances, legal counsel will catch these types of problems after the deal is done. At this point, it may be too late to approach the bargaining table with the same amount of bargaining currency.

Employment contracts represent another landmine for potential legal issues. Understandably, U.S. parties often assume that agreements in a negotiated employment contract will be enforced as written and agreed upon. For example, the contract may give the employer the right to terminate the employee, pay severance, and enforce a post-termination noncompetition covenant. Notwithstanding the fact that both parties have agreed to these covenants and may be eager to enforce them, such provisions are simply unenforceable as written in many foreign countries.

Similarly, businesspeople from the EU erroneously assume that they will automatically incur significant severance obligations when terminating U.S. employees. This inaccurate assumption leads them to start their negotiating position with the amount of severance compensation. Quite the contrary, in most U.S. jurisdictions, employees can be terminated at will. While U.S. counsel to the EU party most certainly knows this fact, he or she may not advise on the issue until the underlying agreement has already been hammered out by the parties. By that time though, the die has been cast, and the negotiating position of the EU party has been weakened. Having agreed to severance, it will be very difficult to then take it off the table without some other concession.

These problems and many others can be avoided. What it takes is up-front training and the physical presence of an international business expert, or both. The expense incurred will prove comparatively insignificant when compared to the need to start over. At a minimum, from the very first stages of negotiation, the team needs to think carefully about their legal assumptions and question whether these assumptions apply before approaching the negotiating table. While legal counsel can assist in this endeavor, ultimately it is each businessperson's responsibility to raise questions and issues in a timely manner as the negotiation progresses.

Negotiation Styles around the Globe

In today's increasingly global marketplace, it's important to restrain from making any assumptions about a person's country of origin. Just because the company you are dealing with is headquartered in Germany doesn't mean you'll be dealing with Germans. Therefore, it's important to be well-versed in the negotiating styles of many nations.

The French are masters in the art of stage management. While their German neighbors rely on substance and the British rely on style, the French rely on effect. In negotiations, they will often play along the opposition, almost for pure pleasure, and then make a theatrical last-minute concession. The Italians, on the other hand, have their own inimitable way of negotiating. As many businesspeople have observed, the Italians do what they want, when they want, and how they want. They will argue at length, disagree empathically, appear to compromise, leave the negotiating table, and then reinvent a new strategy in front of the coffee machine. But they always get it right in the end—honoring their own interests first, but also making an effort to meet the needs of their opposition.

Greece has a long-established tradition of philosophic debates; thus, negotiations include tough bargaining on many different levels, often simultaneously. Generally speaking, Greeks employ a polychromic work style. They are naturally accustomed to pursuing multiple actions and goals in parallel. When negotiating, they take a holistic approach and frequently jump back and forth between topics rather than addressing issues in a logical or sequential order. Negotiators from strongly monochromic cultures, such as Germany, the United Kingdom, and the United States, find this style irrational, unsettling, and just plain difficult. But the lesson here is to be patient and keep track of the bargaining progress at all times, often emphasizing areas where agreement already exists.[2]

Romania, a country with a long history of communist rule, approaches negotiations as an exercise in team problem solving. While their approach works great for businesses they know and trust, it's not so great for newcomers. It takes time and patience to build trust with Romanian businesspeople. They are more reluctant than others to share information with people they perceive as outsiders. There is usually more emphasis on the short-term rather than building long-term relationships. They are straightforward, don't rely on drama, and always focus on the facts. Business in Romania is hierarchical, with decision-making power residing at the top of the company and still requiring several layers of approval. Of course, this is information is crucial for skilled negotiators.

Another country that rose after defeat of communism is Poland. When negotiating any deal with executives from Poland, equip your team with lots of patience to accept delays and changes of direction. At times you will be convinced that conducting business with you is no longer their objective. Don't be naïve. This is just one tactic used by Polish negotiators to wear you down.

In emerging markets, increasing wages and social benefit obligations may not be deal breakers, but it is critical that these and other human capital costs be included and played under several scenarios for a number of years if a buyer is to get a more realistic picture of a target company's value and of future integration issues. The lack of transparency combined with the greater overlap between political, regulatory, and economic policies in emerging markets adds to the nature of unpredictability, and therefore requires more due diligence, data points, and sensitivity to cultural nuances.

The more a country falls into the category of emerging market, the more likely it is that political red tape will slow the pace of progress, as well as labor laws that may vary from one jurisdiction to another. Other issues may include the limit on the number of foreign nationals that can be brought in to assume key responsibilities, and there is of course the issue of local employee loyalty and how to maintain it. U.S. firms face the Sarbanes-Oxley issue, since most companies in the emerging markets are not obliged to comply with that regulation.

All of this means that from the very first stages of negotiation, and certainly before a letter of intent has been entered into, the parties in a cross-border transaction must think carefully about their legal assumptions and question whether they apply before coming to the negotiating table. Legal counsel can certainly assist in this endeavor, but it is up to the businessperson to raise the issues in a timely manner. Such successful negotiations only occur when both sides understand and trust each other and are willing and able to engage in a process of meaningful information exchange. Although it may sound simple, it isn't.

It's generally the case that the average American businessperson assumes that the world subscribes to his or her definitions of negotiation: a process by which two or more interested parties resolve disputes, agree upon courses of action, bargain for an individual or collective advantage, and attempt to craft outcomes that serve mutual interests (as I've said, a win–win scenario). Just look at our foreign policies. We attempt to settle international differences by achieving win–win situations whereby no one loses. In other words, we approach negotiations very purposefully with a specific outcome in mind. Internationally, however, negotiating has much more to do with understanding people, their customs and developing long-term relationships that will prove mutually beneficial, either today or in the future. The specific issues of the deal on the table are just the context of the talks, not the content of the talks.

Bridging the Divide

While experience is always the best teacher, global expansion is too costly an endeavor to leave anything to chance. Consequently, bridging the gap between negotiating domestically and negotiating abroad requires an applied program of education, training, and personal development. It requires a global mind-set, a collaborative attitude, and a panoramic view of the competitive landscape. Training enables employees at all levels of the organization an opportunity to learn and develop sensitivities to cultural differences, especially when they are assessed individually and trained according to their needs. Once the nuances of other cultures are understood, greater success can be achieved when dealing with people from many different backgrounds.

Also, it's important to recognize how American businesspeople are perceived outside of the United States. In many cases, they are characterized as informal, punctual, orderly, arrogant, abrupt, impatient, ignorant, and predictable. Not only are these traits offensive to certain cultures, they often cause U.S. businesspeople to impose unreasonable expectations on international business dealings. For example, approaching a meeting with detailed agendas and predetermined start and stop times will not always work in paving the way to successful negotiations. Instead, U.S. businesspeople need to learn how to function and live with the flexibility and ambiguity that exist in so many other regions of the world. Sometimes it is about your mind-set and your need to embrace these differences and learn how to intelligently integrate them into your daily practices. Only recently I was negotiating a transaction and came fully prepared to the meeting, with a glorious PowerPoint, per the group's guidelines, only to experience that the meeting was very informal and no attention was paid to the PowerPoint. Knowing the culture and taking this possibility into account made this meeting smooth, productive, and enjoyable.

Cultural sensitivity, empathy, personal integrity, and sharing of knowledge are important aspects in global training. Looking ahead, multinational teams are likely to become more commonplace whereby executives are regularly dealing with people from various cultures and where both understanding and being understood are essential to success. Rick Goings, Chairman and CEO of Tupperware, has firsthand experience in this area:

> I think we need to stop looking at companies that are global companies as American companies or companies that have a nationality based on where they have headquarters. My management team and most of my executive committee are from

all over the world. We throw our passports on the table and forget the original nationality of them and transcend nationalism.[3]

In a world packed with businesspersons of various cultural backgrounds, it's important to communicate a corporate-wide sensitivity to culture. Building that sensitivity is imperative for any business that is expanding into international marketplaces. At the same time, this sensitivity and need to compromise must be balanced with the need to preserve personal, corporate, and national integrity.

Pearls of Wisdom

U.S.-based companies have lost the luxury of picking and choosing where they are willing to conduct business and where they will not, or simply leave the negotiations table because it won't go their way and the other party doesn't play by their rules. Like all other nations, U.S.-based companies need to be prepared, ready, and willing to get in the game wherever opportunity presents itself. Once there, they need to get in tune with the culture, and be ready to learn, observe, and accept new ways of conducting business. Inevitably, this new dynamic puts U.S.-based companies up against businesses from other nations with far more international experience. But, that's no reason to hold back. As U.S.-based companies gain experience and master the ability to analyze, assess, evaluate, understand, and negotiate with other cultures, they will become fierce competitors in the world marketplace. After all, the United States is still one of the most competitive nations in the world . . . for now.

In any negotiation, the corporate representatives must fully comprehend their own organizational goals and expectations for a true negotiation success. That means knowing what terms are important, what is negotiable, and what is not. In the international arena, this is still important, but it's complicated by a host of other challenges, and the stakes are high. Accordingly, take no shortcuts, make no assumptions, and go in prepared.

Here are some key points to keep in mind from reading this chapter:

- Negotiation abroad is all about building trust and long-term relationships.
- Relationships are as important, or more important, than any legal document in other international business communities. Tune in and understand your counterpart's culture, language, communication style, ideology, customs, traditions, and political systems. How will you develop an interest to learn from a culturally diverse workforce and to appreciate and embrace the differences?
- Knowing the culture, customs, practices, values, political system, and decision-making process of your counterpart is critical to success. Don't stereotype. Do find creative ways to bridge the culture gap.
- The requisite skills to negotiate successfully in the United States do not necessarily translate to success abroad. Differentiate your approach to global legal proceedings especially because the legal aspects of international negotiations are usually very different from those in your home country.
- Inventory every possible consideration before engaging, and make sure the negotiating team is prepared. The cost of having an unprepared team will far outweigh any expense of preparing them on the front end.
- As competition abroad intensifies, the importance of skilled business negotiators who are equipped to work internationally is critical.
- Never rush through negotiations. Stop, look, listen, and be aware!

Now that you have found insight into the skills you need to hone for sound negotiations, it's time to look at corporate partnerships and the opportunities they present. All over the world, the biggest success stories in history have been less about one individual or one company's triumphs. On the contrary, the top successes have been the result of collaboration.

Chapter 6

Corporate Partnerships

A Match Made in Heaven . . . or Hell?

"It is probably not love that makes the world go around, but rather those mutually supportive alliances through which partners recognize their dependence on each other for the achievement of shared and private goals."

—*Fred Allen*

National Railway Equipment Co. (NREC), headquartered in Mt. Vernon, Illinois, is a privately owned, vertically integrated provider of new and remanufactured locomotives, locomotive products, and wheel services. Founded by Lawrence Beal in 1984, National Railway Equipment Co. has become one of the world's largest suppliers of remanufactured and new locomotives, new and rebuilt locomotive mechanical and electrical systems, and components. The company also provides locomotive field service and technical support. NREC delivers locomotives and services to customers throughout North America and worldwide.

When expanding into new international markets, NREC purposefully capitalizes on its core competencies of engineering, project management, and global marketing and sales reach. Recently, in an effort to grow the business, NREC sought strategic alliances in Croatia, Australia, and India. Each of these marketplaces offered NREC a unique opportunity. The alliance in Croatia and the alliance in Australia allowed NREC to leverage its strategic position as a systems integrator with the ability to manufacture the entire locomotive rather than the numerous components in it. The alliance in India enabled NREC to source key components necessary to manufacture the entire locomotive and better penetrate the growing marketplace in India. "Mergers and acquisitions are becoming a key component in achieving many of our strategic objectives. Cutting edge due diligence of acquisition targets ensures that these objectives are achievable, and that the valuation and expected returns are justified. Due diligence of targets also helps to mitigate risk factors," says Robert Loewer, JD, MBA, MSA, of NREC.[1] In his capacity as NREC's General Counsel and Director of Finance, Loewer has executed a number of M&A, joint venture, and strategic alliance transactions.

Partnerships for Global Expansion

From Wall Street to Madison Avenue to the Silicon Valley, the biggest success stories in the history of U.S.-based businesses have been less about one individual or one company's triumphs. On the contrary, top successes at U.S.-based companies have been the result of collaboration and acceptance of a win-win philosophy. Unfortunately, too many American businesspeople have lost sight of this important lesson and insist on going global solo. By going it alone, they rely on traditional business models like import/export, outsourcing, franchising, and licensing. While these business models are still relevant today, greater success can be accomplished by incorporating corporate partnership models such as collaboration, mergers and acquisitions (M&A), joint ventures, and other strategies more suitable for strategic global expansion.

Regardless of industry, business size, ownership structure, or net equity, every business with a future is looking for growth. And the opportunities for growth in the international marketplace are aptly diverse and unlimited. That's why globalization should be on every organization's to-do list. There is something to be gained by every company. But the actual execution of a global expansion plan can take on many different business forms and stages. For some businesses, going global is nothing more than having the capability to sell a product via a website to a consumer in Europe, Africa, or Asia. For other businesses, it means joining forces with an international organization to leverage strengths in an ever-changing world, being acquired by (whether purposeful or by surprise) or tagging along with a domestic client who took the initiative to explore opportunities abroad.

U.S.-based businesses are increasingly making emerging markets the focus of their global business. In a survey of 247 executives from consumer and industrial product companies with a presence in emerging markets, a Deloitte study revealed that 88 percent of those companies plan to expand their presence in emerging markets. Approximately half of these organizations expect 20 percent or more of their global revenues to have their origins in emerging markets. Equally interesting is their reasoning for establishing functions in these emerging markets:

- Cost savings: 71 percent
- Market expansion: 69 percent

- Speed to market: 55 percent
- Access to talent: 36 percent
- Develop new products: 31 percent
- Develop new service: 28 percent

This information illustrates two key points. First, globalization is not business as usual; second, developing countries are fertile soil for innovative companies looking for growth. No longer satisfied to increase their presence in low-cost regions for the sole purpose of saving money, companies surveyed are seeking innovative ways to maximize their presence and exploit local opportunities to achieve growth and market expansion. In this study, 40 percent of the businesses had established commercial operations that cater to the local market in addition to their manufacturing.

Collaborate, Coordinate, Cooperate

Businesspeople around the world marvel at the tremendous success China has achieved over the past two decades. Want to know a secret? It's embedded deep within the Chinese culture: It's the spirit of cooperation. Winning through cooperation is a core concept of Chinese culture, which has a tradition of highly valuing mutual social obligations. Today, this principle of cooperation is paramount to success when navigating a global marketplace, and it's especially imperative when entering a new market for the first time. Regardless of which business structure is ultimately selected for global expansion, it will require a spirit of cooperation and some level of collaboration. This key ingredient, collaboration, has proven to be a major obstacle for businesspeople who hail from the land of rugged individualism and independence, America.

Certainly, the idea of collaborating between organizations and creating partnerships is nothing new. It's a long-established tool to achieve results one cannot easily achieve alone. In today's global business environment, however, alliances are more important (and more complicated) than ever. Creating new value networks, tapping into new sources of innovation, or driving growth through partnerships are just a few examples of how alliances can help generate success abroad. But successfully creating and managing these business structures requires new skills and a trip up the learning curve.

A collaborative network is an innovative organization that necessitates rethinking structure, governance, and ways of relating among participants. Organizations and individuals that develop expertise in creating and working within collaborative networks represent the future. It's a fact. Complex problems are increasingly solved by leveraging the resources of purposeful collaborative networks, such as strategic alliances and public-private partnerships. Innovation and economic growth of all kinds are occurring through collaborative networks. Unfortunately, traditional roles, policies, and measures can work at cross-purposes when creating an environment conducive to collaborating. The reality is that most people are more comfortable working in the silos of traditional organizational hierarchies and boundaries. Our approach to collaborative network design and governance must acknowledge this fact and make it a priority to demonstrate the increased value a well-functioning collaborative network can provide to all participants. Key elements of this management methodology include fostering effective collaboration and building an environment conducive to achieving the strategic intent. Too often collaboration is misunderstood to mean the simple act of working together, or worse, just being nice. Collaboration is a purposeful and strategic activity that produces results through:

1. Sharing a common goal/vision and willing to partner and collaborate, while seeing the advantages of all parties involved as opposed to going it alone.
2. *Coordinating activities.* The activities of the network must be sufficiently coordinated to plan and execute in a timely manner.
3. *Communicating information.* The right information needs to be communicated to (available to) the right person at the right time to appropriately inform and ensure timeliness and agility in decision making.
4. *Leveraging resources.* The people, knowledge, relationships, resources, and finances of all network members need to be properly utilized in pursuit of the unifying purpose of the network. The management methodology must also support an environment that is conducive to collaborating.

5. *Governance.* Most simply, governance is how collaborating organizations manage joint work. The composition and operation of governing bodies, such as executive committees, operating committees, and working teams, as well as their relationship to one another, are generally all that is thought of as governance. Governance also includes:

- Decision-making processes and authority
- Communication protocols
- Conflict-resolution processes
- Intellectual property procedures
- Evaluation and improvement regimens that encourage excellence

6. *Accountability.* The operating norms of the network recognize the interdependency of the network members and encourage acceptance of responsibility for individual actions and inactions. Accountability functions together with governance to ensure the network is on a path to success.

7. *Trust and transparency.* The network members must operate with the appropriate degree of openness relative to the collaboration intensity the network requires, demonstrate trustworthiness in their actions, and trust that other members of the network will behave in a similar fashion.

Key to network governance and management is the use of common principles, guidance, processes, and tools across the network. This management framework defines "goodness" within the network, but also empowers local participants to do what will further the purpose of the network in a particular situation. This framework is what allows independent, just-in-time decision making to flourish, without jeopardizing the network's agreed-upon strategy. It encourages agility because network members can act without seeking authority. This helps to encourage innovation and balances the strengths and weaknesses of control and decentralization.

A key characteristic of collaborative networks is their ability to bring together the right specialist organizations in a seamless and non-bureaucratic manner. They also recognize and appreciate that collaboration is a continuum, not an all-or-nothing proposition. Thus, each collaborative network has unique features, especially assembled to achieve its purpose. Today, organizations operate as a network of networks accomplishing their purpose by:

- Allowing structure to be determined by strategy. If the strategy changes radically, the structure may need to change. It may also need to evolve as a partnership moves through its lifecycle.
- Forming sub-networks that collaborate to achieve a particular aspect or element of the network's purpose and that disband once the purpose is achieved. The work of the network is accomplished through networks. Some will essentially be permanent because of the nature of their purpose. Others will be much more ad hoc.
- Developing functional excellence in the management of networks.

Think of the organization as a network of networks, each of which exists only to achieve a specific purpose. The governance and accountability dimensions of the management methodology are designed to achieve that purpose with increasing excellence. This is a significant departure from traditional organization design and is indicative of the innovativeness management must demonstrate to achieve its objectives.

Collaboration in Action

Japanese companies have practiced collaboration for centuries, and this has enhanced their global growth efforts. Unfortunately, many U.S. companies fail to understand the purpose or benefits of engaging collaboratively. But there are many. For example, initiating a strategic alliance can help defend an organization from competition or increase effectiveness by learning from (and with) partners in the industry. Internationally, collaboration can radically improve the time to market. Remember, entering any global market requires the same level of commitment and energy as starting a new business from scratch. Never assume that globalization is merely an extension of your domestic business. It is not. Every detail from product design, packaging, distribution, marketing, sales support, and customer service must be modified appropriately for each new marketplace. Consequently, the process of global expansion, especially if going it alone, consumes substantial resources including time, money, and personnel.

To expedite this process, astute business owners and leaders will choose to collaborate with an existing domestic business. Through a strategic alliance plan and implementation process, U.S. businesses gain a deeper understanding about consumer behavior, the culture, and the business practices of a specific market. Equally important, a local partner can offer insight into how a product or service will be used in that culture and can help a company plan for new upgrades and features that may be necessary before moving forward. With this type of collaborative relationship, U.S. businesses are more likely to experience a quicker time to market, a quicker return on investment, and a sure foundation for future ventures.

A successful strategic alliance is created when its purpose is derived directly from the overall strategy of the organization. Thus, it requires initial identification of clearly defined goals and objectives, significant attention to the type of partner needed, and to the long-term implications of a formal alliance. During the life time of any alliance, key skills associated with relationship building, trust, and flexibility must be developed and applied consistently. If done well, the rewards of one successful alliance can easily be invested in future alliances as the learning curve for engaging collaboratively is mastered.

Look at collaboration as a three-step process:

1. *Goal setting.* Be clear why you do this and what you'd like to achieve. What is the problem this will solve or what advantages will both gain? If there is no real advantage, it is not going to work. In this phase, the focus is on convening the appropriate stakeholders, getting a commitment to collaborate, and building trust. Then, together, define the problem, develop a working commitment, secure the resources necessary to move forward, and make sure that the collaboration meets each member's specific interests.

2. *Direction setting.* Why and how are we going to get there? What are the steps, responsibilities, accountabilities, processes, and other measurement activities? During this phase, stakeholders explore the issues/problem(s) in depth and reach an agreement about strategy. The aim of this phase is to define the key issues to be addressed through collaboration by pooling information and perspectives. It's also the time to generate new information, explore options for

working together, establish agreements, and lay the ground rules for working together.

3. *Implementation.* This is the time to make it happen and get deliverables. Are you on task and meeting targets? Or did you make a wrong turn that requires circling back to step one or step two? In this phase, stakeholders follow through on the agreements reached for the collaborative arrangement. The principal concerns are deciding how to structure the collaboration and how to design the process for working together. This includes dividing responsibilities and resources, ensuring that all partners have the support and agreement of their respective organizations and the ongoing systematic management of the collaboration to ensure that all parties fulfill their obligations.

Successful alliances are management intensive and require a significant investment of resources. Time and effort must be invested early in the collaboration to negotiate a shared agenda and ensure that all members believe that they are reaping added benefits from the alliance. Commitment and trust should be a focal point throughout the process.

Preparing the Foundation

People and positions may change in either organizational structure, but the global expansion must continue as planned. Thus, the foundation should include clear, precise documentation that is agreed upon and understood by all parties. The project must not fail just because one person is no longer there and this is the "one" person who was truly committed. When preparing the foundation for alliances, focus written documentation of these key items:

- Goals and objectives
- Structure
- Processes
- Communication
- Resources (human and capital)
- Data/information and a good execution strategy that includes strategic, tactical, operational, interpersonal, and cultural integration

Too often, the crucial role of human processes is frequently over-looked in favor of more tangible considerations. For example, executives often invest more time and effort screening potential partners in terms of finances than in terms of management competence or philosophical harmony. This lack of attention to the human element is the root cause of many cross-border alliances failing before they ever really get started. Defining roles and developing decision-making processes are especially critical across cultures where misunderstandings are more likely to occur as decisions are made based on values, mind-set, and perceptions.

For that reason, a skilled facilitator with expertise and experience in the international marketplace can contribute significantly to ensuring effective process management. Facilitators are particularly useful when the objective is to promote understanding among diverse cultures and to arrive at mutually agreeable solutions. By focusing on the design and management of the collaboration and maintaining neutrality, facilitators can create a comfortable environment for both parties to identify and clarify the problems that must be addressed. Facilitators can also help resolve differences, develop a shared vision, minimize the influence of power dynamics, and reduce the costs and time of meetings.

When collaborating across borders, it is especially important to seek the right foreign partners. In international business, more so than U.S. domestic markets, good relationships that are built on trust and honor are essential for success. Be sure to check your potential partner's financial status, influence, and reputation in the local business community as well as the partner's access to resources and experience in bringing your product to the home market. But it is also important to reach a meeting of the minds. A good and solid relationship will go a long way in accomplishing goals or resolving issues that arise as part of international business. In smaller countries, consider a partner's political influence since politics and business are often closely intertwined. In any case, remember to proceed with caution and weigh the pros and cons carefully before selecting a foreign partner.

The downside to collaboration through partnerships or joint ventures must also be considered. The two greatest sacrifices, of course, are complete control and sharing revenue. But, when looked at in terms of the cost of doing business, long-term benefits often outweigh the associated costs. Plus, as more experience is gained in the marketplace, the risk of "going it alone" is naturally reduced. And, at some point, many international partnerships progress toward wholly owned subsidiaries and eliminate the issues of shared control and shared revenue.

Considering an International Joint Venture

A joint venture (JV) is a classic strategic alliance between two or more entities to engage in a specific project or undertaking. At first glance, partnerships and JVs may appear very similar, but they can have significantly different implications for those involved. A partnership usually involves a continuing, long-term business relationship, whereas a JV is often based on a single business project. It can be long or short term and used for various business activities: engineering, production, and distribution among others. Some contracts are especially designed for small and medium-sized enterprises (SMEs) in emerging economies and developing markets. These relationships take into account the particularities of specific business fields. Both the guidelines and the texts of the model contracts have been reviewed by international trade law experts from various professional, cultural, and legal backgrounds.

Joint Ventures (JVs): A Balanced Assessment

Joint ventures provide a mechanism that allows interested parties an opportunity to share complementary abilities and resources to gain individual benefits by joining forces on a specific project or objective. The objective may be to develop a product, intellectual property, build a distribution channel, or just share the financial burden and risk of any new venture. Legally, a JV is a new entity formed through the participation of two or more companies in an enterprise whereby each party contributes assets (money, land, equipment, buildings) and shares in the equity and risk according to an agreement. A joint venture, like a general partnership, is not a separate legal entity. Revenues, expenses, and asset ownership flow through the joint venture to the participants, since the joint venture itself has no legal status. Once the JV has met its goals, the entity ceases to exist.

JVs are not new. In 1879 Thomas Edison teamed with Corning Glass Works to develop the incandescent light bulb, and throughout the 1800s railroads in the United States formed partnerships for many large-scale projects. The key to a successful joint venture is sharing of a clearly defined common business objective.

International joint ventures can be extremely advantageous since they provide access to income and growth, which may be impossible for one organization to accomplish alone. Also, developing countries give joint ventures preferential treatment because they do not exclude local interests. Rather, a joint venture between a U.S. company and a local business presents the desired mix of foreign technological and capital involvement. In some countries, a joint venture may be the only way that a firm can participate in local markets. For example, India restricts equity participation by foreign firms in local operations to 40 percent, and many western firms use JVs to gain access to Eastern European markets. Another important business reason for participating in JVs is to minimize the risk of exposing long-term investment capital while at the same time maximizing leverage on the capital that is invested abroad. Other advantages of the JV business model include the ability to:

- Provide companies with the opportunity to gain new capacity and expertise
- Allow companies to enter related businesses, new geographic markets, and gain new technological knowledge
- Generate access to greater resources including specialized staff and technology
- Share the risks with a venture partner
- Experience greater flexibility (a joint venture can have a limited life span and only cover a specific objective, thus limiting both your commitment and the business' exposure)
- Provide a creative way for companies to exit from noncore businesses, especially in an era of divestiture and consolidation
- Gradually separate a business from the rest of the organization and eventually sell it to the other parent company (roughly 80 percent of all joint ventures end in a sale by one partner to the other)

Embarking on a JV can provide the ideal opportunity to redirect or reconstruct a business if it fits with the overall business strategy.

As such, it's important to define, review, and measure your business strategy before committing to a joint venture. It's also critical to choose the right partner by conducting a thorough external analysis. To that end, the due diligence in order to investigate the competition, both real and perceived, is crucial to understand how they operate. Also, check out who owns these companies and inventory their connections, market share, and other relevant variables such as local culture, ways of doing business, corruption index, etc.

Next, conduct an internal assessment and be realistic about the organizational strengths and weaknesses. Consider performing a formal SWOT analysis, which will reveal your organization's strengths, weaknesses, opportunities, and threats. Understanding how a business fits into these categories can assist in finding synergy and compatibility with a prospective partner. When the right partners join forces, the sum is greater than the parts as weaknesses are compensated and strengths are made stronger.

But it takes time and effort to build the right relationship and partnering with another business can be challenging. Problems are likely to arise if:

- The objectives of the venture are not 100 percent clear and communicated to everyone involved.
- There is an imbalance in levels of expertise or investment of assets brought into the venture by the different partners.
- Different cultures and management styles result in poor integration and cooperation.
- The partners don't provide enough leadership and support in the early stages.
- The JV is created without thorough research and analysis of the objectives.

Of course, JVs are not without challenges. An example to illustrate that was Fellowes Inc. based in Itasca, IL, confirming that its Chinese joint venture partner, Jiangsu Shinri Machinery Co., Ltd., has blocked all shipments at the Fellowes' Manufacturing facility in Changzhou, China.

Fellowes has had a long and successful 12-year association with its Chinese JV partner. The relationship evolved in late 2006 from a third-party relationship to a cooperative joint venture. At that point Fellowes gained 100 percent control of the operation and the Chinese partner ceased to be involved in the operations. The terms do entitle the Chinese partner to an annual return on its investment. Fellowes has met this obligation each year.

The shipment stoppage was unilaterally imposed in August by the Chinese partner to force Fellowes to radically change the key provisions of the contract and board resolutions with the effect of shifting power, control, and financial gain to the Chinese partner. In spite of Fellowes efforts to negotiate a settlement with the assistance of the government, the demands from the JV partner have continued to grow with no willingness for compromise or common ground.

Problems began earlier in the year when a dispute broke out between the two brothers of the Chinese partners company Shinri. The dispute resulted in Fellowes' long-standing partner leaving the business and his older brother taking over. Tensions mounted over the ensuing months, but the stoppage of shipments came as a surprise to Fellowes as the shut-down dramatically undermines the Chinese partner's economic opportunity.

Fellowes continues to work with Chinese government and party officials with the help of the U.S. government. The Chinese government has assisted Fellowes in this dispute but so far has been unable to lift the blockage.

In the meantime, Fellowes is diligently working to bring up alternate products and new supply chains to bring its affected machines back into the market. Other problems arise from a lack of understanding of the basic rules that govern how business is conducted in different cultures. For example, when working with Japanese colleagues, failing to understand the importance of maintaining the appearance of harmony and agreement (even when neither actually exists) risks creating serious discomfort among co-workers or causing offense at meetings with behavior that would otherwise be viewed as perfectly acceptable in a Western context. Also, in the Middle East, Sharia, or Islamic law, influences the legal code in most Muslim countries. A movement to allow Sharia to govern personal status law, a set of regulations that pertain to marriage, divorce, inheritance, and custody, is even expanding into the West.

When two strong-minded leaders, accustomed to making decisions unencumbered, are obligated to reach consensus on decisions, conflict can arise. The result can be an impasse on critical decisions. On an international level, any conflict is exacerbated by cultural, political, and philosophical differences. Common areas of concern include:

- *Varied management styles.* Management styles, if widely different, sometimes result in stressful partnerships.
- *Government licensing and policy differences.* Government relations and licensing issues may prove challenging if not addressed and resolved at the beginning.
- *Differing financial and marketing strategies.* Depending on the depth of the JV agreement, contradictory strategic philosophy, particularly in the financial and marketing areas, can prove counterproductive to the partners.
- *Business and operations practices.* Operating philosophies, ethical standards, and corporate policy practices sometimes result in conflict among the partners. Address any obvious potential clashes in day-to-day relations early in the process.
- *Communication with employees.* Remember to communicate and consider the employees' perspective bearing in mind that people can feel threatened by a JV.

Unfortunately, the majority of international JVs fall short of their stated goals, leading to costly failures. External forces like the legal system, political system, state of the economy, and partner differences contribute to these failures. However, a large proportion of these JVs fail due to the inefficient management of human resources, the lack of people skills, and the soft skills necessary to manage cultural issues that come with any cross-border activity.

Best Practices: International Joint Ventures

To avoid a costly failure and navigate these areas of concerns, JV partners should agree upon managing the following key issues before the JV becomes an operating entity. While these items do not represent the entire universe of considerations, they are common to all international and domestic joint ventures.

1. *Education and knowledge management.* Partners should establish the level of organizational training, learning, and intellectual capital

management during JV negotiations. Intellectual capital usage and a protection policy must have the sincere agreement of the partners.

2. *Performance standards, measurement, and goals.* Much like knowledge management, performance standards, benchmarking, and joint goals must be clearly stated and require all parties' agreement before operations commence. Most senior executives are already well aware of the misunderstanding potential of performance goals and the measurement thereof within their own organizations.

3. *Globalizing operations.* International JVs include more critical path issues, particularly for the partner new to the country(s) involved. Among important considerations are timing of the physical entry into the foreign market, selecting the best partner for individual foreign operations, analyzing foreign industry conditions, and foreign government influences and policies.

4. *Cultural variances.* Some international JVs are formed when two U.S. firms, one of which has established a foreign presence, decide to partner. Many other ventures involve a U.S. corporation partnering with an organization native to and based in the foreign market. In both cases, those involved with a new JV must analyze cultural, protocol, and other ethnic differences to establish a performance-oriented "marriage" (or is it "engagement")? of the two organizations.

5. *Command and control.* JV partners tend to be strong, confident, sometimes dominant organizations in their primary markets. Their senior management is typically strong, confident, and equally dominant. If the JV structure is divergent in equity participation (e.g., 80 percent versus 20 percent) command, governance, and control issues can become problem areas unless all nuances achieve enthusiastic and sincere agreement.

6. *Valuation of benefits and the JV as an entity.* In order for a valuation of an individual corporation within a JV to be accurate and fair, it takes experts to analyze, digest, and interpret complex data to arrive at a reasonable value for the organization. A JV with two or more equally complex organizations as partners can be a valuation challenge. That is why it is essential to establish a solid value for the access to new resources and knowledge, along with a fair selling price when JVs seek buyers.

Mergers and Acquisitions (M&A) on the Rise

The global recession, technological advancement, and globalization have fuelled and frenzied mergers and acquisitions at home and abroad. Prices are down, technology and innovation are on the rise, and conducting business without borders increases the number of potential customers exponentially. Some companies, faced with continued pressure to grow profits and the added benefit of cash on the balance sheet, see these deals as virtually mandatory. Executives and deal makers surveyed by Accenture across the globe estimate that 20 percent of projected future growth will come from acquisitions. Not surprisingly, the same Accenture survey revealed that the majority of respondents expect their next M&A deal to be a cross-border transaction. However, this research also shows that companies find these deals substantially more difficult than domestic acquisitions.

Managing cultural differences, integrating across borders, and establishing a clear organizational structure and lines of responsibility are cited by survey respondents as particularly difficult yet critical to the success of cross-border deals. Difficult or not, it's clear that global M&A is no longer just an option to ponder—it is part of the new reality. U.S.-based businesses are being acquired by foreign investors, and that brings global competition to your doorstep. It is no longer a choice whether to participate in cross-border business. It's buy or be bought. Engage or be engaged. U.S.-based business leaders can't ignore opportunities abroad any more than foreign investors can ignore the opportunities here, on U.S. soil. But the long-term success of M&A depends on strong leadership, a forward-thinking mind-set, thorough due diligence, cultural awareness, and a well-planned post-merger integration process. Each step is critical to getting it right the first time. When done right, the advantages are numerous.

Advantages of Global M&A

Companies choose M&A for a variety of strategic reasons: to obtain new technology, new brands, complementary products; to gain access to experienced management/workforce; to exert control over the supply chain; to gain economies of scale; improve distribution channels;

or to remove a competitor. Plus, it's a relatively safe and economical strategy when compared to other expansion options. Another significant advantage is the built-in customer base that flows naturally with the purchase of a popular brand. For some domestic businesses, M&A abroad may represent the only tangible option for growing market share in a slumped domestic economy.

In the first decade of the 21st century, global M&A activity has increased substantially as this business model is a natural progression for businesses gaining experience and confidence abroad. The current global crisis is further fueling cross-border M&A with sellers generally more distressed and, therefore, more inclined to work with foreign buyers. Also, there is less competition from buyers in the seller's home country even with prices falling to attractive levels.

When contrasted to building a business abroad from scratch, consider these important benefits of expanding through M&A:

- An existing, successful business is already functioning and properly set up and may require only minor changes to continue successfully.
- The workforce of the business will already be in place and well organized. The buyer just needs to develop a relationship with the workforce and discover what motivates them.
- Marketing initiatives and contacts will be firmly established.
- The customer base and revenue stream will also be set up.
- A well-developed company can ease access to capital if it has a sound business plan and available cash flow.

Challenges to Successful Cross-Border M&A

Pursuing expansion and growth in the global market through M&A requires an entirely new perspective and understanding of due diligence and risk assessment, and that's proving to be a significant obstacle for most U.S. businesses. Acquiring or merging with a foreign company necessitates due diligence that extends way beyond financial numbers and reaching agreeable terms. Rather, the critical (and often overlooked) aspects of any due diligence process should be strategic and cultural in nature. These are the issues that are more likely to cause real problems than numbers alone. Long-term success of an M&A deal is equally dependent upon dealing effectively with differences in corporate cultures; maintaining employee, stakeholder, and customer loyalty in a foreign company; and gaining a workable understanding of that company's human and business values. Due diligence is much more than making sure the numbers work.

Unfortunately, the majority of due diligence, fact finding, risk assessment, and investigative resources are focused solely on fundamental "hard" challenges such as infrastructure, EBIDTA, and ROI. However, over 80 percent of the real risks associated with international M&A are derived from "soft" challenges. Soft challenges originate from cultural differences, corporate transparency, and systems of doing business in a new country such as legal, labor, accounting, and cultural integration issues. Understanding the corporate culture along with the culture of the country or region plays a crucial role in securing the long-term success of any M&A deal. While profits, EBIDTA, and ROI are important matters, these considerations represent just the tip of the iceberg—the visible tip. Underneath the water, and hidden from view, lurk the real dangers someone must expose through extensive research and due diligence.

Some of the professionals commonly found on a due diligence team are focused on the "hard issues." For example, your investment banker who will already have a lot of knowledge about the target and will understand what has been negotiated and what is and what isn't part of the deal. But his/her goal is to seal the deal. Then your attorney, who is the professional primarily responsible for assessing legal risks. For example, he might assess legal risks, such as the potential for product liability or the potential for lawsuits and successor liabilities.

The attorney might also look for undisclosed liens on assets. The attorney will make sure the business is in good standing and that all legal documents protect your interests. The attorney will also draft or review the sale agreement to be certain it properly reflects the deal as negotiated and protects you against known and unknown liabilities. But the attorney is the one representing you and will be gone after the deal is sealed. Therefore, he/she may not be as interested in developing the relationship and trust and understanding the cultural nuances that will lead to successful corporate integration. Attorneys deal with facts, risks, and taking sides, and definitely don't focus on the "soft issues."

Your CPA should be able to review financial records and, sometimes, operational records. He/she might look for unrecorded liabilities and verify that accounts receivable and inventory are accurately stated. He might also verify that product costs and gross margins are accurately stated and also advise you on the tax aspects of the transaction. But your CPA will not be able to inform you about the "ins and outs" of actually distributing your product and other transparency issues or lack of.

You may need to hire technical consultants and other professionals to deal with environmental issues, real estate issues, etc. But again, these people would stick to their expertise and won't be able to advise you on the strategic aspects of the deal, on the integration "soft issues," as well as culture, relationship, and what is underneath the iceberg.

Too often, the real difficulties and challenges of M&A surface months after deals are signed. Then, the tough questions that should have been addressed in the front-end due diligence process start flowing. For example:

- How will this newly acquired enterprise be integrated into the existing company?
- Will it operate independently or as a department?
- How will the integration be made smooth and seamless?
- How will the acquiring company deal with duplicate departments, systems, vendors?
- How will the new business be operated the day after that deal was sealed?
- Will this organization structure produce loyalty?
- Will the employees and managers stay?
- What will the local reaction be to any proposed changes?
- What is the new competitive landscape?

The answers to these questions and many others come from gathering the *right* information from the *right* sources. It's easy to get misdirected or overwhelmed by the staggering quantity of available information. Stay focused on research that includes assessment of consumer demand, consumer profiles, competition, pricing, packaging, foreign regulations, shipping, and distribution, to name a few. In addition, companies need to look internally at their strengths and weaknesses in relation to their action plan. That means evaluating corporate resources, manpower, internal knowledge, and their own culture (perception, loyalty, motivation) before determining whether expansion opportunities are viable and warrant penetration into new markets.

The Perils of Culture, Language, and Distance

While all mergers require bridging the differences between corporate cultures (see Figure 6.1 for the stages of increasing importance of the topics), this exercise becomes even more daunting when you add in the affect of national cultural differences, distance, and language barriers. In many cross-border M&A deals, the effort involved in cultural integration proves more difficult and just takes longer than expected. Part of the problem stems from the strictures of "political correctness," which discourage any overt references to national differences out of a fear of creating offense. Other problems arise from a lack of understanding of the basic rules that govern how business is conducted in different cultures. For example, when working with Japanese colleagues, anyone who fails to understand the importance of maintaining the appearance of harmony and agreement (even when neither actually exists) risks creating serious discomfort among coworkers or causing offense at meetings with behavior that would otherwise be viewed as perfectly acceptable

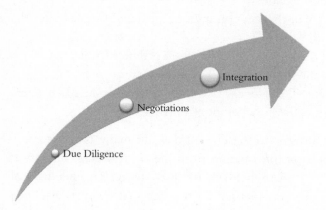

Figure 6.1   Growing Globally through Cross–Border Partnerships: The Stages of Increasing Importance of Mastering Cross–Cultural Fluency
Copyright © 2010. All rights reserved to Mona Pearl, BeyondAStrategy, Inc.

in a Western context. Based on this point, how do you provide timely feedback? What are the right communication modes to use? What are the risks associated with doing that?

Language is another barrier to the successful completion of a cross-border deal. With a few exceptions, it is seldom practical for an acquirer to impose its language on the acquired company. In many cases, enforcing the acquirer's language stirs up resentment that makes cooperation even more difficult. This is especially true when the two countries represented in the deal have a long and troubled history—such a language imposition winds up opening old wounds.

Also challenging is developing a team spirit post-M&A, and physical distance only complicates this important process. Without regular opportunities to meet face to face, misunderstandings can easily arise. This can lead one group to conclude that their remote colleagues are incompetent or, worse, not acting in line with the organization's overall strategy. Add in language differences, culturally driven behavior, and expectations, and the risk of misunderstandings increases, which makes successful cross-border cooperation even more difficult.

A final area of concern is the reaction of national governments and consumers who face losing control over critical strategic assets or iconic brands. For example, when a foreign company was rumored to be considering the acquisition of Danone, the giant French company known for its yogurt, Prime Minister Dominique de Villepin declared that the government would come to "the defense of Danone's interests and the French future of Danone." The flap led to passage of a "strategic sectors" bill, dubbed "The Danone Law." A similar outcry in the United States greeted Belgian brewing giant InBev's proposed acquisition of Anheuser-Busch—makers of the revered American beer Budweiser. However, that deal was finalized.

One of the latest examples is in Egypt, where the new government revoked the license/agreement for an acquisition transaction that was sealed a few years ago.

Integration from the Start

The vast majority of acquisitions fail to meet the pre-acquisition objectives two years afterward. Even three years following an acquisition, only a mere 12 percent of companies report that overall growth has surpassed the pre-acquisition period. In other words, 88 percent of acquisitions are still trying to figure out what went wrong three years after the deal is complete. This failure to succeed, at least immediately, is often the result of limited time addressing and planning important aspects of the cultural integration of the two unique businesses. Typically what happens is that the acquiring company seeks to imprint its own culture on the acquired company and appears surprised by the issues that result—issues that should have been discovered and planned for during the due diligence phase.

But it doesn't have to be that way. Savvy businesspeople can improve the likelihood of success with a more relevant distribution of due-diligence and an emphasis on post-deal integration. If 80 percent of the risk comes from the "soft" issues, that's where the focus of efforts should be directed. By extending the principles of traditional due diligence, businesses can make more informed decisions. Remember, even when the numbers look good, the deal can become a disastrous failure if the soft issues are not properly addressed. Learn about the culture of doing business; learn about the legal system and how it may affect your new venture; and learn about the political environment and any implications on daily business.

While the art of cross-border post-merger integration is still evolving, there are two best practices that can be distilled from observing the most successful deal practitioners:

1. Set clear expectations, and invest in high-quality, two-way communication.

    Clear communications is the basis for post-acquisition cooperation between the two companies' management teams. When cross-border deals go wrong, lack of clarity about goals and objectives, compounded by poor and deteriorating communications, is frequently the cause. In addition, careful attention is needed to ensure that remote companies fully understand the overall corporate direction and have an opportunity to customize the strategy to local requirements.

    For best results, companies should bring together management teams across borders on a regular basis, whether through face-to-face meetings, management rotation, or other methods. For example, critical factors in the successful integration of Abbey National into Banco Santander included a three-year plan with ambitious objectives, strong internal communications, and the assignment of key Santander managers to work with Abbey on a day-to-day basis.

Some key communications strategies include:

- Pay attention to the early integration of key leadership of the acquired company into the appropriate information and decision-making forums. This gives leaders access to the larger corporate context and ensures that local decision making is aligned with overall corporate direction.
- Rely on selective use of management at headquarters to support the leadership of acquired companies, rather than second-guessing or overruling them. These assignments should be treated as both sensitive and critically important for realizing the value of the acquisition and not as an opportunity to offload managers for whom no other obvious role is available.
- Remember that headquarters' attention needs to be focused on critical decisions that will drive value in the acquisition, rather than micromanaging local activities or imposing rules and procedures that may not be effective, efficient, or, even appropriate.
- Make an investment in high-quality, two-way communications between the parent and the acquired company. This provides transparent visibility of performance, early warning of potential problems or changes in direction, and clear roles and responsibilities on both sides for maintaining these links.

2. Acknowledge cultural differences but simultaneously create a common corporate culture with a single goal: achieving high performance.

In an effort to be politically correct, we need to remember that it is bad behavior to refer to national stereotypes or to base expectations of behavior or performance on cultural background. However, there are systematic differences in both values and behavior between countries that will color interactions between individuals of different backgrounds. Understanding these can be extremely useful in avoiding misunderstandings. Here are some examples:

- Germans dislike uncertainty.
- French are inclined to be skeptical and self-critical.

- Japanese place a high importance on correct form and ceremony.
- Swedes prefer decision making based on consensus.
- British have a high tolerance for ambiguity and use humor in ways that foreigners often find puzzling.
- Americans are less formal than Europeans.

One advantage of openly acknowledging cultural differences is that it sets the stage for a broader examination of the larger post-merger company culture and creates an opportunity for the two entities to work toward a single shared culture that is more supportive of high performance. Conversely, the failure to acknowledge and adopt superior practices of the acquired company can result in lost value opportunities, usually accompanied by the departure of key individuals.

One merger in the banking industry, for example, combined two companies with very different attitudes about the organization of international teams. The smaller, acquired company favored a more informal approach, while the larger, acquiring company relied more on formal structures and procedures. Rather than examining these differences and evaluating their relative merits, the large company's approach dominated by default, resulting in the loss of key skills and management, and, ultimately, the closure of several international sites.

Some key points in this area to remember are:

- Conduct cross-cultural training workshops and one-on-one coaching sessions to raise awareness of and sensitivity to cultural differences. These should cover both national differences and those arising from different company cultures.
- Use tools to objectively assess both organizational cultures, from the macro level down to individual functions and departments. The purpose is to establish a baseline against which change can be measured and to identify potential areas where gaps are likely to create integration problems.
- Develop a clear description of the desired post-merger shared culture, one that combines the strengths of both organizations.
- Chart the road map as to how this change management as part of integration will happen. Step by step.

- Implement formal programs for cultural change sponsored and driven from the most senior levels of the organization.

The recent surge in cross-border mergers is part of a broader set of trends that reflect how companies are adjusting their strategies to compete in a world in which customers and suppliers are increasingly global. The best international competitors are simultaneously leveraging the benefits of global scale and configuring activities to ensure a highly tailored response to local customer needs.

For many companies embarking on a cross-border acquisition for the first time, the temptation is twofold:

1. To make as few changes as possible in the structure and management processes of the newly acquired company and
2. To look for the most straightforward way of connecting them to an existing operating model.

While this is often a safe near-term strategy, over time the failure to exploit the benefits of scale can add up to significant lost profit opportunities.

More sophisticated acquirers will move to realize the obvious cross-border synergies, such as leveraging purchasing scale or moving to shared back-office services. At the same time, the continued duplication of management structures, the inefficient distribution of assets, and the dispersion of critical skills across multiple geographies often remain as unexploited opportunities for profit improvement. Companies that develop superior skills in selecting, evaluating, and integrating cross-border acquisitions will benefit from faster growth and higher profitability. Those that struggle are more likely to become acquisition targets themselves.

Cross-Border Strategic Due Diligence

Rigorous due diligence conducted by a team of people that possess a deep knowledge of the local language, customs, and legal requirements is essential. During the due diligence stage, close attention is needed to ensure that the potential value of the target is being fully captured.

In particular, the transfer of rights (including intellectual property) and assets, as well as access to favorable supplier contracts, must be carefully considered in the context of the culture and the way business is conducted in that country. A contract may outline certain terms, but there are other issues, "unwritten rules/agreements" that can be found only when talking to local people and only after establishing a trusted working relationship. Again, anyone can see the tip of the iceberg, but it takes a trained eye to see the real danger hidden under water.

In emerging markets, increasing wages and social benefit obligations may not be deal breakers. At the same time, it is critical for these and other human capital costs to be included and played under several scenarios for a number of years if a buyer is to get a more realistic picture of a target company's value and of future integration issues. The lack of transparency combined with the greater overlap between political, regulatory, and economic policies in emerging markets adds to the nature of unpredictability, and therefore requires more due diligence, data points, and sensitivity to cultural nuances. The more a country falls into the category of an emerging market, the more likely it is that political red tape will slow the pace of progress. One way that this occurs is that labor laws often vary from one jurisdiction to another. Other issues may include the limit on the number of foreign nationals that can be brought in to assume key responsibilities and the issue of local employee loyalty and how to maintain it. Additionally, U.S. firms face the Sarbanes-Oxley issue, since most companies in the emerging markets are not obliged to comply with that regulation.

All of this means that from the very first stages of negotiation, and certainly before a letter of intent has been entered into, the parties in a cross-border transaction must think carefully about their legal assumptions and question whether they apply before coming to the negotiating table. Legal counsel can certainly assist in this endeavor, but it is up to the businessperson to raise the issues in a timely manner. Such successful negotiations occur only when both sides understand and trust each other and are willing and able to engage in a process of meaningful information exchange. Although it may sound simple, it isn't.

Too often, U.S.-based businesses are hastily lured into specific global markets by competitors before extensive due diligence is complete. Many, hungry for market share and quick profits, fail to do their homework. As such, they neglect to ask the right questions, do their research, gather data, and analyze that data carefully in order to establish a detailed strategy and comprehensive plan for international expansion. Erroneously, some businesses just assume they have to expand and fail to consider the long-term versus short-term implications of globalization. Consequently, over half of U.S. global ventures end in failure, and valuable resources are squandered.

International due diligence requires a company to go beyond traditional M&A work and consider variables that are unfamiliar to most companies and most business people who lack cross-border experience. Because "You don't know what you don't know," unintentional mistakes are made and rarely corrected in time. Avoid this by identifying the right team of experienced people—people who can obtain and interpret actionable data concerning the political, national, corporate, and human culture of the targeted company as it relates to the ongoing business operation. Ignoring or misunderstanding these issues will jeopardize a company's M&A initiative.

Companies can prevent late-stage integration issues from derailing an otherwise sound international expansion initiative by following these additional guidelines:

1. *Practice cultural due diligence.* Determine how the target company operates in a broader, human-capital sense. How will customers and employees view a foreign company moving onto their turf? What's the work ethic of its employees? How is productivity viewed, measured, and maintained? What's the management style of its executives? Who are the company's main competitors? How stable is the political environment? Are there any conflicts with the U.S. Foreign Corrupt Practices Act?
2. *Make a strong commitment.* Peter Drucker once said that "Unless commitment is made, there are only promises and hopes . . . but no plans." Management has to be on board 100 percent—on both sides! Developing an international market requires enormous energy, knowledge, managerial buy-in, and an understanding of business practices in other countries. Few, if any, companies have the resources to go it alone. They'll need a non-U.S. view of the world and the assistance of people experienced in global business transactions.

3. *Be humble.* The brash, pushy approach of the rugged U.S. businessperson won't work in the global arena. Successful international business leaders possess a quiet, respectful humility combined with a passion for learning, understanding, and practicing how people in other cultures live, work, and like to be rewarded. Customers in different countries have unique ways of relating to products and services. Their lifestyles vary greatly, along with their values, priorities, and buying habits. Savvy international businesspeople blend in and adapt to the cultural norms of whatever market they're serving. In this respect, cross-cultural or intercultural diversity as a corporate principle is an absolute requirement for business survival and long-term profitability.

4. *Educate your team on cross-cultural communication.* Research shows that communication between culturally different organizations is often plagued by prejudice and stereotyping on the part of the acquiring company's managers. Poor or insensitive communication between managers and the target company's employees can absolutely derail an international venture's chance for success. On the other hand, with proper cross-cultural training, these problems can be minimized or prevented altogether.

5. *Ask for help.* Seek guidance from an experienced, "hands-on" international business expert—someone who thoroughly understands how to do business internationally and in that specific region. Such a professional is sensitive to the national and corporate cultures of both the client and target countries and will be able to guide you and put some of the essential policies in place. For example, what does it mean when foreign business executives become quiet at a key meeting? Are they in agreement? Disagreement? Insulted? Trying to hide their laughter from you? How does the country's ethical system differ from that of the United States? Is corruption rampant? Will the U.S. entity be competing with businesses owned by relatives of the country's president? (If so, good luck!) While there are no guarantees in any business venture, the right international business expert can make a dramatic difference in and increase the chances for ultimate success.

Since almost 40 percent of corporate revenues are spent on people (salaries, benefits, hiring costs, etc.), due diligence must focus on all issues related to human capital in every phase of the M&A process—and the earlier the better. In Japan, for example, a deal that fails to demonstrate tangible benefits for target company employees, not just the acquirer's shareholders, may not get off the ground. In China, wage inflation is becoming a serious problem for owners, and India is fast running short of technically trained people.

It's Your Responsibility: Foreign Corrupt Practices Act (FCPA)[2]

Corruption, while not unique to developing countries, is more common in emerging markets. And any level of corruption will complicate compliance with FCPA rules and regulations. The FCPA prohibits payments to foreign officials for certain purposes; however, it can be difficult in certain developing countries to know whether an individual is a private businessperson or a foreign official. Regardless of local enforcement, it is a violation of the FCPA to induce a foreign official to commit any act in violation of their duty to uphold local law. The FCPA does exempt certain payments to foreign officials who "expedite or secure" the performance of routine governmental action. However, many more facilitation payments are a matter of due course in some developing countries. As you can see in Figure 6.2, corruption is a result of different ethical standards in different countries and cultures. In some cases, people won't follow the FCPA simply because

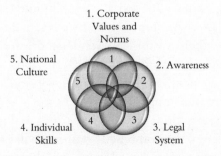

Figure 6.2 Ethics Across Borders Tend to Be Relative in Meaning and Enforcement

they are not even aware that corruption is perceived by others as illegal or immoral. Cultural differences affect the values, norms, and even the level of awareness.

When examining target companies, ensure compliance with the FCPA by asking the following questions:

- Has the target company (or its principals, directors, or key managers) been publicly sanctioned or come under suspicion for corruption?
- Have background checks and other forms of due diligence been performed on key members of management, customers, agents, etc., to identify potential government links?
- To what extent does the target company rely on third parties to conduct business?
- What are the total amounts of retainers, commissions, and expenses paid to third parties in connection with sales?
- Has the target company distributed a compliance policy to all employees and agents?
- Has the policy been assessed as to whether it is regularly enforced and records maintained?
- To what extent does the target company maintain written agreements for all international agents regarding FCPA and anti-corruption clauses?

Creating Sustainable Value: Post-Merger Practices

Acquisition integration is defined as the combining of two companies through changes of ownership such as mergers, acquisitions, and takeovers, to include their customers, vendors, organizations, processes, products, and employees to form a larger, more powerful organization. But this is only accomplished when the goals and objectives, which should have been well framed, identified, and set, fully materialize. Without proper integration, the "day after" the deal is signed as well as future performance of the combined company will not justify the purchase price and sometimes even destroy shareholder value. Common consequences of failed integration include loss of customers, loss of employees, loss of morale, operational difficulties, lost opportunities and impaired reputation, brand equity, and culture clash, to name only a few. Companies must execute a successful integration to realize the synergies indentified before the transaction.

Shamefully, 65 percent of cross-border M&A fail. Some deals never emerge from the initial phase of negotiations and due diligence, while others fall apart in the latter stage when the acquisition is being integrated into the mission, vision, and values of the acquiring organization. For these latter failures, the cause is a lack of foresight. Too often, dealmakers are so consumed by making the numbers work that they fail to establish a front-end strategic integration plan that details how the business will operate post M&A. Instead, consider integration at the outset of any talks. It's never too early to start thinking about integration and what issues it may trigger.

Companies making their first international acquisition must realize that integrating a foreign business into an organization that has been optimized for operation in a single country will require additional resources. For example, the volume of work required to accommodate multiple currencies, reporting requirements, and local employment laws is often underestimated, leaving the acquirer poorly prepared to operate as an integrated whole. The transaction itself is only the beginning of a long process of combining two companies. The real hard work begins after the transaction is completed and can take years to complete. The results of the post-transaction integration process will ultimately determine whether or not a merger is successful.

So get this right:

1. *Communicate the vision and business logic of the deal.* Employees and other pivotal stakeholders, including investors, must understand the strategic rationale, business objectives, and post-merger integration milestones and targets. Senior management should lead the implementation.
2. *Separate the post-merger integration from the core business.* Post-merger integration needs its own organization with a dedicated team of executives and faster than usual governance and decision-making processes. The correct allocation of resources is especially important where there are mission-critical functions.

3. *Monitor core business performance.* Establish early-warning systems to alert management to any falloff in revenue or profitability in the core business.
4. *Proactively manage the soft issues.* Post-merger integration isn't just a numbers game. The process involves complex organizational and cultural changes. Identify key staff and design strategies to keep them on board as they are the value of the franchise. Handle new appointments with care.
5. *Move before the close of the deal.* There are a lot of actions that can be taken in advance (prior to the close) that enable you to realize the benefits of the transaction immediately after it is finalized.

When a post-merger integration is successful, the payoff can be striking. A rigorous approach may enable an acquirer to exceed synergy expectations and earn the shareholder's respect and confidence in the company. A word of caution here: Do not rely on the CPA, the attorney, or the investment banker to plan the strategic integration plan. First, this team of dealmakers already received its payment in full (whether a lucrative commission or hefty fee) when the transaction was officially completed and no longer has a vested interest in the success of the transaction. Second, the essential questions are strategic in nature and require the foresight of a global business expert—someone who can ask the right questions, gather the requisite data, and evaluate the information in a cross-border context.

Because businesses operate so differently in other countries, it's critical to address integration issues as early as possible when crossing borders. For example, a business in Malaysia cannot be run the same way a business is run in the United States. In addition to cultural differences, there are environmental, political, and legal differences that need to be understood and factored into an overall risk analysis. In some countries, for example, the government has tremendous influence on how, when, where, and if business can be conducted. The government may also reserve the right to retroactively institute changes that could result in land, buildings, or certifications being revoked. Without cause, some governments can simply eject a company from the country with no explanation. In one recent example, a mining company with operations in Africa was conducting business as usual on Monday. By

Wednesday, it was shut down and management was told to leave the country. Their mining certificate was revoked, and they were provided no explanation.

Pearls of Wisdom

Innovative, collaborative, and forward-thinking competitive strategies are the key to success in the future. Don't settle for the same old cookie-cutter global expansion plan that your competitors are already utilizing. It will only skim rewards off the top. Take the initiative to thoroughly evaluate potential markets, get to know the local people, and design a custom business model that will maximize the opportunities of those markets and deliver on your globalization goals. Plan, commit, act, and execute with confidence to achieve success.

The recent surge in cross-border alliances, especially cross-border M&A, is part of a broader set of trends that reflect how companies are adjusting their strategies to compete in a world in which customers and suppliers are increasingly global. This trend cannot be ignored. Start now and build the skills necessary to success in today's global marketplace.

Here are some key points to keep in mind from reading this chapter:

- As international collaboration grows in occurrence and complexity, consider alliances/partnerships as a key to achieving sustainable cross-border growth and a competitive advantage.
- Can you craft flexible business models that leverage your strengths in conjunction with the unique circumstances of target markets? Remember, collaboration is a three-step process: goal setting, direction setting, and implementation.
- It takes time and effort to build the right relationship, and partnering with another business can be challenging.
- The foundation for global expansion must include both collaboration and strategic innovation.
- Joint ventures provide a mechanism that allows interested parties an opportunity to share complementary abilities and resources to

gain individual benefits by joining forces on a specific project or objective.

- International joint ventures provide access to income and growth that may be impossible for one organization to accomplish alone.
- Cross-border M&A is no longer an option or a luxury. It is the new reality. Have you considered the advantages of M&A? In addition, can you conduct effective international due diligence?
- Prevent late-stage integration issues: Practice cultural due diligence, make a strong commitment, be humble, educate your team, and ask experts for help.
- Beware of the Foreign Corrupt Practices Act (FCPA).
- There are best practices for global M&A—apply them!

In addition to considering and evaluating external partnership structures, we can't forget to look at growing from within. That means focusing on innovation, entrepreneurship, business clusters, vertical integration, and sourcing abroad all are components that we'll address in Chapter 7.

Chapter 7

Corporate Business Models

Growing Your Business from Within

"Globalization has changed us into a company that searches the world, not just to sell or to source, but to find intellectual capital—the world's best talents and greatest ideas."

—*Jack Welch*

When PFW, a small German aerospace parts manufacturing firm, first ventured outside its homeland searching for growth opportunities, it chose the Aegean Free Zone in Izmir, Turkey. Joining a government-sponsored endeavor, or cluster, can provide immediate access to the "right" contacts, including government officials and inspectors, permits, tax advantages, and an established talent pool. PFW chose this location because the industrial park was designed specifically for the purpose of creating an aerospace industry cluster.

"The free zone was very attractive because we were inexperienced at outsourcing and it was easier for us to start our expansion in the Aegean Free Zone," says Mr. Viehrig, Managing Director of PFW, Turkey. The zone works to improve collaboration between the university and local businesses to strengthen education and skills. And it's working: PFW receives 200 qualified applicants for every advertised position. PFW began operations in Izmir with 20 employees. Currently, it employs about 120 with plans to increase that number to 500 within the next four to five years. "Our success in Turkey is due to several factors including proximity to European markets, a well-trained workforce and the absence of quality problems," adds Mr. Viehrig. Furthermore, the Aegean Free Zone offers superior amenities such as childcare, improved working conditions, and a pleasant work environment, which make the company an attractive employer compared to those outside the zone.[1]

Innovative Models for Tomorrow's Success

Unlike traditional business models, emerging models are not mutually exclusive, and the PFW story is a great example of combining clusters, innovation, and entrepreneurship in a global context. It's a matter of blending various aspects of traditional and emerging business models to customize an approach that best links the goals of corporate strategy with the circumstances that exist in a specific prospective market. That said, no one business model is inherently right or wrong. Yet, when presented with a specific set of facts for one business and one geographic area or region, it becomes remarkably clear which business model will deliver the desired results. Likewise, it is equally clear which business model will only lead to trouble.

When choosing a business model, it's always a tradeoff between control and risk. Increased control demands greater financial resources, which opens the door to financial risk. In addition to financial risk, it's equally important to consider market risk. Market risk results from holding back the resources necessary to achieve success in the new market. Driven by fear of financial risk, many businesses inadvertently mastermind their own failure by withholding adequate financial resources. For example, a business might select the least-expensive mode of market entry, such as indirect distribution, to minimize financial risk. However, with indirect distribution, the seller is removed from important consumer information such as buying behavior and product feedback. Ultimately, the distance between the end user and U.S. business entity could result in lost opportunities and increased market risk.

In any case, every enterprise should choose the business model that best links its goals and objectives, taking into consideration, of course, the unique circumstances of the target market. As we've already discussed, two models that are gaining in popularity are M&A and joint ventures. But there are many other options, such as joining a business cluster, vertical integration, or sourcing abroad.

Regardless of the option selected, savvy business leaders must learn how to implement aspects of collaboration and innovation to differentiate their presence in a foreign marketplace. Before committing to any business form, however, it's important to recognize that continued growth may require a business to transition from one business model to the next as internal or external conditions change. That ability requires flexibility, agility, and a keen eye for marketplace opportunities.

With a rapidly changing global marketplace, it's also vital to be able to craft flexible business models that leverage the strengths from each global marketplace. For instance, some U.S. businesses may consider returning certain functions, like high-tech manufacturing, to the United States in order to stay competitive and protect intellectual property. On the other hand, they will collaborate with global partners on new ways of outsourcing, generating future innovations, and product upgrades. Through this paradigm shift in mind-set and strategy, businesses can create and foster long-term success.

Innovation: The Secret Ingredient

No business model is complete without innovation. Innovation is like that coveted secret ingredient in a cherished family recipe. When skillfully added at just the right time, or as a corporate strategy, in the right way and in the right quantity, it never fails to win the blue medal. But discovering how to deliver innovation to the global scene requires great insight into a specific market, its culture, the business environment, and the competition. For example, consider the traditional business model of outsourcing. For decades manufacturers flocked to China for low-cost sourcing. But how many businesses truly maximized the potential of their investment in China? Not many. Very few U.S. companies were forward-thinking enough to foresee the local Chinese citizens as potential consumers and cater to their growing needs, desires, and discretionary income. Of the few forward-thinking businesses that did, even fewer were innovative enough to exploit those domestic markets.

Wikipedia defines innovation as "a new way of doing something." It may refer to incremental, radical, or revolutionary changes in thinking, products, processes, or organizations. A distinction is typically made between invention, an idea made manifest, and innovation, ideas applied successfully. Peter Drucker, noted writer and management consultant of the 20th century, viewed innovation as the tool or instrument used by entrepreneurs to exploit change as an opportunity. While he never agreed to a theory of innovation, he realized enough was known to develop it as a practice—a practice based on when, where, and how one looks systematically for ground-breaking new opportunities and how one judges the chances for their success or the risks of their failure. From Drucker's perspective, systematic innovation consisted of the purposeful and organized search for changes and in the systematic analysis of opportunities.

Innovation Comes in Many Forms

Necessity is the mother of innovation, and it comes in many forms: meeting a need through product modification, creating a need through expert marketing of a global brand, or solving current market problems like Procter & Gamble (P&G) did in Eastern Europe. When P&G chose Eastern Europe as a target market, these formerly communist countries were beyond undeveloped; they were collapsed markets. Still, in spite of the lack of any local resources, P&G saw opportunity and enormous market potential. To get started, P&G had to solve a number of local market problems, like the absence of any distribution system. To that end, the company funded distributor businesses in the form of vehicles, information technology, working capital, and extensive training.

The experience P&G gained in the trenches of the local marketplace developed into a significant competitive advantage. In Russia, for example, P&G gained access to 80 percent of the entire population. While this plan was fraught with risk, the risk was calculated, assessed, and assumed only after it was contrasted with long-term gains. Considerable investment was required of P&G to develop this network from the ground up in a country with renowned distribution challenges, but by tackling the issue head-on rather than waiting for the enabling condition to develop, P&G gained huge leads in market share.

P&G's approach to Eastern Europe clearly illustrates the tradeoff between control and risk. It also demonstrates the long-term rewards of understanding the local marketplace, its culture, and the needs. Through a willingness to collaborate, the ability to innovate, and sheer determination, U.S. businesses can reap greater rewards in foreign markets. For businesses already on the ground in foreign markets, like China, the possibilities to expand market base and achieve growth are just waiting to be discovered.

In 2004, William Lazonick, Professor in the Department of Regional Economic and Social Development at the University of Massachusetts Lowell and Director of the Massachusetts Lowell Center for Industrial Competitiveness, coined the phrase "indigenous innovation," which is the development of a collective type of learning within the organization. Another offshoot is "disruptive innovation," which improves a product or service in ways that the market does not expect (e.g., lower prices, designed to appeal to a new customer). Coined by Clayton M. Christensen in his 1995 article "Disruptive Technologies: Catching the Wave," co-written with Joseph Bower, disruptive innovations are predominantly intimidating to existing market leaders because they represent competition coming from an unexpected direction. The concept of disruptive innovation carries on a long practice of recognizing radical technical change in the study of innovation by economists.

Another method for practicing innovation involves the antithesis of what Drucker called systematic innovation. It is based upon the concept of "accidents happen." Innovation cannot always be planned, which is why this approach emphasizes how many important innovations are the byproducts of accidents. It is expecting the unexpected and always taking into account that this is a variable within your equation. Popular innovations discovered by accident include cellophane, corn flakes, nylon, penicillin, Teflon, Post-it notes, and so many more.

Innovation and Entrepreneurship in the 21st Century

These examples demonstrate how innovation evolves and adapts to a changing business landscape. Looking back, it's interesting to observe the strides innovation and entrepreneurship have made. For starters, innovation has become a necessity in today's global business setting, regardless of a company's market scope. This is due to the new reality that competition for any business extends way beyond its local area. In fact, companies that recognized this early on and nurtured innovation as the ultimate source of competitive advantage are surely reaping the benefits today.

With the proliferation of elaborate think tanks and R&D facilities overseas, it is evident that companies today are striving for an innovative climate. Yet based on a comparative study of innovation practices, the practice of innovation is not without its extreme challenges.[2] The study was completed using a series of interviews with corporate executives and senior innovation officers in four of the largest Chicago-area, publicly traded companies,[3] and one government agency. The intent of the study was to learn how individuals, groups, leaders, and the organizational culture are influenced by creativity (generating an idea) and risk-taking (taking action on the idea). Interview questions were based on the Innovation Equation model, Innovation = Creativity + Risk-Taking.[4]

The study's findings showed a key difference between those companies that referred to their culture as "highly innovative" and those that did not. All of the highly innovative companies had innovative processes in place. While each process had its strengths and weaknesses, the simple act of articulating a process was enough to communicate the importance of innovation to the whole company.

In 2009, most American businesses were forced to shift back as the economy was brought to its knees at home and abroad. Although entrepreneurs are known for turning such conditions into opportunities, this crisis hit hard. In the book *Webs of Innovation: The Networked Economy Demands New Ways to Innovate*[5] authors Alexander Loudon and Roel Pieper argued that even during recessionary times, the need for innovation persists. He recommended a concept of "networked innovation" as the way to help corporations adapt to carrying out innovation in the Information Age. Companies with ongoing commitment to innovation, he noted, are both able to take greater advantage of new markets and opportunities during boom times and to maintain and grow existing business during downward cycles. "Companies that don't take charge of their innovation processes cannot expect to profit from innovation," he concludes.

If entrepreneurs are going to be an integral part of the answer to the world's turbulent times, if they are destined to be the opportunity diggers and job creators, then it will probably come from those who lean more to the creative side. According to Professor Jean-Claude Larreche, Professor of Marketing at INSEAD in Fontainebleau, France, creative entrepreneurs can weather this crisis better than traditional companies can. "It's not the creative entrepreneurs, but it's the large companies that are being challenged. Creative companies can survive any condition," says Larreche.

Speaking at the World Knowledge Forum in Seoul, South Korea, on November 19, 2008, Larreche used Virgin Atlantic as his shining entrepreneurial example. Richard Branson, founder and entrepreneurial architect of the Virgin Group, embarked on his first business venture in 1967 at the age of 17. Branson started his second business three years later. It was a mail-order retail record company: Virgin Mail. Three years after that he expanded to establish Virgin Records.

What can now be called a Virgin empire contains a conglomeration of wholly owned subsidiaries and outside partnerships. Branson actually maintains a controlling interest in every company he starts. What gives him such a unique entrepreneurial spirit? For one, he advocates social responsibility by sticking to his belief that employees' personal needs come first (social responsibility) and, while others cannot figure out how, he still manages to avoid layoffs. Also, Branson believes in the power of informal communication. Each of his companies is kept small and controllable even though they're run under a conglomerate structure. Virgin is diversified in countless directions, with interests in airlines, retail stores, a travel group, an entertainment group, a hotel enterprise, financial services, cinemas, radio stations, and much more. The man is doing something right, and many believe a large part of it is his earnest consideration of his employees.

Innovation on a Global Scale

Innovation as a practice has come a long way since Drucker shared his ideas in the 1980s. For starters, any present-day discussion about innovation is likely to include references to international initiatives. Also, due to the global economy, measuring innovative performance has moved to the top of corporate executives' agendas. In fact, global innovation now has a formal means of measurement. The Global Innovative Index (GII), conceived and developed by INSEAD Business School and World Business, is a formal model built to better see which nations are currently meeting the challenges of innovation. The GII ranks the world's best and worst performing economies from the standpoint of innovation, as well as providing insights into nations' strengths and weaknesses in their innovation-related policies and practices.

Because entrepreneurship and innovation are so closely aligned, it's equally important to measure a country's entrepreneurship. For example, there are countries that have enormous success with innovation, yet they often have trouble getting these products to market. To get actionable information, we need to look at entrepreneurship and innovation interchangeably and develop an index to reveal the linkage between them on a global basis. Mounting concern over the lack of access to global entrepreneurial measurements became the catalyst for the Entrepreneurship Indicators Project (EIP). Today, this index measures entrepreneurship across the globe based on number of patent acquisitions, new startups, and number of publicly traded companies as a starting point. But there are missing links that the EIP seeks to fill as it develops comparable measures of entrepreneurship and the factors that enhance or impede it.

Global Innovation and Entrepreneurship: Future Forecast

Based on the current information available, innovation and entrepreneurship will continue to expand in the future across borders, because of the existence of these six circumstances: global market conditions, entrepreneurial mind-set, eroding confidence in established institutions, shifting business environment, international collaboration, and environmental/technological advancements.

1. *Global market conditions.* Trade barriers are easing. Economies are interdependent. Communication via the Internet has never been easier or more accessible. These conditions drive political reform, cultural transparency, social progress, and a great deal of wealth creation.

2. *Entrepreneurial mind-set.* Entrepreneurs have the ability to see, understand, and take advantage of evolving markets. The entrepreneur's ability to think differently, use insights, see what others don't, envision what doesn't yet exist, and identify opportunity when it's ripe—these are the prized qualities of today's entrepreneur. Wayne Gretzky of national hockey fame helped state it succinctly when he said, "I skate to where the puck is going to be, not where it's been."

3. *Eroding confidence in established institutions.* The recent world economic meltdown is removing any last confidence that most people

had in governments, large enterprise banks, and other financial entities. The resulting mistrust will lead to reinventing ourselves as individuals, communities, countries, and societies. As such, many more entrepreneurs will be joining the field.

4. *Shifting business environment.* Large-scale firms are synonymous with bureaucracy, which tends to stifle innovation. In response, the business environment is shifting to accommodate the needs of its rapidly changing market players. Innovation and entrepreneurship are beginning to flourish around the world and will likely take the form of much smaller, yet bolder companies. Knowing and catering to this is how entrepreneurial ventures beat corporate giants to the punch. Any company, large or small, that continues down the same path it has always taken will find it to be a losing proposition.

5. *Entrepreneurial collaboration.* Also, on a global scale, there will be more entrepreneurial collaboration, which in turn will make shared innovation between countries a far more common occurrence at the company to company level—not just at universities and research institutions. One of China's approaches for creating an innovative nation is the Technology Business Incubator (TBI). China's mission is to nurture "technopreneurs" and technology-based startups. Business incubation is considered a viable option for countries that want to expand economic opportunities.

6. *Growth of environmental and sustainable engineering technologies.* A growing consciousness about the value of protecting our world will fuel the demand for products and services that can accomplish this goal.

In Drucker's world and for the past couple of decades, an exodus of people moved "west" for a good education and often ended up staying because of the rich opportunities that existed. But now, these opportunities are not limited to the West. Opportunities are international in scope, and people are choosing to return to their homeland to utilize their newly acquired talent in order to build fortunes and elevate global competition. The demand for innovation on an international scale and for the entrepreneurship that accompanies it will focus increasingly on being more purpose-driven. With intention at the helm, innovation and entrepreneurship will adapt to accommodate the changing focus of the drive to live a better life, do good, save the planet, and make money. It's about building a better world and a better life through innovation with a purpose.

Business Clusters: Safety in Numbers

Clusters represent another avenue for business development and growth through more formal international alliances. Generally speaking, a cluster is any geographic concentration of interconnected businesses, suppliers, and associated institutions in a particular industry. In some countries, business clusters are a long-established tradition. In Japan, for example, the term *keiretsu* refers to a grouping of affiliated companies that form a tight-knit alliance working toward each other's mutual success, often with government support. It's an intricate web of relationships linking banks, manufacturers, suppliers, and distributors with the Japanese government. This Japanese tradition includes recognizable names like Toyota, Toshiba, and Sony.

In Korea, the term *chaebol* refers to a more exclusive system of interlocking ownership. Chaebols are primarily controlled by founding families, have centralized ownership, and dominate Korea's business sector. Among the top 10 players in Korea's IT sector, only one (a subsidiary of state utility Korea Electric Power) isn't affiliated with a chaebol. Throughout many industries in Korea, chaebol affiliates dominate the scene. "The chaebols have become so dangerously powerful that you must put a bridle on them," says Lee Dong Gull, a former financial regulatory official who teaches economics at South Korea's Hallym University and fears chaebol's' affects on future innovation.[6]

Less formal versions of industry-based clusters are found throughout the United States in areas such as Detroit (automobiles), Pennsylvania (chemicals), and North Carolina (furniture). California's Silicon Valley is a classic example of a cluster. This concentration of high-tech businesses began in the mid-to-late 1990s and generated some of the world's most successful technology spinoffs. The region developed a reputation as the premier global innovation hub and attracted venture capital firms, more entrepreneurs, and a plethora of talent. In hindsight, it's easy to see how many small businesses were catapulted into success with location as their competitive advantage. Today, despite technological advances in the virtual world, physical location remains central to competition.

In certain countries, and in specific industries, businesses have the unique opportunity to participate in strategic industry-based clusters. Comparatively, entering a new market through a cluster is less risky than entering that same market independently. That's because clusters allow a company to take a developed product into unfamiliar markets with the support of existing infrastructure and established relationships. Ultimately, the advantages of strategic clusters reduce risk while increasing the prospect for international growth and market longevity. Whether the goal is to expand, relocate, or collaborate, an understanding of clusters offers innovators, manufacturers, and service providers a new way to scan the world for opportunities.

Advantages of a Cluster

Winemakers know that the best wine starts with grapevines that were planted just close enough together to be forced to compete for nutrients in the soil. Stress causes the plants to put more energy into their reproductive processes, increasing the quantity and quality of the grapes. It turns out that similar businesses located together in clusters also demonstrate better results.[7] Clusters have been shown to increase productivity, drive innovation, and foster an entrepreneurial spirit that ultimately leads to new business creation. They also provide greater access to human capital and informational resources, closer cross-industry relationships, and financial incentives, which can easily translate into a significant competitive advantage. Other benefits of clusters include the following:

- Greater collaboration and sharing of infrastructure and transportation hubs
- A more economical supply chain
- Increased access to information about the competition
- Consistency with green initiatives to reduce corporate footprints on the environment
- Multiple opportunities to reduce operating costs

Clusters are particularly well-suited for companies that require a workforce with specialized knowledge in areas such as biotechnology, medical devices, food technology, or pharmaceuticals. Most important, clusters provide a strategic weapon for companies that are venturing into global markets for the first time.

When coupled together, the power of clusters, innovation, and entrepreneurship are clearly illustrated through the extraordinary development of Israel in the past 50 years, which has attracted the attention of many academics and professionals, as evidenced by the success of the recently published book *The Start Up Nation: The Story of Israel's Economic Miracle*. Today, Israel is a technological powerhouse in the fields of biotechnology and medical devices. The emergence and rapid growth of companies, independent from their industry alignment, demonstrate that Israel is not simply a set of industrial clusters where the innovation advantage is limited to specific industries. Rather, Israel's success is best understood as an evolution and extension of the Porterian industry cluster theory whereby innovation and entrepreneurship become the norm. Early adoption is the rule and thinking "out of the box" is a daily phenomenon.

To date, clusters of innovation have been understood as a fundamentally geographic phenomenon. However, these clusters are becoming more and more global as they develop relationships between international centers of influence and create a web of relationships. For example, in alliance with politicians, entrepreneurs, and companies in Israel, Denmark, Japan, and France, Shai Agassi (founder of Better Place Inc.), an Israeli-American businessman based in Palo Alto, California, is promising to upend the car industry by going electric. This collaboration of investment dollars, people, ideas, and innovation across the world has the power to solve problems that could never be solved by one country or one business. By tapping into innovation incubators around the globe, the potential is truly unprecedented.

To Cluster or Not?

Still, clusters represent just one global expansion strategy or growth model, and not necessarily the right strategy for every business. Before joining a cluster or embarking on any global expansion effort, it's critical to perform an internal assessment of the current organizational infrastructure and its ability to support swift international growth. Next, conduct an external investigation. Perform the research and analysis necessary to identify potential markets while being realistic given the region's culture, infrastructure, legal environment, standard of living, economic and political stability, and attitude toward foreign direct investment. Then, filter all viable locations through a comprehensive risk analysis whereby potential risks are identified and mitigated through proper planning. In every stage of this analysis, the focus should be on creating a competitive advantage with sustainable growth.

The advantages of a cluster can tip the scale in favor of one region over another. When examining the feasibility of joining or creating a cluster, it's important to understand both regional and global trends. While one market may be prosperous today, what do established trends reveal about future prospects? Remember, today's actions are a result of yesterday's decisions. Just like the stock market, the biggest rewards are reserved for those who are in tune with the future and willing to act first. As such, be prepared to answer the following questions in terms of today and the future:

- Who and where are my suppliers?
- Who and where are the businesses/customers I supply?
- Where is the best labor pool?
- Where can I save on operating costs and still be efficient: transportation, wages?

Don't dismiss the idea of establishing a new cluster in a more desirable location. While it is easier for large multinational organizations to create the foundation for a new cluster, smaller businesses can generate the required critical mass with the right amount of planning, collaboration, and financing.

On the other hand, clusters can be a significant disadvantage— particularly when your business is "on the other side." For example, in Korea, where clusters are more exclusive, U.S. businesses will face insurmountable barriers to entry. Clusters can also drive up costs as companies compete for land, workers, and infrastructure. Clusters are also hard to relocate when the world shifts as the cluster businesses are invested in infrastructure, labor forces, and years of experience.

Available Resources on Clusters

To encourage and support U.S. businesses in global initiatives, a number of resources are available on business clusters. The real challenge is navigating and interpreting the available information rather than becoming overwhelmed by its abundance. As a general rule, first establish what information is required. Information needs should be guided by an in-depth understanding of the organization's strategic goals, internal resources, and overall appetite for risk. The Institute for Strategy and Competitiveness at Harvard Business School has several projects underway to help businesses identify specific clusters both at home and abroad. The Cluster Mapping Project has assembled a detailed picture of the location and performance of industries across the United States. For a global resource, the institute has created Cluster Profiles. These profiles provide standardized descriptions of more than 800 industry clusters in 52 countries. Cluster examples include everything from watches in Hong Kong and tufted carpets in Southwest Flanders to wine in Napa Valley.

Vertical Integration Model[8]

Vertical integration is the merging of one or more companies along a product's supply chain. It can occur anywhere along the chain from a business involved in providing the raw material all the way to a company involved in retail sales. Vertically integrated companies in a supply chain are united through a common owner. Usually, each member of the supply chain produces a different product or (market-specific) service, and the products combine to satisfy a common need. An expansion strategy based on vertical integration occurs when a business grows through the acquisition of companies that supply the intermediate goods needed to produce its product, market its product, distribute its product, or all of the above. This form of expansion is strategically desirable because it secures the inputs needed at various stages of the supply chain.

　　The objective of vertical integration is the creation or enhancement of market positioning—upstream or downstream the supply chain—within particular markets and for the development of a better supply chain. The underlying reasons for vertical integration are to exercise greater control, create more value, decrease costs, increase revenues, or all of the above. Through vertical integration, companies can gain control over any stage, from product development through the retail function.

This control allows for greater product quality and eliminates the duplication of profit margins being paid at each stage. In certain cases, vertical integration provides an avenue for businesses to leverage organizational capabilities, gain greater operational flexibility, develop a more defensible market position, reduce the potential threat of opportunism, and establish a competitive advantage. If properly executed, vertical integration will also enhance selling advantages that lead to business growth.

In a fully integrated organization, every stage from the acquisition of raw materials to the production of goods and, finally, the retailing of the final product are controlled by one company. The three most common forms of vertical integration are *backward, forward,* and *balanced.* Backward vertical integration occurs when a company controls subsidiaries that produce some of the inputs used in the production of its products. A company will be inclined to utilize forward vertical integration when it wants to control distribution centers and retailers where the products are sold. Balanced vertical integration is used when a firm controls all components, from raw materials to final delivery. These three varieties are general concepts. In reality, businesses use a wide variety of subtle variations. For example, suppliers can be contractors instead of legally owned subsidiaries. This allows a business to effectively control the supplier without requiring the investment of capital to actually buy the supplier.

Utilizing the lessons learned about M&A in the previous chapter, organizations can integrate through vertical acquisitions. Vertical acquisitions can also be used to achieve economies of scale, reduce costs, and gain market share, which may lead to market dominance. Acquisitions can meet a number of goals if approached and executed as part of a long-term strategy. Some of the typical reasons to initiate a vertical acquisition include the following:

- To enter an adjacent market space
- To accelerate revenue growth

- To expand into a new geography or obtain a physical footprint in a new location
- To access new customers
- To access technology
- To strengthen the pool of talent and capabilities
- To complete or augment a product or service line
- To reduce costs
- To capture market share
- To prevent a competitor from gaining these advantages

To decide on whether to adopt this model as part of corporate strategy, ask (and answer) these three questions: Where is vertical integration positioned in the corporate hierarchy and organization? What is the balance between functional managers that have part-time vertical integration management responsibilities and full-time dedicated experts? How will the roles and accountability be defined?

Advantages of Vertical Integration

A company should consider vertical integration into those business activities in which it possesses valuable, unique, and costly to imitate resources and capabilities. To vertically integrate is to enhance your market positioning and better control costs as well as "harvest" a portion of the multiple margins. Cost enhancement is dependent on comparison of the cost to outsource versus the investment in and the cost of administering the same activities internally. Vertical integration will also have an effect on the intensity of competition upstream and or downstream and the associated price-cost margins and profits. For example, when a company vertically integrates and self-supplies with some "input," other potential suppliers are in some sense precluded from providing those inputs to the vertically integrated firm and will experience a competitive disadvantage. These vertical integration affects must be factored into the front-end analysis.

In general, vertical integration offers the following advantages:

- Captures and owns the upstream suppliers and/or downstream buyers as well as the resulting profit margins.

- Creates access to down or upstream diverse "distribution" channels.
- Lowers transaction cost that in turn may lead to increased margins/profitability.
- Leads to expansion and development of core competencies either within the company by driving change and innovation or through M&A. In many ways, it develops a modular structure, easier to control. Improves supply chain coordination. This involves the ability to more flexibly synchronize the supply and demand along the chain of products in a more effective and efficient manner, while customizing the process and adapting it to changing needs.
- Creates strategic similarity between the vertically related activities, which later can lead to an enhanced production model, being price competitive, and hard to duplicate.
- Develops economies of scale.
- Provides opportunities to differentiate and create a competitive edge as well as improved market positioning.
- Increases entry barriers to potential competitors and secures the company's position in certain markets.

Vertical Integration Pitfalls

While the advantages to vertical integration are appealing, this approach is not without difficulty, risks, and challenges. So carefully weigh the benefits against the potential for trouble. For example, because vertical integration strategies typically require that one business be integrated with an existing business (in the case of an acquisition), integration naturally presents some challenging management issues. Consider flexibility. When a business integrates with another, it's necessary for one organization to expand its oversight to include multiple activities. It also mandates changes to organizational structure, administration, control systems, compensation practices, as well as many other areas to reflect the new organization. All of these changes require substantial effort, time, and commitment from both organizations.

Never vertically integrate into activities where the business lacks the resources to achieve a competitive advantage or achieve a cost-effective result. The integration must be backed by the requisite financial resources and management infrastructure in order to achieve a successful integration strategy. Before making the decision to vertically integrate, give these issues careful consideration:

- The ability to create value through vertical integration is not rare and can be imitated.
- Developing new core competencies may compromise existing competencies.
- A company that monopolizes the market may be perceived by many as a competitor rather than a partner, which can lead to a decrease in collaborative opportunities.
- The core competencies between the integrating activities are often very different.
- This approach can result in a decreased product variety if significant in-house development is required.
- The potential for increased general and administrative expenses can offset desired gains.
- The potential for higher operating costs such as materials, marketing, etc., can affect feasibility.
- The addition of a new activity can place the firm in direct competition with other businesses whose cooperation is required for ongoing success.

The practice of vertical integration is a relatively new discipline that has yet to fully establish itself in most industries. Given the increasing importance of vertical integration and M&A, there is little doubt that the ability to manage them well is essential. The costs of not doing so, which can include stalled development efforts and lost time to market, as well as inability to compete for desirable market share, are too great. The specifics of crafting the right move and implementing it, however, depend greatly on each company's portfolio of collaborative relationships.

As companies proceed with vertical integration activities, it's essential for the strategy and goals to be crystal clear and based on objective data that substantiates what they do well, what value they bring to the table, and what they don't do well. Most important, it must be communicated. Internal stakeholders including team members, directors of supporting functions, and senior executives must all share the same information and understanding. Management practices and tools should become more consistent and systematized, so that good business practices survive the inevitable turnover. It is essential for the value and purpose of the vertical integration capability to be established, communicated, and ingrained in the organization's psyche. Without it, stakeholders are at risk.

Sourcing Abroad

Ever since the offshore shift of skilled workers sparked widespread debate and a political firestorm, it has been portrayed as the killer of good-paying American jobs. But sourcing abroad can boost profits and lead to a more competitive position. Further, it can create great jobs here in the United States, just different ones. The trend was to hire software engineers, computer help staff, and credit-card bill collectors to exploit the low wages of poor nations. U.S. companies suddenly faced a grave new threat, with even highly educated tech and service professionals having to compete against legions of hungry college grads in India, China, and the Philippines willing to work twice as hard for one-fifth the pay. And without doubt, big layoffs often accompany big outsourcing deals.

The changes can be harsh and deep. But a more enlightened, strategic view of global sourcing is starting to emerge as managers get a better fix on its potential. The new buzzword is "transformational outsourcing." Many executives are discovering offshoring is really about corporate growth, making better use of skilled U.S. staff, and even job creation in the United States, not just cheap wages abroad. True, the labor savings from global sourcing can still be substantial. But it is nominal compared to the enormous gains in efficiency, productivity, quality, and revenues that can be achieved by fully leveraging offshore talent. Sourcing abroad is a chance to turn around dying businesses, speed up their pace of innovation, or fund development projects that otherwise would have been unaffordable. More aggressive outsourcers are aiming to create radical business models that can give them an edge and change the game in their industries. Old-line multinationals see offshoring as a catalyst for a broader plan to overhaul outdated office operations and prepare for new competitive battles. And while some want to downsize, others are keen to liberate expensive analysts, engineers, and salesmen from routine tasks so they can spend more time innovating and dealing with customers.

Some even believe "Big Business" is on the cusp of a new burst of productivity growth, ignited in part by offshore outsourcing as a catalyst. In theory, it is becoming possible to buy off-the-shelf practically any function you need to run a company. Want to start a budget airline but don't want to invest in a huge back office? You can. But as companies work out the kinks, the rise of the offshore option is dramatically changing the economics of reengineering. With millions of low-cost engineers, financial analysts, consumer marketers, and architects now readily available via the Internet, CEOs can see a quicker payoff. Those savings, in turn, help underwrite far broader corporate restructuring that can be truly transformational.

Creative new companies can exploit the possibilities of offshoring even faster than established players. Also, smart use of offshoring can fuel the performance of established players, too. Manufacturers and technology companies are learning to capitalize on global talent pools to rush products to market sooner at lower costs. Such strategies offer a glimpse into the productive uses of global outsourcing. The winning companies of the future will be those most adept at leveraging global talent to transform themselves and their industries, creating better jobs for everyone.

Pearls of Wisdom

World economies are becoming more and more interdependent. Communication via the Internet has never been easier or more accessible. Easing trade barriers, entrepreneurial mind-set, eroding confidence in established institutions, shifting business environments, and environmental and technological advancements are collectively opening doors for U.S. businesses to engage not only with the world's consumers, but also with the world's businesses. These conditions are driving political reform, cultural transparency, social progress, and a great deal of wealth creation. Don't miss this chance to find the right opportunity for your business to leverage these changes and gain unprecedented growth.

Here are some key points to keep in mind from reading this chapter:

- Traditional business models will no longer deliver optimal results. Scan emerging markets for opportunities.

- U.S. businesses are looking to emerging markets for future growth, not just low-cost labor and sourcing. Take a fresh look at your goals and align them with global growth models.
- Future success requires flexible business models that leverage your strengths in conjunction with the unique circumstances of each target market.
- Clusters offer safety in numbers and another avenue for business development and growth through more formal international alliances. Inventory the value your organization can bring to a cluster and what strengths you could access and develop.
- Clusters provide access to human capital and informational resources, closer cross-industry relationships, and financial incentives, which can easily translate into a significant competitive advantage.
- Vertical integration is an expansion strategy whereby a business grows through the acquisition of companies that produce the intermediate goods needed by the business or help market and distribute. Continually seek relevant information about how global business models are operating in your industry and seek opportunities to grow through them.

In sports, coaches and managers teach players to keep their eye on the ball in order to be successful. The same is true in business. When companies are focused on success, the organization will track in that direction. If they take their eye off the goal, even for a minute, they risk failure. As we'll discuss coming up in Chapter 8, the way to stay focused requires setting clear objectives, identifying relevant metrics, and continually measuring, tracking, and managing people and assets.

Chapter 8

Focusing on Success

"You must have long range goals to keep you from being frustrated by short term failures."

— *Charles C. Noble*

A multinational food company jumped at the opportunity to acquire an extremely successful business in the international marketplace. Although the acquisition was not in the purchasing company's main business line, the acquisition was a great opportunity for a great price. By most conventional standards, it had the potential to be a great venture—"a sure thing." But within just five years, this company, once regarded as an ideal acquisition, found itself on the chopping block and being divested. What happened? The acquired company was never properly integrated into the overall organization. Even after a significant expenditure of effort and resources, there was still a "disconnect" between corporate strategy and business development. In a short period of time, the product line lost its position as a market leader and the acquired company was sold for 22 percent of its original purchase price. This scenario can happen to any business. It is about focus on strategy and success and not just what may seem like a good opportunity at the time.

Keeping Your Eye on the Ball

Whether the sport is golf, baseball, football, soccer, or tennis, one key to success is keeping your eye on the ball. When your eye is squarely focused on the ball, your body will naturally make contact. Take your eye off the ball, and you either miss a perfect opportunity to score or, worse, you take an unexpected hit to the head. It's a simple but powerful lesson—a lesson that is equally important for CEOs and business leaders responsible for global expansion. Keep your eye focused on success, on your strategic goals, and the organization will track in that direction. Take your eye off, even for a minute, and you risk failure.

For decades, management productivity researchers have developed new models for the implementation of strategy with the goal of improving organizational performance. Unfortunately, progress has been slow. Most of the new models introduced have never been adequately tested. Even reasonably intuitive propositions designed to increase the alignment of strategy, structure, and systems, which should lead to improved performance, have not been proven. As a result, we have very few clear-cut results to help us understand what drives organizational success. However, a few things are certain. Achieving success requires the establishment of clear objectives, taking the pulse of current events and trends, identifying relevant metrics and continually measuring your strategic accomplishments, and tracking and managing both people and assets.

Don't Go on Autopilot

Here's a typical scenario. After months, perhaps years, of preparing to enter the global marketplace through extensive market analysis, identification of a target market, product modifications, negotiations, training, collaborating, and the deployment of a flawless market entry strategy, you're in. Better yet, sales are growing and the team is looking for the next great global opportunity. Stop. At this point in the expansion game, it's tempting to engage autopilot, sit back, or move on to the next challenge. Either can be fatal.

In today's rapidly changing world, it's critical to constantly review corporate strategy and make any minor or major adjustments necessary to keep the organization tracking toward success. Consider a pilot preparing for flight. It's possible to chart a course from point A to point B, select the flight plan, and engage autopilot. But with no adjustments for changing winds and other conditions, the aircraft will never arrive safely at its destination.

Even the "sure things" can fail without an ongoing strategic plan to ensure their success, since current events may cause a 180-degree turn on your plans and unless you monitor real-world current events, economic, political, or cultural, you are going to miss your target. That means a living, breathing plan that is constantly monitored for changes in both the internal and external environment—not a plan that is created, shelved, and covered in dust. (See Figure 8.1 for a visual representation of the components for sustaining success.) Domestically, this is a major challenge and frequent obstacle on the path to success. Internationally, the challenge is further complicated by the speed of change and the added complexity of dealing with foreign surroundings.

Because strategic planning is often confused with corporate strategy or, incorrectly, used interchangeably, it's important to clarify the difference. Strategic planning is a process whereby a company's leadership team sets objectives, goals, and direction for the next several years. Strategic planning creates the vision. Corporate strategy evolves from the strategic planning process. The strategy is a detailed set of actionable steps and activities that bring the corporate vision to fruition and steer the company toward success. Before effective strategic planning can occur, a business must understand the external environment, internal assets, internal weaknesses, and what resources are needed to move forward. That awareness helps companies identify any existing gaps within the organization and fill those gaps ASAP. If you can't make the necessary changes, at a minimum, plan for the consequences. From a global perspective, success depends on following everything discussed in the previous chapters of this book, and more.

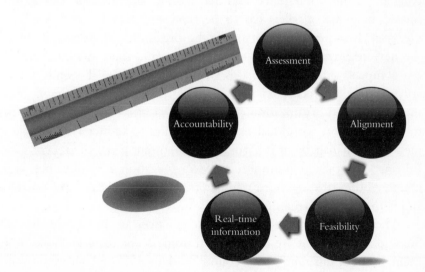

Figure 8.1   Sustaining Success

Developing Cross-Border Best Practices

A central goal of strategic management is to understand why some organizations outperform others when it comes to developing and implementing a successful global strategy. As in any strategic development, there needs to be a link among strategic resources, strategic orientation, performance, and reality. Then managers can allocate resources and invest appropriately in areas such as technology, innovation, quality, and human resource management, all in context of the local market needs, culture, and interpretation of data and events.

A company that operates internationally has the ability to reap the benefits of its various and often far-flung operations. The drill is to identify the best practice—such as an innovative product, an efficient IT system, or a fast delivery process and then replicate it, within context, across the full organization to maximize the impact, while addressing cultural and regional differences. Then what happens? The company, in effect, raises the whole enterprise to a new, more standardized best-practice level of performance.

When companies cannot replicate their successes, they not only leave money on the table, they also miss an opportunity to make the company a more integrated and manageable organization. But again, success in global markets has to be replicated through the development of "best practices" to match the organization's culture in HQ, the new organization in the target market, and then integrate this in the company as a whole. In this way "best practices" become standard practices, the accepted way of doing business. The benefits of a more integrated organization can range from increased scale efficiency to better support for global product launches to tighter risk management. Risk management is particularly important given the recent global financial crisis. A more integrated organization across business and country boundaries is more transparent and less likely to have isolated and perhaps even rogue operations.

There are many reasons why best practices are not easily shared. Some objections that are often voiced inside a company include: "our business line is different," "our country is different," or "our regulations are different." Unspoken reasons may include the "not invented here" refrain and perhaps conflicts with lesser initiatives already underway.

While there is often some slight truth to these concerns, they are used more often to create roadblocks than to find solutions.

The 4Ps Business Model

In business, another way of keeping your eye on the ball is to adopt the 4Ps business model. That means focus on planning, process management, problem solving, and people.[1] By this approach, companies create a common language to share best practices and develop new regional processes across different countries and regions.

Applying the 4Ps in a global context means having a common language for each of the following:

1. *Planning.* Business plans should have quantitative targets for each area with the measures defined consistently for all countries. This allows easy and clear communication across management areas and across countries. However, the cultural context has to be kept in the plan and, therefore, setting up and milestones that measure not only the progress by HQ standards, but also by the local reality and current market trends in the country/region.

2. *Process management.* Countries are all required to achieve a basic level of process sophistication. All countries are expected to consistently define process scope, monitor, and share process performance. Any key process with performance below target becomes a candidate for improvement. However, expectations of performance and rewards, and how to encourage and execute varies among countries and cultures. Attending to the softer skills and issues need to be taken into account when looking to design and implement process management.

3. *Problem solving.* When identifying process performance gaps, a problem-solving methodology is applied to reach objectives. By having all countries using the same methodology, it's easier to collaborate and share new improvement initiatives. However, the team needs to be careful not to "push" certain practices that may not be understood, followed, or may even cripple the operation in a certain country or region, not to mention create resentment.

4. *People.* Employees are developed through shared leadership in regional cross-departmental and cross-funtional teams. These teams

are established for major process areas such as the customer service process. These teams have explicit responsibilities and accountabilities to share best practices and develop region-wide initiatives. Values and corporate behavior may be different, depending on the country or region. Loyalty, a soft skill usually neglected by U.S. corporations, may play a critical role.

So what happens when you actually put these measures in place? You generate:

- *Synergy.* Adopting a standardized, customer-centric global platform across local operations, while still maintaining corporate process as well as customizing specifics for the local markets. Synergy is accelerated because the replication of local improvement projects is greatly simplified by having just one standardized process and one set of measurements for all businesses. Therefore, a local improvement can create a rapid multiplier effect across the organization as a whole, and can be measured across countries and disciplines and against corporate strategy.
- *Scale.* The global standardized platform can ultimately operate across borders, when processes that originate in one country can be adopted, followed, modified, and handled by another business unit in a different country.
- *A competitive advantage.* Creating these models that support global strategy becomes a foundation for the implementation of strategic vision and action. It enables a company to successfully manage and initiate more global opportunities. Chapter 4 in this book discusses the different competitive advantage models.
- *Managing risk.* These benefits will include significant improvement in cost, speed, and customer satisfaction while mitigating other risks such as FCPA and more.

Considering the Strategic Elements

When developing and evaluating corporate strategy, validate that your strategy is suitable, feasible, and acceptable. Suitability ensures that the action steps you have determined in your strategic planning sessions address the major strategic plans and initiatives. For example: Are you ready to go global? Is your product suitable and ready? Does the strategy make economic sense? Would the organization obtain economies of scale? Does it make sense in terms of the internal and external environment?

A feasibility analysis will ensure that the resources required to implement the strategy are available and accessible in the right quantity and at the right time. Resources include staff time, financial capital, informational resources, and any other key inputs required by the corporate strategy. For example, suppose you have a great water purifying product that is suitable for markets in Africa. Some of the questions to test feasibility include: How will you get your product to the customers? How much can they pay for it? What are the barriers to entry in these countries (corruption, government regulations, and logistics)? Are the resources easily accessible or do they need to be developed over time? These questions have to be asked on more than just one occasion, at the beginning, since some of the answers to these components may change with time, political change, or many other reasons I have mentioned in previous chapters. Predictable and constant are not the norm or the baseline to operate from in the global business arena.

Acceptability examines the corporate strategy from different angles. Most critically, the strategy must be understood from the perspective of every identified stakeholder: mainly shareholders, employees, customers, and key vendors so they can buy in and perform accordingly. Then the question is: What are the desired outcomes of your strategic plan, and will they be acceptable to these groups, within the reality frame your company has to operate in? The buy-in is very important to ensure future success. The desired outcomes may include outsourcing certain activities, creating an impact of stock prices, or merging with a competitor. None of these corporate strategies occurs within a vacuum, and each will have implications for key stakeholders. Stakeholder reactions should be anticipated and managed proactively. For example, shareholders may oppose the issuing of new shares of stock that dilute their holdings. Employees may oppose outsourcing for fear of losing their jobs, and customers may have concerns about a merger's impact on quality and support. Therefore, performance is going to be down, or a company may even run the risk of losing key employees. In planning global growth strategies, one of the main issues could be the inability of the stakeholders to grasp the opportunities, function within this new environment, all impeding on the proper decision-making process, therefore contributing to embarking on a shaky path.

Synchronized Strategy: A Top 10 Approach

Corporate strategy must be continually evaluated and synchronized at three levels of the organization: corporate, business development strategy, and functional. In general, companies are engaged in one of three corporate level strategies: grow, stabilize, or divest. The tactics to accomplish the corporate-level strategy are performed at the business level strategy and involve things like M&A, alliances, and collaboration. At the functional level, it's all about making the strategy work on a daily basis. In a vacuum, this would be simple. But the global marketplace is anything but a vacuum. As rapidly changing external forces dictate change on one level of strategy, timely adjustments are required on other levels in order to maintain synchronization. When strategy is no longer synchronized, corporate-wide focus on success is lost.

Michel Moulin, a serial CEO based in France, comments:

> After the hard work on how to define a structured growth strategy, the hardest is to come . . . "not losing focus on success" which means, measuring, tracking and managing people and assets for success in global markets. To capitalize on the new strategy it's really all about the team and its ability to understand the key milestones of the new road map, the clear indicators which will guide everyone on the way forward or the need to rework the actions required and the new methodologies to apply to challenge the status quo. Clearly based on my experience either be in Europe, USA or Asia, the failure lies in not being disciplined enough and respecting enough the team involved . . . and the issue becomes: how to move from being just involved to completely committed?

Strategic planning can be viewed as bottom-up, top-down, or collaborative processes. In any case, clearly defined and communicated objectives help set the pace and keep everyone focused on the task at hand: success. As the leader, one option to consider is the Top 10 approach. In this scenario, the CEO/president establishes 10 inter-mediate (three to five years) objectives. These objectives are care-fully targeted at three core groups of any organization: shareholders, employees, and customers.

What makes the Top 10 approach work for the entire organization is deployment and visibility. After these top-side corporate objectives are clearly communicated by the leadership, each level of the organi-zation is required to propose 10 subobjectives specific to its areas of accountability that will move the organization toward accomplishing this corporate strategy. From the vice presidents to the line managers, everyone's objectives are synchronized. By linking department-specific objectives back up to the overall corporate strategy, the entire organi-zation is tracking in one direction, gaining momentum, and making progress toward success. To keep the momentum going, objectives should be graphed, charted, and placed in highly visible locations throughout the organization. At regularly scheduled status meetings, discuss progress, and when necessary, any realignment of subgoals. This is what makes a living, breathing, viable strategic plan.

Documenting the strategic plan brings credibility to the objectives and builds corporate-wide acceptance, which helps identify the process and implementation steps necessary and fundamental to achieving results. Thus, every objective should be identified in writing. Pay close atten-tion to the wording. Accurate wording can make all the difference between whether a goal is actually understood and achieved. Also, objectives should focus on solutions, not problems. For example, if business in Asia is experiencing unexpected losses, this may qualify as the special project. But the objective should not be worded as "Stop losing money in Asia." Rather, the objective should focus on solutions and understanding the cultural and geopolitical factors that come into play in Asia. One solution may be to divest, another may be to modify operational tactics or initiate a close examination of the competitive landscape. In any case, the objectives must be clear and measurable. And the research to find the right solution must go deep into under-standing the market, the competition, the culture, and anything that could have an impact on success.

Is Your Strategy Working?

It's a fact. Successful businesses constantly assess themselves in order to improve on all dimensions of the operations and achieve success. They continually ask, "Is the corporate strategy working?" It's a simple but important question—a question that every successful CEO should be equipped to answer, provided the company is using the right metrics. Metrics are the cornerstone of the assessment process. Measure the right things, and measure them the right way. However, in global initiatives, when there are so many cultural clues as well as geopolitical issues, the answer is more complicated. Sometimes, the answer is "yes," but you may be losing money because acceptance into some foreign markets is slow. So, it's the right metrics interpreted correctly for the market.

Metrics generally fall into two categories: performance metrics and diagnostic metrics. However, in the global arena we need to add another dimension: measuring within a country/region context. Performance metrics are high-level measures that assess overall performance in the areas being measured. They are external in nature and closely tied to outputs, customer requirements, and business needs for the process. Diagnostic metrics are measures that reveal underlying causes of why a process is not performing as expected. They are internally focused and associated with internal process steps and inputs received from suppliers. The context connects the dots and make sense out of cultural, geopolitical, and other dimensions that fall more into the softer skills and qualitative components. These are often overlooked and are usually critical deal breakers. In order to keep track of what is new, what needs to be changed, and what can leveraged, companies need to monitor success, as you'll see in Figure 8.2.

The best place to begin a corporate assessment is with the customer. Looking at an organization's performance through the eyes of a customer can be very enlightening. Next, consider other critical groups such as shareholders, employees, and vendors. Examine these areas first as a whole and then drill down by department, by country, by region, and by product line. Here are some suggestions as to what should be measured in each core group.

1. Customers
   • Performance against requirements
   • Customer satisfaction

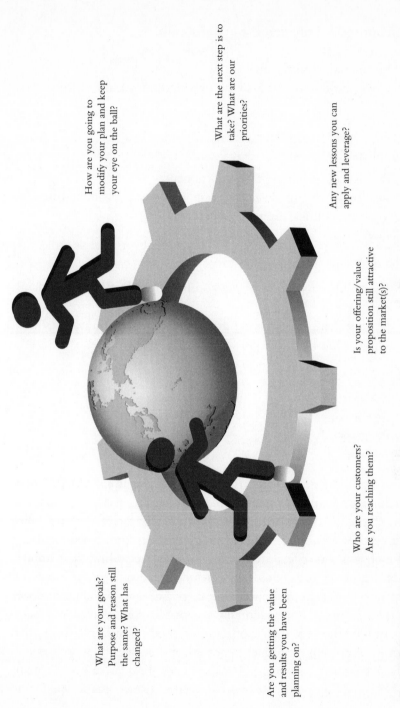

What are your goals? Purpose and reason still the same? What has changed?

Are you getting the value and results you have been planning on?

Who are your customers? Are you reaching them?

Is your offering/value proposition still attractive to the market(s)?

Any new lessons you can apply and leverage?

What are the next step is to take? What are our priorities?

How are you going to modify your plan and keep your eye on the ball?

Figure 8.2 Monitoring Success

- Performance of internal work processes
- Cycle times
- Product and service quality
- Cost performance (could be productivity measures, inventory, etc.)
- Loyalty

2. Suppliers

- Performance against your requirements
- Reality in the markets and ease of getting product based on logistics, politics, supply, and demand
- Loyalty

3. Shareholders

- Profitability (could be at the company, product line, or individual level)
- Market share growth and other standard financial measures
- Understanding of the global goals and initiatives

4. Employees

- Satisfaction
- Performance
- Progress
- Loyalty

To measure these areas the right way, consider using SMART metrics, which are defined as specific, measurable, actionable, relevant, and timely. "Specific" refers to metrics that directly target the area being measured. For example, in order to measure customer satisfaction, a good metric is direct feedback from customers regarding their impression of a product or service. Understand, however, that in some cultures you will not get an honest assessment because providing feedback or offering criticism is not culturally acceptable. Also, you cannot gauge satisfaction by the U.S. metric of returned products since, in most other countries, returning a product is not an option, legally as well as culturally. Some of us may remember the Lands' End lawsuit in Germany in 1998, involving the company's unconditional guarantee for its garments sold anywhere in the world. Local competitors had challenged the guarantee in the German courts citing a 1932 law under which the guarantee could be defined as a separate product given customers for free and, thus, in violation of the law. A lower court ruled for the U.S. cataloger but a higher court ruling overturned the decision. The court held that the company could offer the guarantee but couldn't advertise it. Lands' End turned it into a brilliant marketing campaign, but not without going through growing pains. While returns and complaints are "internal" measurements, they are indirect measures of customer satisfaction and, as such, can produce misleading results.

"Measurable" refers to an ability to collect data that is accurate and complete. "Actionable" means that the metrics are easy to interpret and can result in actionable steps. For example, when performance is charted over time, it should be obvious which direction is "good" and which direction is "bad." But be prepared to analyze results with a global perspective that accounts for the fact that launching products internationally takes much longer. The solution is having the right people on your team who can interpret the measurements in the context of the country, market, culture, and other pertinent parameters. Ideally, actionable metrics will also make the corrective steps more apparent. "Relevant" simply means that the metric is important. A common downfall of process professionals is a desire to measure everything. This approach obscures key metrics and bogs down the team with unnecessary data gathering and analysis. Instead, take time to carefully select relevant metrics upfront. "Timely" metrics refer to measurements for which you can get the data precisely when the data is needed.

The goal for any set of metrics is insight—insight into whether the organization is moving toward achieving goals and objectives. Additionally, the goal should include insight on how effectively these goals and objectives are being attained. Therefore, step back and ask yourself these questions: Do the metrics make sense? Do they form a complete set (i.e., Do they cover areas of time, quality, cost, and customer satisfaction?)? Do they reinforce the desired behavior for today and the future?

Developing effective metrics, however, is a challenge. In the proc-ess, it's common for some organizations to fall into the following traps:

- Using metrics for which you cannot readily collect accurate or complete data, especially in the global arena where the data requires honed interpretation skills. If your sales are up, does it mean that the trend is up? Or did the customers find another use for this product/service? If your launch is unsuccessful, does it mean that there is no need for your product/service? Or was there a problem with the marketing message?
- Adopting metrics that measure the right thing but cause people to behave contrary to the best interest of the business to "make their numbers."
- Generating so many metrics that the process is a burden and cre-ates excessive overhead. The metrics must be purposeful and con-nected to milestones and actions.
- Relying on metrics that are too complex and difficult to explain to others. Never develop metrics that are so complicated they actually shift the focus from success onto the mechanics of the measuring process. Keep it simple so the focus stays where it needs to be, on results.

Selective Benchmarking

When used properly, benchmarking can improve performance by keep-ing the organizational eye on success. A carefully designed assessment process is the key to getting the most from any benchmarking effort. Basically, benchmarking is a three-step process. First, it involves an out-ward analysis such as the examination of competitors' businesses and programs to learn how they are approaching certain practices and poli-cies. The next step is an honest self-assessment as to how your organiza-tion measures up to current industry standards. After getting a sense for your organization's place in relation to competitors, the benchmarking process is conducted by recommending adjustments to either practices, policies, or both.

These basic guidelines will help kick-start a solid benchmarking process:

1. *Ask the right questions.* Obviously, there are thousands of data points that can be compared in any benchmarking assessment. An effective assessment, however, will focus in on those variables that deliver the greatest "bang for the buck" or the processes that offer the greatest amount of leverage. This will maximize the utility of the evaluation process and move the organization towards success.

2. *Compare apples to apples.* Even the best designed benchmarking assessment won't improve performance if the data points are not comparative. The best matches for benchmarking are competitors with comparable locations, markets, and size. In some specific circumstances, "out-of-the-box" assessments look outside the industry for fresh ideas. For the most useful information, stick to analyzing the performance and practices of leaders in your industry.

3. *Use accurate, detailed, relevant, and timely data.* Start with an internal company knowledge base search, then add the Internet search and then fill in the gaps with information from academic and business libraries, government labor statistics, surveys, public filings, trade associations, professional publications, site visits, and vendor partners. More recent and complete data will improve the chances of improving performance with best practices in the industry.

4. *Act continuously on the findings.* Once the analysis is complete, take a slow, measured approach to developing recommendations for new policies and practices and set your next point of measurement. Consider what will work in your organization's unique circumstances. In other words, what needs to be changed, what change management or processes need to be implemented to improve, leverage, and grow capabilities? Schedule periodic reevaluations (every three to six months) to track progress and reprioritize goals as necessary.

Value-Driven Focus

The fundamental objective of every successful leader must be to maximize the delivery of value to the organization by maximizing the value delivered to the customer. Hence, if the product delivers value to the intended market, it will naturally generate success for the business.

However, when faced with myriad everyday issues, it's easy to get side-tracked and focus more heavily on making the machine operate more efficiently than why the machine operates in the first place.

For that reason, it's helpful to organize the business around key constructs of a value-driven organization. This helps everyone focus on success by providing visibility and control over how value is managed, provided to, and perceived by customers. By focusing on what matters most, the organization can deploy core strengths more rapidly and capitalize on new opportunities that help meet or exceed strategic goals and objectives.

Becoming a value-driven organization requires a continual assessment of what value means to your company, what are the values your company stands for, what does it mean in a global context, how value can be increased through the optimization of products and services delivered to the consumers while maintaining the perspectives of both internal and external stakeholders. Use these five key constructs to help focus on common sense elements of delivering value:

1. *Assessment.* Because value is highly subjective, assessment is a foundational element to becoming a value-driven organization. Cultural fluency and correct interpretation of the business environment, trends, and geopolitical cues must be undertaken in order to understand value from the target market's perspective. As such, an organization must assess and understand the critical markets it serves by capturing and analyzing relevant demographic information. Only with an intimate understanding of a market can an organization deliver value. The goal for assessment is to gain a deeper understanding of what a market values today and what it will value tomorrow. Stay current and plan for tomorrow as the concept of value evolves and changes over time.

2. *Alignment.* To stay aligned, every item from product requirements to delivery should be checked against your goals. Those items that are not aligned should be removed from scope or, at the least, given a lower priority so that those items that can be aligned are given the attention they deserve. Understandably, there are times when nonaligned items must be included to meet short-term revenue targets or regulatory issues. These, too, are

aligned because revenue generation and regulatory compliance are clearly represented in your corporate goals.

3. *Feasibility.* Equipped with an understanding of the target market through the assessment process and an understanding of how all the pieces fit and align, it's time to take a reality check. As new ideas enter the pipeline, evaluate them against all existing and proposed product/service ideas and consider "opportunity cost." This is the cost of things that will not occur based of what was previously chosen to move forward. At any point during the lifecycle of one product, if another product comes along that is a higher priority or can provide better benefit, consider it. Give it the right-of-way and appropriate the critical resources needed to make it successful. Too many companies are afraid to "kill" a product in the development stage once it has started. In the end, this often strangles their competitive capabilities.

4. *Real-time information.* For any person involved in the decision-making process, access to accurate data is critical. Without this information, lobbying, politics, and personal agendas will rule the day and negatively impact the organization's ability to succeed. Many organizations address this issue by using product teams and committees to communicate. Others use information portals that provide real-time visibility to critical information. Regardless of the technique used to provide accessibility, it will help the organization embrace a value-driven approach.

5. *Accountability.* The final key to becoming value driven is accountability. Accountability helps organizations focus on actual results, results that make a difference, rather than superficial actions that keep an organization busy. When results are aligned with value, the entire organization will focus on delivering value through its activities and understanding how to improve value in the future. Accountability is not an opportunity for finger pointing. Instead, accountability introduces an opportunity for learning how an activity may be performed better and used to deliver greater value in the future.

By leveraging these five keys to becoming value driven, your organization will stay focused on success.

Pearls of Wisdom

In order to keep your eye on the ball and focus on success, remember to:

- Rely on internationally experienced executives and experts who understand global management and know how to navigate the waters.
- Think locally, act globally, and remember the company's big picture as well as its parts.
- Learn to deal with extreme conditions, unpredictability, fluctuations; plan for the unexpected.
- Measure results in terms of U.S. standards as well as the customs and cultures of other countries in order to evaluate global strategy and direction.
- Offer the same high level of quality in all markets, but the same doesn't mean same as in the United States. If you are a high-quality/ top brand, be the top brand in another region, although the measures can be different.
- Focus on the customer.
- Look to the future. Know where you are going, what the trends are, and how to direct the business to arrive at the destination.
- Be a value-driven business.

Organizations can achieve enduring high performance by creating an environment in which the development of strategic goals is reinforced by processes that educate, organize, and align the enterprise's activities with those goals.

Here are some key points to keep in mind from reading this chapter:

- Keep your eye focused on success and the organization will track in that direction.
- A strategic plan links corporate goals to corporate strategy and must be continually synchronized throughout the organization.
- Consider a Top 10 approach to establishing an effective corporate strategy.
- Continually monitor strategy based on suitability, feasibility, and acceptability. What process does your organization follow to

establish its corporate strategy? Ask yourself if your strategy is on autopilot.

- Measure progress using SMART metrics. Do these metrics elicit the desired behavior?
- Selectively benchmark against the competition.
- Success will follow a value-driven approach.

The journey that led to this book, *Grow Globally,* is a personal journey as well as a corporate one. As an entrepreneur who started and operated international companies, I know firsthand what it takes to be successful. Throughout my journey, I've learned to set aside fear, be inquisitive, open my eyes, listen, explore, and grow. The truth is that what people want is to be heard, understood, and respected. This is true throughout the world, which is what makes building and understanding this platform essential for conducting international business and contributing to the development of a better world. The new reality is more change than continuity, and we'll take a look at this topic more in Chapter 9.

Chapter 9

Looking into the Future

New Players, New Rules, New Game

"Telling the future by looking at the past assumes that conditions remain constant. This is like driving a car by looking in the rearview mirror."

—Herb Brody

Business leaders today confront a new reality of political and economical power. The rise of emerging economies, a globalizing world market, and a historic transfer of relative wealth from the West to the East are shaping a new international system and repositioning the world's center of gravity in terms of economic power. This transfer of power is being fueled by an economic slowdown in the Western world in contrast to the continued acceleration of emerging economies where consumer consumption is growing exponentially.

Other forces reshaping the balance of power include access to oil and other natural resources. These forces have generated windfall profits for the Gulf state countries as well as for Russia. Another key force is access to lower operating costs and better capital efficiencies. Additionally, cheap labor and favorable government policies have shifted both manufacturing and many service industries from the West to the East. This reality is our future.

Power Shift

For evidence of the power shift, just look at the meaning of "10 percent." In China, 10 percent equals the rate of economic growth. In the United States, 10 percent equals the rate of unemployment. That's quite a contrast! If current trends continue on the same trajectory, in just 10 years the economies of the emerging world will exceed $20 trillion, which is equal to the size of the U.S. economy today. This is the new world order. Naturally, some will look at this shift as a threat. But look again.

The former Secretary of Commerce and current U.S. Ambassador to China, Gary Locke just stated that 95 percent of consumers are going to be outside the United States in 10 years: "With traditional drivers of U.S. economic growth like consumer and business spending facing stiff headwinds, it has never been more important for our companies to increase their sales to the 95 percent of the world's consumers who live outside the United States," said Locke.[1] But what's good for the world's population is also good for the United States if we take advantage of the opportunities this rebalancing of power presents.

While the West faces some real challenges, it still constitutes more than 60 percent of the global economy, supports the world's global institutions, and possesses fundamental strengths such as strong innovative capacity, large open markets, strong rule of law, and the world's best higher education institutions. For these reasons, the United States is likely to remain the single most powerful player. However, the United States' relative strength—even in the military realm—will decline and U.S. leverage will become more restricted as emerging powers rise up and compete for dominance.

In addition to changing players, the game itself is changing with emerging transnational issues such as changing climate, growing demand for energy, food, and water, and an aging population in the developed world. Individually, any one of these emerging issues would change the nature of global business play. Combined, these issues promise to turn the playing field upside down in what could be a historically unprecedented age of prosperity, especially for those who develop solutions for these and other global issues. These solutions will be the foundation for continued global prosperity.

Transnational Change: Challenges and Opportunities

Diminishing natural resources and rising temperatures will make it necessary for businesses and governments from around the world to combine forces and work collaboratively. Solving future shortages of water (which will become the new oil), energy, and food will not be possible by any one government or any one business. So the ability to collaborate across borders and across sectors will be an important skill to hone as will cultural fluency, cross-border negotiations, strategic planning, and entrepreneurship.

For example, realizing the energy potential that could arise from the efficient use of technology is an amazing global business opportunity. One reason is that all current technologies are inadequate for replacing the traditional energy architecture on the scale needed. In many cases, the efficient use of technology will yield rewards that far exceed the benefits of renewable energy sources. The challenge is that consumers are not fully engaged, and utility companies lack a strong incentive to encourage energy efficiency among their customers. Regardless, this will be an area of focus and growth when the right people, companies, and governments come together out of necessity to invest and pursue long-term solutions to avoid a future energy crisis.

Perceptions of scarcity, however, may drive some countries to take action to assure their future access to natural resources. This could result in transnational conflicts if government leaders deem access essential for maintaining domestic stability and the survival of their regimes. In some cases, perceived scarcity could contribute to terrorism, proliferation, and conflict as resource issues move up on the international agenda. Terrorism is unlikely to disappear anytime soon, but its appeal will diminish if economic growth continues and youth unemployment is mitigated in the Middle East. Economic opportunities for youth and greater political pluralism will dissuade some from joining terrorists' ranks, but others—motivated by a variety of factors, such as a desire for revenge or to become "martyrs"—will continue to turn to violence to pursue their objectives. As the world has advanced in technology and other aspects, human nature didn't and won't change. There have always been, and always will be, radical groups that use any means necessary to support their cause.

Economic and political empowerment of women is also transforming the global landscape and creating a new breed of leaders with a different, more focused, more global lens. It's also increasing the world's productivity. The explosion in global economic productivity in recent years has been driven not just by advancing technology but also by fostering human resources particularly through improvements in health, education, and employment opportunities for women and girls. The predominance of women in Southeast Asia's export manufacturing sector is a key driver of that region's economic success. Women agricultural workers now account for half the world's food production—even without reliable access to land, credit, equipment, and markets. This creates a new target consumer with a slightly different focus and mindset. On a corporate level, there will be a need to go beyond diversity talks to a full integration, adjustment, and integration of women, their roles, capabilities, and styles.

Women in much of Asia and Latin America are achieving higher levels of education than men, a trend that is particularly significant in a human capital-intensive global economy. Improved educational opportunities for girls and women are also a contributing factor to falling birth rates worldwide—and by extension a better maternal health. The long-term implications of this trend will include fewer orphans, less malnutrition, more children in school, and other contributions to societal stability.

Women will be the ones helping to show the way to greater social assimilation and reducing the likelihood of religious extremism. The well-known quote from William Ross Wallace's poem, "the hand that rocks the cradle is the hand that rules the world," recognizes the power of women as a preeminent force for change in the world. As more women are educated, empowered, and gain influence, there is tremendous opportunity to make great strides in addressing global challenges. The question is: How will this trend impact your business? Does it provide a new opportunity?

The Era of Reasoning and Collaboration

In addition to transnational concerns such as widening economic inequalities, failed governance systems, cyber security, and resource scarcity, globalization has introduced an overall heightened sense of volatility. This volatility can only be contained and managed through foresight, reasoning, and purposeful collaboration across borders. As such, the world's largest economies must accept and recognize this interdependency and collaborate in order to face the challenges of this new reality.

The world is at a turning point, and dialogue among leaders from all sectors is imperative to forge a sustainable future and keep pace with emerging challenges and the acceleration of globalization. The world needs, and businesses must accept, more collaboration and more dialogue among all stakeholders, including governments and multinational businesses. Global leaders need to take a more forward-looking approach, exploring every possible option to proactively address complex risks and associated opportunities.

The emerging trend here is the use of alliances to reinforce not only the country's political standing but their markets as well. Consequently, the U.S. tendency to forge ahead autonomously will no longer be an effective strategy. The United States must learn to play in the sandbox with other nations. This is a change from the past where the United States led and dictated to other nations in order to regain its economic leadership and take advantage of opportunities for growth in the global marketplace. While high-level government agreements will become more of a necessity before taking advantage of opportunities that involve transnational issues, businesses and NGOs (non-governmental organizations) will still be looking for pragmatic ways to contribute by developing and consenting to internationally accepted norms for processes, policies, and practices.

Fortunately, massive online collaboration has become a popular way to tackle projects of all sizes. One reason is that people from all over the world can work on different aspects of the same project simultaneously, contributing their strengths and compensating for weaknesses. The real issue is scaling large projects appropriately and developing the necessary infrastructure for coordinating such efforts on an international basis. This requires the skill of cross-cultural communication and leadership, working with virtual teams, and managing multi-country projects where the cultural fluency will be a winning skill. With technological advances and the increased capabilities in communication, smaller countries that have long been overshadowed by some of the larger ones will now have equal opportunity to showcase their talents and contribute to solving the world's problems.

As regional integration becomes more prominent, it will lead to blocks of countries with specific interests and specific abilities. As such, companies must develop the geopolitical experience and knowledge to leverage these blocks of talent. Regionalization will present new opportunities and challenges to conducting cross-border business transactions in the future.

Trends in 3D: Look Up, Look Out, and Look Around

It's easy for today's business leaders to become transfixed by the demands of short-term operations and lose sight of important happenings outside the walls of their business, outside the walls of their industry, and outside the walls of the United States. When this happens, however, tremendous opportunities can pass right by unnoticed.

Planning for the future in today's high-speed environment requires everyone to develop a predictive awareness and super-sensing capability of what is coming next. This means monitoring global trends and developing business foresight with an eye toward a long-term strategic view. New opportunities will come to those companies that see the future first and become future-ready by anticipating, adapting, and evolving ahead of the competition.

For example, a few of the latest trends that every business leader should be aware of include:

1. *Fast. Cheap. Good.* It used to be that you had to choose two out of the three features. Now, we have gotten to the age that accessing cheap tools anywhere, anytime to get a job done, and with relatively good quality, is our reality. It makes it possible for smaller business to take advantage and grow globally in ways that were unthinkable before. They now can connect, share, explore, and make money while "giving birth" to global products.

2. *Social networking.* It is happening every day and every minute as we witness revolutionary and diverse online action. The virtual gathering of crowds and armies will form before our eyes and draw us into their mission. Look at Egypt and the rest of the Middle East and ask yourself: Would this all have happened without the social media networks where people could express, explore, gather, and change the course of their future, and in this case, their country's history? As trust in government diminishes, groups will encourage people to solve their own problems in the world, and we will be empowered to take action in real time. This gives the platform for action, and people no longer feel helpless or hopeless. The problem is that it may also provide a platform for revolutionary action that ends up creating change that is not for the best.

3. *Technology in the driver's seat.* In addition to social networking that aims to connect beyond borders, the technology of smart phones makes it possible. This is the tool that broke the rules and set new standards for technology developments, human interaction, how, where, and when we do business, socialize, decide on vacation venues, and so much more to come. Our lives are changing: being able to remotely monitor the temperature in our homes, start our cars remotely, monitor our health vitals, and so much more . . . and all with this small device that we used to call a phone and have now turned into a central command center. Thomas Friedman said "the world is flat," and the new reality established that, and right in the palm of your hand.

4. *China will become what Japan was.* Some of us may remember when Japan used to "borrow" innovations and replicate them into a cheaper version. But China may take it one step further and improve on innovation to fit their local market and other niche markets, as well as add features and create new products. Look at the Chinese version of the iPhone, which is extremely successful in China and is a fierce competitor to Apple. Does this approach present potential for entrepreneurs as well as existing manufacturers? Combining innovation with global collaboration may be the "next big thing." Are you ready to get in the game? Do you know the new rules?

5. *Internet and beyond.* It is becoming about real-time, instant, and constant. People want to know more, almost in an obsessive way, about what is going on in other parts of the country and the world. While experts looked at this trend and forecasted less travel, I would dare say that the more people know, the more they would want to "see it for themselves" and the trend to travel globally will increase, with one stipulation that it is tightly connected to the world economy and jobs.

6. *Managing complexity.* More than ever, the top skill that everyone will need is managing complexity in a global economy and a global marketplace. The complexity of dealing with immense and rapid changes, the economic crisis, the job market, global competition, and new technologies will require a high level of complexity management. Survival may well be dependent on how well one can

manage details and competing priorities. This goes for individuals, companies, governments, and everybody on this planet. What's needed is right-brain thinking for strategizing and problem solving, which needs to become the focus of schools, company training sessions, and other activities to breed, equip, and mold tomorrow's leaders with the right skills. Daniel Pink is making the case of why right-brainers will rule the future, as so many professions, such as accountants, lawyers, doctors, are of the past.[2]

7. *The global connection.* Information will connect everyone in business—everywhere and all the time. This includes customers, vendors, and partners across borders as well as businesses up and down the supply chain and across industries. Everyone will be linked together. Entirely new business models, supply chains, customer care networks, markets, and industries will be born from this always-on global connectivity. New business models that deliver real-time value, all the time anywhere and everywhere, will redefine markets.

8. *The megacity consumer.* From China and India to Latin America and the EU, there is a new consumer demographic that is emerging and being driven by massive urban migration. These consumers live in megacities and are highly mobile and transnational. Megacity consumers are the new middle class: tech savvy, highly mobile, and entrepreneurial. They are driving up demand for products and services that could reach more than 120 countries, generating billions of dollars by 2035. This new global middle class seeks the prosperity and quality of life that is defined by the consumer marketplace.

9. *Global market conditions.* Trade barriers are easing. Economies are interdependent. Communication via the Internet has never been easier or more accessible. These conditions drive political reform, cultural transparency, social progress, and a great deal of wealth creation.

10. *Entrepreneurial mind-set.* Entrepreneurs have the ability to see, understand, and take advantage of evolving markets. The entrepreneur's ability to think differently, use insights, see what others don't, envision what doesn't yet exist, and identify opportunity when it's ripe—these are the prized qualities of today's entrepreneur, and when adding the ability to do all that across borders, cultures, and technologies, we are clearly witnessing a new exciting,

challenging, and demanding era. Wayne Gretzky of national hockey fame helped state it succinctly when he said, "I skate to where the puck is going to be, not where it's been."

11. *Eroding confidence in established institutions.* The recent world economic meltdown is removing any last confidence that most people had in governments and large enterprise banks and other financial entities. The resulting mistrust will lead to reinventing ourselves as individuals, communities, countries, and societies. As such, many more entrepreneurs will be joining the field. These changes also take a different turn in the Middle East as people, for the first time in this region's history, rebel against the government and institutions.

12. *Shifting business environment.* Large-scale firms are synonymous with bureaucracy, which tends to stifle innovation. In response, the business environment is shifting to accommodate the needs of its rapidly changing market players. Innovation and entrepreneurship are beginning to flourish around the world and will likely take the form of much smaller, yet bolder companies. Knowing and catering to this is how entrepreneurial ventures beat corporate giants to the punch. Any company, large or small, that continues down the same path it has always taken will find it to be a losing proposition.

13. *Entrepreneurial collaboration.* Also on a global scale, there will be more entrepreneurial collaboration, which in turn will make shared innovation between countries a far more common occurrence at the company-to-company level—not just at universities and research institutions. One of China's approaches for creating an innovative nation is the Technology Business Incubator (TBI). China's mission is to nurture "technopreneurs" and technology-based start-ups. Business incubation is considered a viable option for countries that want to expand economic opportunities.

14. *Growth of environmental and sustainable engineering technologies.* A growing consciousness about the value of protecting our world will fuel the demand for products and services that can accomplish this goal.

15. *The changing demands of the consumer.* With the rising prices of gas and the shift in lifestyle, consumers have been using the convenience of shopping online. This is nothing new. What may be new and a trend to watch is the vacuum that this trend will create in

the retail industry and how it will affect the urban as well as suburban landscape. We will still see quite a few retail storefronts around the world, but the United States is going to resort to more "big box" shopping as well as chains, while an increasing focus will be on the online experience.

16. *Borderless companies.* We are not talking anymore about global corporations and multi-national enterprises. This is a new structure and concept where the company is incorporated in Switzerland, the R&D is in Israel, the CEO is in the United States, the director of marketing is in Asia, and the business development team may be on a different continent. Sound confusing? It is a reality for some of us. These are not virtual companies. These are companies that take advantage of the best resources available and borders do not present barriers any longer. Boards of directors are composed of a variety of nationalities and expertise and the main purpose is to create a successful company that is competitive, sustainable, and recruits the best worldwide. You may want to ask a few questions, such as: What legal system does this company adhere to? What are the HR practices to follow? But these questions and others belong to the "old" mind-set. Think anew and program your existing mind-set to include new rules, new players, and new opportunities.

Together, these trends speak to larger changes within the business world that are not relegated to a single location, country, company, industry, or sector. These transcend borders and are truly global trends with global implications that require corporate America to redefine its definition of management success. Today, management success tends to be synonymous with short-term goals such as maximizing profits for shareholders without any consideration for long-term goals such as sustainability. But, sustainability isn't an issue for just resolving conflicts or winning tradeoffs. Rather, it is a fundamental key to achieving success today and into the future. Starting with our educational institutions, it's time to redefine management success to encourage a long-term perspective and the ability to invest in global opportunities. Looking at all these global trends, how is your company and its people positioned to successfully compete and contribute to the new world order and the new economy?

Europe's Change of Direction

With a proud history of innovation and democracy, this region will thrive at becoming a risk-taking investment culture with a recipe for growth that includes a Europe-wide patent scheme, tougher stress tests, killing off of sovereign debt, and the removal of crushing regulation. Also, the Euro has delivered much-needed price stability and will continue to do so under German leadership.

As more Eastern European countries join the EU, previously overlooked players like Poland are discovering untapped potential. Even long-established countries like Germany are benefitting from the Eurozone. German industry has dramatically increased competitiveness over the past 10 years as the German Deutschmark has stabilized. There is also a moral obligation of Germany, German politicians, and German industrialists to give support to countries like Portugal or Greece that will bring growth to that region of the world.

Focus on Latin America

Aided by growing exports coupled with increasing local demand, Latin America is experiencing its longest period of sustained growth in more than a generation. As hosts to the World Cup in 2014 and the Olympics in 2016, Brazil will contribute a positive impact to the entire region. As such, the opportunities to benefit from doing business in Latin America are endless.

Throughout Latin America, there are two significant changes that are likely to produce unprecedented growth for international businesses. One relates to sheer numbers. The portion of the population, referred to as "Bottom of the Pyramid Consumers," represents over 400 million citizens. With an income of nearly $600 million, this fast-growing sector of lower-income consumers is experiencing a huge surge in purchasing power. Second, technology infrastructure projects are underway. The increased collaboration in building a modern network of telecommunications, power grids, and undersea fiber optic cables will set the stage for more efficient and effective communications in this large geographical area.

Ready to jump in? Not so fast. While many countries in Latin America represent strong potential markets for global expansion, choosing the right country is not always easy. First, growth rates are not expected to be evenly distributed in the 36 countries that comprise this region. The pro-market economies such as Chile, Colombia, Panama, Peru, Costa Rica, Brazil, and Mexico will likely see their fortunes improve, while the economies of Venezuela, Ecuador, Bolivia, and Nicaragua may not. Second, there is a huge difference between doing business in North America versus South and Latin America. Latin America and South America do not consist of a homogeneous population. Each of the 36 countries that comprise the region is unique in terms of language, culture, traditions, government, legal system, and business etiquette. Although many countries share certain commonalties such as a relaxed approach toward time and the need for relationship building before deal making, there are important differences. Sometimes these differences may appear subtle to an outsider, but awareness of the nuances is critical to success. More important, success requires knowing how to access and interpret information. Since each country has unique strengths and weaknesses, a thorough investigative effort is required. That means targeting markets that match corporate needs and fit into overall strategic plans. Factors such as product brands, market strategy, sourcing, transportation, manufacturing, labor, or core competencies are a few key areas to consider. Leveraging one or more of these factors in the global marketplace increases the likelihood of long-term success.

Before engaging in Latin and South America or any other region, research the unique aspects of potential target markets. As mentioned in Chapter 3, one important resource to consult is the Ease of Doing Business Index (EODB). With one glance, EODB makes it possible to have a foundation that helps evaluate and compare every country in the region on the same criteria in a consistent manner. It's not surprising, however, that the aggregate scores for Latin and South American countries range from 40 (Chile) to 125 (Brazil) based on a scale of 0 to 185. For comparison, the United States is ranked 4, and the lower the score, the better for business.[3]

Another resource we mentioned in Chapter 3, alongside the EODB, is called the Opacity Index. The scores for Latin and South America range from 26 (Chile) to 49 (Colombia and Venezuela) compared to the United States' score of 22.[4]

While these resources offer helpful information, the real value comes when the data is interpreted correctly and then applied appropriately in order to achieve corporate goals. The right application of this information can be used to answer specific questions such as "Is this market a good fit for our company? How can we incorporate this market (country) into our overall strategic plan?"

Brazil is the largest country in South America with a culture as diverse as its geography. The culture blends Portuguese, African, and indigenous Indian heritage. Long known for its production of sugar, coffee, and soy beans, Brazil has emerged as a global powerhouse. It is the fifth largest economy in the world. For companies that want to get in on the action, it is important to understand Brazilian business culture and etiquette. Like many South American societies, trust means business and relationships have unprecedented importance. By cultivating close personal relationships and building trust over a long time, companies will have a greater likelihood of success in Brazil's diverse economy.

Colombia, the fourth largest country in South America, is one of the continent's most populous nations. After gaining independence from Spain in the late-nineteenth century, there was more than a century of violent political unrest. Conflict became the norm as governments fought to be the ruling power, and insurgent groups became more prevalent. Today, despite a turbulent past, Colombia's efforts to improve current economic policy and democratic security strategies have given rise to an increased confidence in the economy and business sector. Colombia's main industries are natural resources, agriculture, and textiles. Colombia's substantial oil reserves and natural resources provide numerous business and trade opportunities for foreign investors.

Often overlooked as a player in the global economy, Peru is determined to prove that it is more than just llamas and Machu Picchu. Its 9.8 percent growth rate in 2010 was one of the world's fastest expanding economies. In addition, record commodities prices and demand for raw materials are helping this mineral-rich nation. Peru predicts that the construction of a new road between its Pacific coast and Brazil will replace the Panama Canal as the main passage for trade with China. "South America in general, and Peru in particular, are the region and country of the future," says Francisco Sagasti, a senior associate at FORO, a development think tank based in Lima.

The opportunities for benefiting from doing business in this region are endless. Still, they can be very difficult for outsiders to navigate. Remember, each country has its own idiosyncrasies. Never assume that what works well in one country will translate into another country. For that reason, it is important for companies to proceed with caution and strategic logic. Working with an expert, someone whose finger is on the pulse of these markets and opportunities, is likely to conserve valuable resources and ensure future rewards.

South and Latin American countries that seem to present a stable ground for Foreign Direct Investment (FDI) are Chile, Argentina, Colombia, Costa Rica, and Brazil. Those countries are showing good economic growth for the most part. Mexico, which has the second-largest economy in the region, should also be on the list of investment opportunities even in the midst of a drug war.

Still drawing major headlines of its own is Venezuela, as President Hugo Chavez continues to exert what some call "hostility to private enterprise." The socialist movement in Venezuela, Bolivia, and Ecuador provides great risk for investors. While there are opportunities to generate profits in these countries, they are offset by great economic and political uncertainty. Many multinational companies operating in Venezuela have seen their earnings negatively impacted by unexpected devaluations of the currency and they've struggled to find methods to expatriate those earnings.

Focus on Africa

Some spell opportunity A-F-R-I-C-A. As a whole, it has a population of 900 million people earning the highest returns on FDI worldwide and residing on the second-largest continent brimming with valuable commodities. Of course, Africa's emerging markets, like all up-and-coming markets, present significant challenges and risks. But the mere presence of risk should not stop U.S.-based businesses from entering this region. On the contrary, the key is to remain focused on the opportunities and develop methods to manage and mitigate the risks. And hurry! China is already channelling more investment dollars into this region than the World Bank or any other nation.

By examining economic stability, political maturity, openness of trade, and the quality of education, Goldman Sachs has identified the Next-11, commonly referred to as N-11. These N-11 emerging economies are expected to ignite the future international business scene much like the BRIC countries (Brazil, Russia, India, and China) did over the last decade. Not surprisingly, included in the N-11 are two African countries, Egypt and Nigeria. Egypt makes analysts very nervous lately, but we cannot ignore the economic potential as long as calibrated for the long term. Yes, the turmoil points to a lot of risk, but learning from the steps and mind-set in the previous chapters will guide many companies as to making the right decisions in this country, while not becoming risk averse, but using the information to form new partnerships, plan accordingly, and wait for the right time and form to enter or re-enter the market.

Remarkably, throughout the recent economic downturn, only two regions in the world continued to grow. One of those regions was Asia; the other was Africa. In fact, from 2000–2008, Africa's economy grew at two times its pace during the 1980s or 1990s. And it's not just petroleum.

According to the Overseas Private Investment Corporation (OPIC) and the UN Trade Agency, Africa offers the highest return on direct foreign investment in the world and unsurpassed growth. In 2010, Africa's economy is expected to grow over 5 percent, which is considerably higher than the global average of 3 percent. For comparative purposes, Africa's collective gross domestic product (GDP) is $1.6 trillion. That equals the current economies of either Brazil or Russia.

Neville Isdell, Former Chairman & CEO, The Coca-Cola Company explains:

As business leaders with a wealth of experience working on the continent, we know that Africa is rich in business opportunities that yield high rates of return for investors as well as increased opportunities for the people of Africa. U.S. business leaders should take a fresh look at Africa and the significant growth taking place there, or risk being left behind.[5]

Isdell's optimistic outlook is supported by a recent report from McKinsey & Co titled *Lions on the Move*.[6] In this report, McKinsey bullishly informs business leaders that Africa's growth in recent years is more widespread than generally recognized. Specifically, four groups of industries are projected to reach a combined total of $2.6 trillion by 2020. Those industries include consumer goods (telecom, retail, banking), infrastructure, agriculture, and natural resources. It takes just one look at the explosive growth in the telecommunication sector to appreciate the magnitude of opportunity. In the year 2000, Africa had 350,000 working phone lines. Today, there are 60 million. From 1994–2004, cell phone use grew at an annual rate of 58 percent. Since 2000, the cell phone market has grown to over 316 million users. That's more new users in Africa than the entire U.S. population.

Unfortunately, many U.S. business leaders have a very limited perception of Africa—one that is focused solely on the segment of its population that exists on less than one dollar per day. This view of Africa ignores the remaining half of Africa's citizens who have the resources and purchasing power to buy products and services they desire. The reality is that Africa has an expanding consumer class with a taste for luxury goods. This simply can't be ignored.

Another misperception is the magnitude of risk. Kim Jaycox, CEO of Emerging Markets Partnership's Africa Fund, the largest fund investing in Africa, offers encouragement by noting that "the perceived risk is actually much greater than the real risk. And, as risk goes down, so do the returns." The largest risk factor is culture, and this must be incorporated into the overall risk assessment. Yes, it may require a different skill set to operate effectively in Africa, but these skills can be acquired through international experts that understand the region and local business practices.

To provide a glimpse of what's happening across Africa, let's highlight three countries that were ranked in the top 10 according to the 2009 African Competitiveness Report.[7]

1. Egypt—Arab Republic of Egypt (pop. 77 million; GDP $128 billion/per capita $5,400)

Egypt, a middle-income country, is home to Africa's largest city, Cairo. As a result of its unique geographical location, Egypt has developed a very diverse culture that combines influences from the Mediterranean, Africa, and the Arab world. But diversity is not limited to the culture. There's also economics. In addition to its vast natural resources and tourism, Egypt's agriculture and light manufacturing industries are substantial. With the latest new developments in Egypt there may be an economic vacuum for a while, as political tensions keep on affecting this country. They were fighting for democracy, but really have to define what it means for them and how it will look in Egypt, where democracy was always just a word, and never in its history, part of the life of Egyptians. From early biblical days it has been tightly controlled and ruled.

2. South Africa (pop. 48 million; GDP $283.1 billion/per capita $9,767)

In 1994, South Africa transitioned from apartheid to democracy and has successfully concluded four general elections, the most recent in April 2009. This country has the largest reserve of gold in the world and major reserves of diamonds, platinum, and other nonprecious metals. In addition to its natural resources, South Africa has a well-developed infrastructure of roads, railways, and air services that will all receive a boost from a $114 billion infrastructure investment project that was approved in the 2010/2011 budget.

In addition to this project, the government has established a Medium Term Strategic Framework (MTSF) for 2009–2014. In this framework are 10 priorities, including (1) more inclusive economic growth, decent work, and sustainable livelihoods; (2) economic and social infrastructure; (3) rural development, food security, and land reform; (4) access to quality education; (5) improved healthcare; (6) the fight against crime and corruption; (7) cohesive and sustainable communities; (8) creation of a better Africa and a better world; (9) sustainable resource management and use; and (10) a developmental state including improvement of public services.

3. Nigeria (pop. 150 million; GDP $167 billion/per capita $2,027)

Nigeria is the most populous country in Africa. It began democratic rule in 1999 with a seven-point agenda that focused on improving infrastructure, food security, land tenure, national security, wealth creation, human capital, and the Delta region. At the same time, the government worked diligently to eradicate corruption. This ambitious reform agenda has produced results as evidenced by Nigeria's rapid ascension toward middle-income status and GDP growth, which doubled from just 2005 to 2007.

Nigeria is the twelfth-largest producer of petroleum in the world and supplies 20 percent of all U.S. oil. While petroleum accounts for almost 40 percent of GDP, a number of other industries are growing rapidly. Nigeria is one of the world's fastest growing telecommunication markets. In addition, it has a highly developed financial services sector with the second-largest stock exchange in Africa. Despite huge deposits of natural resources, Nigeria's mining industry is still in its infancy and many minerals remain underexploited. As a result of the oil discovery, Nigeria's agriculture industry slipped into neglect, and large areas of arable land remain underutilized. To illustrate the extent of neglect, in the 1960s, Nigeria was a net food exporter growing 98 percent of its own food. Today, it imports these same cash crops.

As Africa continues to make progress in the area of increased political stability and a reduction in violent conflicts, its economic performance is certain to improve and spur even greater opportunities. Nelson Mandela once said, "It always seems impossible until it's done." Let that statement serve as a wakeup call to U.S. businesses. We cannot afford to walk away from the opportunities in Africa because they seem impossible. Instead, we should challenge our entrepreneurial expertise and discover ways that we, like the Chinese and Europeans, can be helping to build Africa's future.

Focus on the Middle East

The Middle East sits strategically where Africa, Asia, and Europe meet and includes 20 distinct countries and several world-class cities. Fortunately for U.S. businesses, much of this region is highly dependent on outside expertise and foreign imports to meet the growing demand for products and services. European and Chinese companies have already forged closer ties to this region and are reaping a disproportionate share of opportunities while U.S businesses struggle to sort out political and business concerns. An understanding of the full potential is best illustrated with a glimpse at a few countries in this region.

The latest uprising in the region came as a total surprise to most observers, but so was the fall of the Berlin wall and the transformation from communism in Russia and Eastern Europe. Both created amazing business and other opportunities. While the events in Eastern Europe were focused on social reforms, the Middle East uprising is driven by the quest for financial reforms.

1. Dubai—United Arab Emirates (pop. 4.6 million; GDP $228.6 billion/$40,200 GDP per capita)

In the early 1970s, seven sheikdoms came together to form what is currently known as the United Arab Emirates (UAE). Geographically, the UAE sits squarely in the center of the Arabian Gulf, with extensive natural petroleum reserves and a relatively relaxed society when compared to its neighbors. Today, the UAE is a thriving business center with lucrative opportunities for foreign investment.

The markets in the Middle East and North Africa (the MENA region) are growing rapidly. Dubai, one of the seven Emirates, has well-established industries in telecom, financial, shipping, construction, and real estate. The high-tech industry is growing slowly but gaining momentum thanks to government initiatives. Ray Milhem, Chief Technology Officer at Dubai Silicon Oasis Authority (DOA), notes:

> We are building a "Hi-Tech Eco System" and have attracted many high tech companies from this region, Europe and the Silicon Valley. The Government here is supportive of investments in many sectors including technology and pro- vides generous incentives, tax breaks, and facilities. We've learned to leverage the fact that we are both a regional and global "hub" between the east and the west.[8]

In terms of conducting business, the UAE was ranked 33rd globally and fourth regionally in the World Bank's Ease of Doing Business (EODB) index. As noted previously, this index provides a quantitative measure of regulations for starting a business, dealing with construction permits, employing workers, registering property, get- ting credit, protecting investors, paying taxes, trading across borders, enforcing contracts, and closing a business. However, it ranked 18th in the 2010 World Economic Forum's Enabling Trade Index, just behind the United States' 16th place, which demonstrates the UAE's ongoing effort to increase foreign direct investment.

Understanding Emirati culture, Islam, and business etiquette are essential for success. Age, money, and family connections are all key determining factors of a person's status. In direct contrast to the U.S. mind-set, who you are is more important than what you have achieved. Also, the organizational structure is typically a vertical hierarchy with one person owning, operating, and making all the decisions. In addition to these cultural issues, U.S. businesses must exercise caution with regard to Sarbanes-Oxley issues and conduct a comprehensive risk analysis and weigh those risks against the potential for growth.

2. Saudi Arabia (pop.: 25.7 million; GDP $379.5 billion/$24,200 GDP per capita)

As Ahmed S. Islam, Regional Director for the Americas, International Operations of the Saudi Arabian General Investment Authority (SAGIA), explains:

> Investing in the Kingdom of Saudi Arabia gives our partners an ideal opportunity to benefit from the unique trade heritage of a country that constitutes more than 80 percent of the Arabian Peninsula and more than 30 percent of the regional GDP. We are among the prime investment destinations of choice in a global economic milieu of burgeoning costs and dwindling margins.[9]

As the world's fastest reforming economy, the momentum behind this economic transformation is undeniable. In recent years, Saudi Arabia has risen from 76th to 13th position in the EODB index and is currently ranked number one, regionally. Adds Ahmed Islam:

> With the current focus on creating four "green" economic cities and our clear intent to migrate from Oil Capital of the World to Energy Capital of the World by developing an entire value chain from upstream to downstream, there

is no better time for businesses who wish to benefit from the unmatched costs of production and unparalleled incentives being offered in these new, revolutionary, smart cities. In total, the investment opportunities for these projects alone are quantified at $300 billion over the next ten years. All in all, over one trillion dollars of investment opportunities from both the public and private sector are to be realized over the next decade. So, as you can imagine, we're already quite busy.[10]

While opportunity abounds in Saudi Arabia, only businesses capable of navigating the Arab world will succeed. Generally speaking, the Arab world's form of communication is classified as "high context." That means that a message is often conveyed heavily by cues, body language, eye contact, and silence rather than verbally. In fact, people from this region frequently make assumptions based on what is not said rather than what is said. Also, knowledge of the Kingdom, its culture, and the Arab world are more essential to success than product and price and will require some sensitivity training for U.S. businesspeople.

3. Israel (pop.: 7.2 million; GDP $215.7 billion/$29,500 GDP per capita)

In stark contrast to the Arab world stands Israel, which offers a unique set of opportunities for business development in the Middle East. The main reasons to invest in and look for opportunities in Israel are the highly educated workforce, academic excellence, and the military influence. These conditions and others might be why more than 8,000 entrepreneurs have built an array of diversified high-tech companies in Israel. As Warren Buffett once said, "Americans came to the Middle East looking for oil, so they didn't stay in Israel. We came looking for brains, so we stopped." With the highest number of engineers per capita (double that of the United States and Japan), Israel is a nation of innovation and home to the highest concentration of high-tech companies outside of Silicon Valley. To illustrate the extent of Israel's' potential consider the following facts:

- 400-plus Israeli companies have subsidiaries or headquarters in the United States

- 200 new startup companies are created each year
- 500 high-tech firms earn annual revenues over $20 million each
- 80-plus fortune 500 global corporations conduct R&D in Israel
- Israel has the highest number of non-U.S. companies on NASDAQ
- Israel is in the top five countries for patents per capita
- Israel is the largest export market in the Middle East
- Israel's EODB rank is 29th globally and third regionally

With a strong link to the United States and a long-established European influence, Israel appears culturally familiar compared to its Arab neighbors. However, looks can be deceiving. Israel, like any country, has an established business culture that must be understood *before* jumping in. Because Israel is a very tight community, there's little need for formality. Accordingly, Israelis' interactions are very direct. This directness can be perceived as "pushy" to an outsider. From an organizational perspective, the typical corporate hierarchy is flat, and business is carried out in a collaborative, highly polychronic style with constant reprioritization of tasks.

Walid J. Tamari, a business litigation attorney with Tamari & Blumenthal, LLC and national chairperson of the Commercial Law League's Complex Commercial Litigation Committee, is optimistic about opportunities for U.S. entities conducting business in the Middle East. According to Mr. Tamari, "rising oil prices have created significant businesses opportunities in the Middle East. U.S. firms that structure their business correctly, while minimizing the various regional and local risks, can find meaningful and profitable opportunities."

Global success requires today's expansion to be based on future opportunities, not yesterday's reality. Forward-thinking businesses will explore the Middle East for new markets and pave the way for future growth. They won't wait until all conditions are right. Think back. Did U.S. manufacturers establish operations in China because the culture was familiar, the location was right, and the risks were low? No! They entered China in response to unparalleled opportunities. Similarly, the Middle East today represents an area of enormous potential. Equipped with accurate market analysis and risk assessment, U.S. businesses can also penetrate the Middle East with success.

From the well-established, high-tech giant of Israel to the future "green cities" of Saudi Arabia, the Middle East is open for business. And success is attainable for any U.S. company with the ability to identify a well-matched opportunity, assess the risks, and plan accordingly. Consider the opportunities that existed when cities in China, Canada, or Germany were sketches on paper. Even greater opportunities exist today in the Middle East for U.S. businesses willing to invest the resources necessary to learn the culture and how to navigate the Arab world. After all, it is these countries that have elaborate plans for the future and the financial resources to make it happen. All they lack is what we have: expertise and resources.

Opportunities in China

China is poised to have a greater impact on the world than any other country. If current trends persist, by 2025 China will have the world's second-largest economy and be the largest importer of natural resources. In recent years, China's economic mission has shifted from sourcing and manufacturing to outbound and domestic investment, indigenous innovation, and domestic consumption. This could be extremely beneficial for those U.S. businesses already in China. When evaluating opportunities here, think about these key issues:

1. Made in China: price versus quality

The initial surge of U.S. investment in China was fueled by businesses looking for cheap labor and excess manufacturing capacity. For any company competing primarily on price, discovering China was the equivalent of striking gold. On the contrary, for businesses competing on quality, the result was quite different. After a series of scandals involving tainted food, toys, and other products manufactured in China, the international community began to question whether Chinese exports met minimum quality standards. Companies like Apple even began labeling their products "Designed by Apple in California. Assembled in China."

Going forward, one of China's main ambitions is domestic investment. As China invests in infrastructure, education, and social welfare, it will no longer be the best source of cheap labor. However, this shift might result in a heightened commitment to quality thus providing previously unavailable opportunities for U.S. businesses. On the other hand, China will always strive to protect its own brands, leaving no guarantee of benefit for foreign companies. While it is still too soon to tell what impact this change will have, one point is clear: U.S. businesses need to continually reevaluate their international strategy with a fresh perspective on China coupled with a look at emerging markets.

2. Outbound Foreign Direct Investment (OFDI) and implications for intellectual property rights

China's OFDI has attained a level that is challenging international investment norms and affecting international relationships. Prior to China's "go abroad" policy, which started in the late 1990s, China's OFDI was minimal. In 2007, OFDI grew to $25 billion and reached $50 billion in 2008. On the positive side, by investing so much abroad, China is forced to recognize the importance of intellectual property rights and the consequences of product piracy. Ideally, by exposing themselves internationally, China will be encouraged to adopt the necessary laws to protect foreign investments. Hence, U.S. businesses unwilling to risk technology transfer may want to give China a second look in the future.

3. The impact of distance

Culturally and geographically, the United States and China are as distant as the east is from the west. Culturally, the divide is fraught with additional risk when considering language, social and business customs, level of formality, the meaning of relationships, and time. Interestingly, a study conducted by Grant Thornton found the top five barriers to cross-border transaction were cultural issues, regulatory environment, legal environment, intellectual property protection, and due diligence—each are monumental in China.

Geographically, China's relative distance to emerging markets may become problematic. Strategically, a U.S. manufacturer operating in China might soon discover that a better market has

emerged in Brazil, Eastern Europe, or Africa. In that case, manufacturing in China may prove too distant and increasingly more
expensive relative to other emerging markets.

4. Political landscape

While young people in China aspire to a more Westernized
culture, some things might never change. China is still a centralized economy that obstructs business with problematic issues such
as regulations, intellectual property, standards, taxes, market access,
currency manipulation, and corporate laws that regulate mergers
and acquisitions. For that reason, China rates comparatively low
in terms of opacity scores and ease of doing business, which ultimately act like a hidden tax. Furthermore, economy and politics
are interrelated, and China–U.S. relations will experience heightened tension as China continues to engage with countries like Iran
and North Korea.

5. Weighing the pros and cons

It's true that many U.S. businesses continue to report tremendous success in China and are committed for the long term.
However, with sweeping change in China and rapid development
of other emerging markets, it's essential for businesses to analyze
accurate and timely data before making any global decision. Don't
go to China because the competition did, and don't stay in China
because that was the five-year plan. Choose China when a thorough strategic analysis indicates that China is the best market to
meet your specific business goals. Look again: Is China the best
place for your business?

Pearls of Wisdom

Obviously, no one can predict what the future holds. Nothing is
certain. But as business leaders today we must start asking the tough
questions. For example: What kind of future do we want? What kind
of company do we want to build? What can we contribute to creating the reality we desire? Equally important, recognize that, long term,
it's in the West's best interest to collaborate with countries like China,

India, Brazil, Russia, as well as those emerging markets, to make sure they grow in stature and become constructive international players.

When you look at the 21st century, it's not about who will replace the United States in terms of economic power and value leadership. No country can or will in the foreseeable future. The real danger is that no one will. Without world growth, the U.S. economy will stagnate because American businesses will lack new markets and the necessary global partners for international growth. Therefore, it's important for businesses of all sizes to explore innovative ways to enter global markets on the right path that minimizes risk, generates the highest rewards, and builds a stronger world.

With this in mind, here is a list of key points to keep in mind from this chapter:

- Political and economical power is shifting from the West to the East.
- Transnational issues such as potential energy, water, and food shortages will fundamentally change the way business is conducted. How will new global players, the new playing field, and the new rule book impact your business?
- Globalization has created a sense of volatility and unpredictability that requires reasoning and collaboration across borders. How will transnational issues such as diminishing natural resources, cyber security, widening inequality, and the increased proportion of women in the work forces impact your global plans?
- Planning for the future requires increased awareness of global trends. Is your organization prepared to collaborate with other regions of the world to collectively solve the world's problems? Does your long-term planning take into consideration global trends?
- Latin America is experiencing its longest period of sustained growth in more than a generation and offers lots of opportunity in Brazil, Colombia, Peru, and others.
- The Middle East is highly dependent on outside expertise and foreign imports to meet the growing demand for products and services, and these countries have no shortage of capital.

- China's new economic mission has shifted from sourcing and manufacturing to outbound and domestic investment, indigenous innovation, and domestic consumption, which offer new opportunities for U.S. businesses.

Coming up in Chapter 10, I will wrap things up by looking at how growth in business is a journey and how, in many ways, personal growth and growth in business go hand in hand. I'll also offer some of the most common mistakes that businesspeople make when looking to expand their businesses in a global capacity.

Chapter 10

Growth and Discovery

"Only the ignorant try to imitate the behavior of others. Intelligent men don't waste their time over such things: they develop their own abilities. They know that in the forest of a hundred thousand trees there are no two leaves alike and that no two journeys along the same road are the same."

—*Paolo Coelho*

Many years ago, a shoe manufacturer was searching for opportunities to expand its reach into new regions of the world. After scanning the globe for potential markets, the firm settled on the Australian bush. Two of the firm's newly hired business school graduates were then dispatched into Australia's rugged interior. Their goal was to locate new markets for shoe sales and possibly develop new product ideas for the Aborigine market. For efficiency's sake, the two split up and explored different villages. After a day of meeting and observing the natives in one village, the first employee contacted headquarters and said, "There are no prospects of future sales in Australia's interior. The natives don't wear shoes of any type." Minutes later, another message was received by headquarters. The second employee told headquarters, "Send all possible shoe stock. We are sure to dominate this market since the natives have no shoes."

Seeing opportunities in the global marketplace requires the right perspective. Acting on those opportunities requires the right skills and entrepreneurial instincts. Both of these, perspective and skill, take time plus experience to develop and mature. Most important, they require intentional learning and curiosity to explore. Learning should be a deliberate response to every experience, every environment, and every opportunity. Then, through daily business activities, develop a global lens that transcends culture, borders, and mind-sets.

A Personal Journey: Learning to Negotiate across Borders toward Expansion

I am fortunate to have been exposed to a multicultural life, having lived on three different continents with frequent travels to many international destinations. Purposefully, I use every experience to familiarize myself with different aspects of various cultures around the world. From a business perspective, I have the experience of being both an entrepreneur and a COO, having started and sold three separate businesses from manufacturing to technology to consulting. I work across many different industries ranging from manufacturing and technology to homeland security, hospitality, and transportation.

Throughout my life, I've fostered a love for intellectual curiosity and ongoing learning. With each new experience on my journey, whether good or bad, positive or negative, I add another dimension to my understanding of people, cultures, and how to best penetrate the global marketplace. I use these experiences and knowledge to impart insight and wisdom for the benefit of my clients, my students, and my work.

For example, when I started a manufacturing business, I learned how to negotiate across borders to deliver the best possible product for markets in both North America and Asia. I maximized the value of a global supply chain by sourcing abroad and working collaboratively with other businesspeople from around the world. Ultimately, the product was developed in Germany (German top engineering), designed by Italians (Italian top design and style), and made in the United States (American quality). I also learned the importance of protecting products and intellectual property in the global arena. If you are not exceptionally careful, your product will be stolen. I learned this the hard way when my high-tech product was reverse engineered by the Koreans.

Today, as a global expansion expert, I combine my acquired business skills with my unique global perspective to help clients navigate through the global expansion process. Throughout my years in business, I have discovered that the business deals themselves are seldom the problem. Business leaders today have the skills and finesse to identify and execute great deals. It's the soft issues that surface on the international stage that cause unanticipated and disastrous problems.

Additionally, I've noticed that companies get into trouble when they have a false belief that simply expanding the domestic execution strategy will translate into a successful international expansion. Rather, when there is a lack of understanding with regard to the business culture and customs of the local people and a lack of international due diligence, that causes most of the challenges.

Because I have worked with some of the world's leading multinationals and I communicate in several foreign languages, I'm able to interpret how a U.S. business proposal may be perceived and help that business customize its approach depending on the target market, as well as help with the negotiation's message, style, and strategy. I also work with foreign businesses to help them access U.S. markets. Working both inbound and outbound, I'm uniquely skilled to anticipate stumbling blocks and develop contingency plans to eliminate surprises. That is my competitive edge and my passion: using my versatile expertise, multicultural lens, and laser-focused listening to help businesses leverage their strengths and take advantage of endless opportunities in foreign markets.

Avoiding Costly Mistakes

Clients tell me that my strength comes from taking the guesswork out of going global and helping them to avoid costly mistakes. Some of the most common are described in the next sections.

Mistake 1: Underestimating the Time to Market for Your Product/Services

Don't put expansion plans at risk by budgeting too short a time line. When this happens, inevitably, the business depletes available capital and the upfront investment of time and money is wasted while your international reputation is blemished. Resist the temptation to be overly optimistic, and then anticipate time to market very conservatively. It's simply impossible to predict how long it will take to build the necessary relationships and establish the right network and the right channels of distribution. Look at the Ease of Doing Business (EODB) index[1] for planning purposes, and focus on interpreting that information correctly and analyzing how it will affect your specific business plans. You cannot put a time frame on building trust.

Mistake 2: Lacking Clear Objectives

In his book *Winning*,[2] Jack Welch dedicates an entire chapter to "Change." Appropriately, it's subtitled "Mountains Do Move." Welch's wisdom for bringing about change is clearly stated in four principles. The first principle is to attach every change to a clear purpose or goal, since creating havoc and change for change's sake is stupid and enervating. I've watched many global expansion initiatives fail due to a lack of clear objectives for going global in the first place. In some cases, I've watched businesses go global because that's what everyone else is doing, but riding into a foreign market on the coattails of the competition cannot be a smooth ride!

The reason to go global must come from a legitimate need to change that is based on accurate data, starting with the present and looking into the future. It begins with asking the right questions. Don't skip this critical step. You can significantly increase your likelihood of success by researching the market and the competition; setting clear objectives, timelines, milestones, and metrics; and using this research to create a road map to success. And of course, all this information has to be analyzed and interpreted in context. Data alone will not suffice. Make sure you define the right target market(s) for your product or service and choose the appropriate mode of entry.

One domestic coffee company has done a great job entering a saturated market in Turkey by banking on the idea that as a foreign brand, it will enjoy product differentiation and therefore have a competitive advantage over local brands. In order to maintain that success into the future, this company must focus on the next step. Will the trend of drinking foreign brand coffees get old? Will political unrest affect consumer loyalty and behavior? If so, when and how can this company prepare for that today?

Mistake 3: Inaccurately Assessing Risk

Understand your exposure to risk without becoming risk averse. Reveal risk, assess that risk, and have a contingency plan to mitigate the potential for risk.

When conducting transactions across borders, you will be faced with government restrictions and unanticipated government involvement since the lines that divide business and government are not so clearly defined in the international arena. This adds another element of unpredictability to an already unpredictable environment. But, that's no reason to ignore the world's markets. Instead, discover ways to cope with uncertainty and work within the limits imposed by governmental interventions. The rewards often outweigh the risks. For example, in some countries, it's nearly impossible to repatriate your money out. While a qualified CPA can help you structure it correctly, good planning will help you recognize this obstacle *before* you select this market so that you are aware and prepared.

Mistake 4: Focusing on Quick Sales Rather Than Long-Term Business Development

Don't be short-sighted. In the United States we have a tendency to make decisions based on quarterly profits. Unfortunately, this approach fails to generate the best long-term strategy, and going global should be a long-term commitment. How you enter a market, who your partners are, and the way in which you generate your first sale will set the stage for future business and have a profound effect on overall success. As a general rule, begin with the end in mind. Focus on developing the right strategy, the right relationships, and the right tactics for sustainable success, not short-term gains. Consider how you will position, brand, and grow your business for the long run.

Remember when McDonald's failed miserably offering one cuisine across the world? Its international efforts were disastrous until they learned to adapt to local preferences and local tastes. Apparently Kellogg wasn't paying attention, as well. It also failed when the company attempted to introduce cold cereal to India in the 1990s. It's just not part of the Indian culture to eat from a box, and it is unthinkable to have a breakfast out of a box! Both these organizations would have benefited greatly from up-front market research and cultural sensitivity rather than a superior attitude about U.S. products. Or they should have adopted a long-term strategic vision that set out to create a need and change habits over a long period of time, like Starbucks did in the United States. In many ways, the success of Starbucks was a willingness to forgo short-term profits in favor of a long-term strategy and business development that did change the way Americans enjoy their coffee.

Mistake 5: Forgetting the Fundamental Importance of Cultural Differences

Be sensitive to cultural nuances. I've witnessed many business transactions that come to a screeching halt and fall apart due to cultural misunderstandings and cultural ignorance. Don't assume anything, and do your homework. Businesspeople in an international business environment must not only be sensitive to differences in culture and language, but they must also learn to adopt the appropriate policies and strategies for coping with these differences.

For example, it's increasingly commonplace for multinational teams to engage in virtual communication rather than face-to-face meetings. This situation magnifies existing language and cultural barriers. Relying on e-mail is even more challenging since words can be interpreted in many different ways with no intonation or facial expressions to help dissect the message in "real time." Given this reality, what is your company's response: training exercises, more frequent virtual meetings to help build the skills necessary, annual face-to-face visits? There must be a plan to bridge the cultural and language divide caused by virtual communication.

In terms of designing or modifying U.S. products for global markets, never assume those products will be used in the same manner. A U.K. product first introduced in 1780, Altoids were originally marketed to relieve stomach discomfort. By the 1920s, the original cardboard box had been replaced by the more durable distinctive metal tins of today. The irreverent, quirky personality of Altoids has led Altoids Peppermint tins to be a top-selling mint in the United States. How does your current brand, supply chain, and strategic plan fit into this target market? Can you, like Altoids, innovate and discover a better match for your product?

Mistake 6: Making Decisions Based on Widely Known Information

From one market to the next, there is no one size fits all, and product modification or product adaption must be built into the front end of the planning process. Start with a strategy that best fits your product/ service, business objectives, and corporate culture, then match it with the appropriate country or region. Next, be prepared to modify your product to fit the precise needs, tastes, and preferences of the intended market. Differences among countries require that an international business vary its practices to meet the expectations of each individual region. Marketing a product in Venezuela may require a different approach from marketing the same product in Argentina, even though they are both in Latin America.

Also, managing U.S. workers might require different skills than managing Egyptian workers. Maintaining close relations with a particular level of government may be very important in Mexico but irrelevant in the U.K. If you disregard one component, you are sure to dramatically decrease your chances for success.

Mistake 7: Being Overconfident in Your Global Expansion Skills

Remember what Bill Gates said: "Success is a lousy teacher. It seduces smart people into thinking that they can't lose." People who have developed and grown successful domestic businesses are frequently fooled into thinking they can transfer those skills abroad and become the next big international craze. If it were that simple, more U.S. businesses would be achieving success abroad. Instead, try a dose of humility. Humility goes a long way in combating the problems associated with overconfidence. Remember, what made you successful in your domestic market, in most cases, won't make you successful in the international marketplace.

At the most fundamental levels, differences arise from the simple fact that countries are different, people are different, and expectations are different in every market. From culture, political systems, economic systems, legal systems, levels of economic development to openness to foreigners, countries are very different. Many of these differences are very profound, and some are subtle. So, seek professional advice to navigate the unknown and use other peoples' experiences to help you develop a road map destined for success. Even if it is to just validate your approach and planned activities, ask for help.

TNN, a successful global corporation, recently acquired a local Chicago company. As a precaution, TNN senior management requested assistance from me to prepare their managers who would be coming to the United States. Through a series of questions and training, I made sure that the company was sending the most suitable people to conduct business here in the United States. I equipped these managers with the training and education necessary to be successful in their new roles. In addition, I developed a special program for their U.S. counterparts to help them deal with this new management group, which would become part of the daily business environment. What I offered was the perspective needed to craft a strategy, vision, mission, and risk assessment by understanding the U.S. markets for their product lines.

Looking at the Facts: Evidence-Based Decisions

When I ask companies to explain why they chose to move operations to or source from China, the common answer is that China is cheaper. On a hunch that the decision lacked adequate due diligence and the business was just "following the crowd," I challenged one client to illustrate the savings. After pouring over the financial statements, the calculated savings was one dime per unit. The payback period to cover the costs of going to China wouldn't be recovered until the business sold one million units, which would take years, assuming everything went forward as planned with no currency, logistical, legal, or management hurtles. Given the unpredictable nature of the global environment, these are dangerous assumptions. In retrospect, it was a poor decision, and my doubts were validated.

However, if their intent was to reach new markets in Asia and therefore save on logistics, this could create a competitive advantage and make business sense.

It's Global Business, Not Show Business

Along the same lines, another problem I see is business executives playing the Hollywood game. They become more enamored with advancing their own agenda, boosting egos, and creating the right corporate image. I call this the "Go-Hollywood" virus, and it's often complete with buzzwords, special effects, superstars, and other glitz. It creates a corporate buzz based in fiction, not fact. Too often these fads come at the expense of proven processes such as SWOT analysis (looking into your strengths, weaknesses, opportunities, and threats analysis) and good old-fashioned common sense.

Some companies struggle because they have a genuine, but misplaced, desire to innovate. New initiatives fail to deliver when innovation focuses on management processes rather than on designing products with the right features for a changing and diverse global market. Customers, not authors and industry gurus, are the best business advisors a company can access. Before introducing any product ideas, conduct market research, look around, and see what is needed. But also know what and how to ask so you get the right answers/data to help you make an informed decision. Too often, engineers and R&D fall in love with a product, but the product never sells because it doesn't serve the needs of the local market and sales.

The Value of Relationships

When all else fails, recognize that a solid foundation of trusting relationships in the target market and around the globe will ease the difficulties of going global. Personally, I have benefited on numerous occasions because I took the time to cultivate long-term relationships based on trust and mutual respect. By definition, relationships in the United States are different from relationships in other parts of the world. In the United States, people tend to be very open to casual friendships, and the word "friend" is used frequently. But these friendships often lack the depth necessary to offer real value in times of crisis. Internationally, relationships can take years to build, but the result is loyalty that can last a lifetime. For visual effects, I used to compare the first as a peach (a soft exterior that stops at a hard core) and the latter as a coconut (a hard exterior that may be tough to break, but when done, it is as smooth as can be).

I have always been intrigued by different people, and I have a keen and genuine interest in people and a natural curiosity that helps me explore the nuances of each person I meet. I make it a priority to learn how to engage each one in a conversation, gain his or her trust, and develop a long-term relationship that may or may not lead to business. The global network of meaningful, long-lasting, inspiring, and thought-provoking friendships I've developed around the world has certainly added to my global experience and helped me become a successful player in the global arena.

To build relationships, understand that people want to be heard, understood, and respected, not judged, benchmarked, or ridiculed. This is universal. My first client, a major German company, could have hired anyone or any company from around the globe. But they hired me. We had a relationship that originated in cultural fluency that developed into trust and mutual understanding. This is when I truly learned the value of relationships and cultural fluency in the international marketplace. Knowing the target market's language is helpful, but cultural fluency at the level of strategy is what separates the good business deals from the great ones. For example, the CEO of a U.S. company doesn't have to learn Portuguese if he or she wants to do business in Brazil, but he or she needs to know what will work and what will not. And this is best accomplished through commitment, a global mind-set and the establishment of local relationships.

Final Pearls of Wisdom

The great success of U.S.-based businesses in the domestic marketplace has made them slow to react to changes in the global marketplace and less willing to seek opportunities abroad. As a result, most U.S. executives have some catching up to do with regard to developing international experience and a global perspective. My years of acquiring international experience and assisting companies involved with business beyond U.S. borders have produced valuable insights that allow me to simplify the global expansion process for my clients. Also, as a third party, it's easier to evaluate situations and offer objective advice based on facts, not emotions. To share some advice I give to every client, consider the following:

- *Pack your bags and travel.* A key to my success is time spent outside the United States in developing regions around the globe.

So travel. But travel with the intent and commitment to observe, learn, question, and not just be another tourist. How can a business leader or member of the board of directors make sound decisions about a global strategy without first visiting the country? Still, this is a frequent occurrence. If you are considering a certain market, go there. See and experience it with your own eyes but with a global lens; get introduced, and meet people that may become your business partners; create and establish relationships. Put boots on the ground.

- *Be flexible.* Learn to adapt to new ideas and new ways of conducting business. Listen with both your ears and your gut. Instincts are very important, and experience perfects these instincts.
- *Have a realistic vision.* Spectacular visions look great on PowerPoint presentations, but they are not always actionable. Many companies fail because they follow a vision with no consideration for the appropriate context. Never assume that what works in the United States will work in other parts of the world. It won't.
- *Reach beyond your comfort zone.* In many cases people are too conservative, too afraid of change and of the unfamiliar, and therefore, they resist global opportunities out of fear. The key to growth is to let go of fear.
- *Conduct a needs assessment.* Identify the issues, define the scope, and audit existing resources.
- *Set goals and expectations.* Define tasks and plan the work to be done while establishing tools to coordinate and eliminate uncertainty and ambiguity.
- *Provide vision and strong leadership.* Make sure the roadmap is followed and stay on task by implementing the activities.
- *Choreograph simultaneous actions of the various players and stakeholders.* Set the agenda and make sure that all parties involved are communicating and working in concert.
- *Monitor and communicate progress.* Use metrics to measure results, deliverables, and progress.

Since there is no one formula that works in every situation, my main objective is to help clients understand their unique situations.

Now It's Your Turn

With 95 percent of the world's population living outside the boundaries of the United States, the potential for business leaders who can apply these lessons to their unique circumstances is beyond measure. Now is the time to start. You have an opportunity to grow revenues and profits faster than the U.S. market will ever support. Just look at the numbers.

With a world population of over six billion people, it only takes approximately 5 percent of that market to equal the entire U.S. population. Whatever the size of your business, the global market has much to offer you and, although you may not realize it, you have a lot to offer, too.

Notes

Chapter 1

1. National Summit on American Competitiveness, Chicago, 2008.
2. Tackling the Risks of Going Global, KPMG.
3. The Organization for Economic Cooperation and Development (OECD), May 26, 2010.
4. Interview with Ed Morris, Clifton Gunderson LLP.
5. Grant Thornton, "Bridging the global, cross-border transaction gap: What more middle-market dealmakers need to know about global M&A," www .grantthornton.com/staticfiles/GTCom/files/ACG%20reports/Bridging% 20the%20global%20cross%20border%20transaction%20gap.pdf.
6. Joel Kurtzman and Glenn Yago, "Opacity Index," April 21, 2009, www .milkeninstitute.org/publications/publications.taf?function=detail&ID= 38801192&cat=ResRep.

Chapter 2

1. World Economic Forum, "The Global Competitiveness Report 2010–2011," www3.weforum.org/docs/WEF_GlobalCompetitivenessReport_2010–11 .pdf.
2. Gary Hamel, www.garyhamel.com.

3. Lou Kacyn, YouTube, Nov. 15, 2010, Global Boards.

4. Mona Pearl, "Global Expansion," www.manufacturing-today.com/cms2/index
.php?option=com_content&view=article&id=923:global-expansion-
&catid=121&Itemid=80.

5. "The Future Paradigm in People Decisions: Developing and Retaining
Global Talent" www.egonzehnder.com/global/clientservice/executivesearch/
article/id/83700258.

6. "What Makes a Global Leader," www.wharton.universia.net/index.
cfm?fa=printArticle&ID=1426&language=english.

7. Ibid.

8. Ibid.

9. Deborah Wince-Smith, National Summit on American Competitiveness,
Chicago, 2008.

Chapter 3

1. The World Bank Group, "Economy Rankings." Visit www.doingbusiness.
org/economyrankings for a full report.

2. Milken Institute, "2009 Opacity Index: Measuring Global Results." Visit www
.kurtzmangroup.com/pdf/InstituteOpacityIndex_Apr8.pdf for a full report.

3. Transparency International, "Corruption Perception Index," www.transparency
.org/policy_research/surveys_indices/cpi.

Chapter 4

1. "How to Hit a Moving Target," *Business Week,* August 21, 2006.

2. "Outgreening Delivers Sustainable Competitive Advantage," *Business Week,*
December 5, 2008.

Chapter 5

1. Jeswald W. Salacuse, "Making Deals in Strange Places: A Beginner's Guide
to International Business Negotiations" (pages 5–13), http://onlinelibrary
.wiley.com/doi/10.1111/j.1571-9979.1988.tb00441.x/abstract.

2. Lothar Katz, *Negotiating International Business: The Negotiator's Reference Guide to
50 Countries Around the World,* Booksurge Publishing, Charleston SC, 2008.

3. National Summit on American Competitiveness, Chicago, 2008.

Chapter 6

1. Rob Loewer, General Counsel, NREC.

2. The United States Department of Justice, Foreign Corrupt Practices Act,
www.justice.gov/criminal/fraud/fcpa/

Chapter 7

1. Lara Williams, "Busting the Cluster Myths," *fdi Magazine,* October 15, 2009.

2. S. M. Harper and S. W. Becker, "On the Leading Edge of Innovation: A Comparative Study of Innovation Practices," *Southern Business Review,* Spring 2004.

3. Chicago Tribune Top 50 List, January 2003.

4. Paul Lockwood Brown and Jacqueline Byrd. *The innovation equation: building creativity and risk taking in your organization.* Practicing Organization Development. San Francisco: Jossey-Bass/Pfeiffer, 2003.

5. Alexander Loudon, Roel Pieper, *Webs of Innovation: The Networked Economy Demands New Ways to Innovate,* Prentice Hall, 2001.

6. Moon Ihlwan, "Do the Chaebol Choke Off Innovation?" *Businessweek,* December 3, 2009.

7. Richard Mammone, "How to Take Advantage of Business Clusters," *Businessweek,* December 8, 2009.

8. Please note the sections on vertical integration have been written in conjunction with research from Marco V. Galante, Principal, J.H. Chapman Group LLC, and parts of the research were published in the *Nutrition Business Journal,* June/July 2011 | newhope360.com pages: 28–31.

Chapter 8

1. 4Ps were invented in 1960, by Jerome McCarthy (Jerome McCarthy and William D. Perreault, *Basic Marketing: A Global-Managerial Approach,* McGraw-Hill, 2005). They were made leading-edge by Philip Kotler in his book *Principles of Marketing* (Prentice Hall) in 1967.

Chapter 9

1. "Commerce Secretary Gary Locke, Senator Sherrod Brown Highlight Administration's Effort to Boost Exports and U.S. Jobs in Ohio," Commerce.gov, www.commerce.gov/news/press-releases/2010/03/22/commerce-secretary-gary-locke-senator-sherrod-brown-highlight-adminis.

2. Daniel Pink, *A Whole New Mind: Why Right-Brainers will Rule the Future,* Riverhead Books, 2005.

3. The World Bank Group, "Economy Rankings," www.doingbusiness.org/economyrankings for a full report.

4. Milken Institute, "2009 Opacity Index: Measuring Global Results," www.kurtzmangroup.com/pdf/InstituteOpacityIndex_Apr8.pdf for a full report.

5. E. Neville Isdell, "CEO Blog: Take a Fresh Look at Africa," http://www
.cnbc.com/id/38521047/CEO_Blog_Take_a_Fresh_Look_at_Africa.

6. McKinsey Global Institute, "Lions on the Move: The Progress and Potential
of African Economies," June 2010, www.mckinsey.com/mgi/publications/
progress_and_potential_of_african_economies/index.asp.

7. World Economic Forum. See www.weforum.org/en/initiatives/gcp/Africa
%20Competitiveness%20Report/index.htm for the entire report.

8. Ray Milhem, Chief Technology Officer at Dubai Silicon Oasis Authority
(DOA), in an interview.

9. Quote from Ahmed S. Islam, Regional Director for the Americas,
International Operations, used with permission.

10. Ibid.

Chapter 10

1. The World Bank Group, "Economy Rankings," www.doingbusiness.org/
rankings.

2 Jack Welch, *Winning*. HarperBusiness, 2005.

Suggested Reading

Alimienė, Monika, and Rita Kuvykaitė. 2008. Standardization/Adaptation of marketing solutions in companies operating in foreign markets: An integrated approach. *Engineering Economics* 56 (1):37–47.

An idea whose time has come. 2009. *Economist* 390 (8622)(May), special section:6–9.

Arnold, Pamela. 2011. What's culture got to do with diversity? What's diversity got to do with culture? *Profiles in Diversity Journal* 13 (2):16.

Black, J. Stewart, and Mark Mendenhall. 1989. A practical but theory-based framework for selecting cross-cultural training methods. *Human Resource Management* 28 (4)(Winter):511–539.

Brandl, Julia, and Anne-Katrin Neyer. 2009. Applying cognitive adjustment theory to cross-cultural training for global virtual teams. *Human Resource Management* 48 (3)(May):341–353.

Brannback, Malin, and Alan Carsrud. 2008. Do they see what we see? A critical Nordic tale about perceptions of entrepreneurial opportunities, goals and growth. *Journal of Enterprising Culture* 16 (1)(March):55–87.

Burksaitiene, Daiva. 2010. Cross-border mergers and acquisitions in developed countries: A study in 2008–2009. *Economics & Management:* 32–38.

The case for going global. 2009. *Marketing* (February 18):29.

Coeudacier, Nicolas, Robert A. De Santis, and Antonin Aviat. 2009. Cross-border mergers and acquisitions and European integration. *Economic Policy* 24 (57) (January):55–106.

Daste, Matteo, Robert C. White, Jr., Jim Dimitriou, Jack Purcell, Robert Comment, Mahesh Krishnamurti, and Maria Ebel. 2010. Got jobs? *Mergers & Acquisitions: The Dealermaker's Journal* 45(11)(November):40–41.

De la Hera, Maria Luisa, Mayor Blázquez, and Mónica Garcia–Ochoa. 2009. Technological innovation clusters in Latin America. *GCG: Revista de Globalización, Competitividad & Gobernabilidad* 3(3):16–33.

Enderwick, Peter. 1989. Multinational corporate restructuring and international competitiveness. *California Management Review* 32 (1)(Fall):44–58.

Engel, Jerome S., and Itxaso del-Palacio. 2011. Global clusters of innovation: The case of Israel and Silicon Valley. *California Management Review* 53 (2) (Winter):27–49.

French, Warren, Harald Zeiss, and Andreas Georg Scherer. 2001. Intercultural discourse ethics: Testing Trompenaars' and Hampden-Turner's conclusions about Americans and the French. *Journal of Business Ethics* 34(3/4)(December):145–159.

Fuchs, Barbara. 2007. Learning from Toyota: How action learning can foster competitive advantage in new product development (NPD). *Action Learning: Research & Practice* 4(1)(April):25–43.

Gandossy, Robert, Rejeev Peshawaria, Leslie Perlow, Fons Trompenaars, and Daisy Waderman Dowling. 2009. Driving performance through corporate culture: Interviews with four experts. *Journal of Applied Corporate Finance* 21 (2)(March): 67–73.

Global companies with global boards. 2008. *NACD Directorship* 34(5) (October/November):28–30.

Goehle, Donna G. 1989. Going global: Turning strategic vision into operational reality. *International Executive* 31 (2) (September/October):9–13.

Going global: Easier said than done. *Pharmaceutical Executive* 28 (10):15.

Hampden-Turne, Charles, & Alfons Trompenaars. *Riding the Waves of Culture: Understanding Cultural Diversity in Global Business*. Irwin Professional Publications, 1997.

Hofstede, Geert. *Culture's Consequences: Comparing Values, Behaviors, Institutions and Organizations Across Nations*. Sage Publications, 2001.

Hopkins, H. Donald. 2008. Cross-border mergers and acquisitions: Do strategy or post-merger integration matter? *International Management Review* 4 (1) (June):5–10.

Iordache, Carmen, Iuliana Ciochina, and Mihaela Asandei. 2010. Clusters—Tourism activity increase competitiveness support. *Theoretical & Applied Economics* 17 (5)(May):99–112.

Isaksen, Arne. 2009. Innovation dynamics of global competitive regional clusters: The case of the Norwegian centres of expertise. *Regional Studies* 43 (9) (November):1155–1166.

Jaemin Jung, John. 2004. Acquisitions or joint ventures: Foreign market entry strategy of U.S. advertising agencies. *Journal of Media Economics* 17 (1):35–50.

Jie Shen, Lang, and Brant Lang. 2009. Cross-cultural training and its impact on expatriate performance in Australian MNEs. *Human Resource Development International* 12(4):371–386.

Karier, Thomas. 1994. Competitiveness and American enterprise. *Challenge* 37 (1)(January/February):40–44.

Kennedy, Debbe, and Jessica Roemischer. 2010. Global leadership gathering: The art of connecting across cultures, time, and distance. *Integral Leadership Review* 10 (5):1–7.

Knibb, David. 2008. Border crossing. *Airline Business* 24 (5)(May):58–60.

Kok-Yee Ng, Linn Van Dyne, and Soon Ang. 2009. From experience to experiential learning: Cultural intelligence as a learning capability for global leader development. *Academy of Management Learning & Education* 8 (4)(December): 511–526.

Lawrence, William J. and Weidong Sun. 2010. A cluster approach towards enhancing Chinese-American trade opportunities. *International Journal of Business & Management* 5 (2)(February):44–51.

Lucas, Matthew, Anita Sands, and David A. Wolfe. 2009. Regional clusters in a global industry: ICT clusters in Canada. *European Planning Studies* 17 (2) (February):189–209.

Moon, Chris J., and Peter Wooliams. 2000. Managing cross cultural business ethics. *Journal of Business Ethics* 27 (1/2)(September):105–115.

Munley, Almarie E. 2011. Culture differences in leadership. *IUP Journal of Soft Skills* 5(1)(March):16–30.

Neto, Paula, António Brandão, and António Cerqueira. 2010. The impact of FDI, cross-border mergers and acquisitions, and greenfield investments on economic growth. *IUP Journal of Business Strategy* 7 (4)(December):24–44.

Pearl, Mona. 2011. Cross-border mergers and acquisitions: Making them work. *Manufacturing Today* (Spring):10–13.

Pearl, Mona. 2011. Planning today for success tomorrow. *Management Today* (Winter):32–35.

Pearl, Mona. 2011. Strategic clusters: A vehicle for global growth. *Manufacturing Today* (Winter):8–10.

Pearl, Mona. 2010. Africa spells opportunity. *Management Today* (Fall):16–19.

Pearl, Mona. 2010. China: Time to re-evaluate. *Management Today* (Spring): 14–16.

Pearl, Mona. 2010. Going global: Seize your company's international opportunities. *U.S. Business Review* (Winter):40–41.

Pearl, Mona. 2010. Going global: What is your competitive edge? *Manufacturing Today* (Winter):12–15.

Pearl, Mona. 2010. Is the Middle East on your radar? *Management Today* (Summer):24–27.

Pearl, Mona. 2010. The new frontier: Latin America—myth or reality? *Management Today* (Spring/Summer):150–153.

Pearl, Mona. 2010. Plan for action—models for global expansion. *Manufacturing Today* (Summer).

Pearl, Mona. 2010. Seal the deal: Bridging the international divide. *Manufacturing Today* (Spring):8–11.

Pearl, Mona. 2009. Dollars and sense of taking your business global. *Manufacturing Today* (Fall):8–11.

Pearl, Mona. 2009. Global expansion: Get it right the first time. *Manufacturing Today* (Spring):10–13.

Pearl, Mona. 2009. Going global: How to make the decision. *Manufacturing Today* (Winter).

Pearl, Mona. 2009. Making the decision to go global. *US Business Review* (April/May):98–99.

Pearl, Mona. 2009. Successful global business expansion: *Don't discount the data. Manufacturing Today* (Summer):6–9.

Pearl, Mona. 2007. Creating a competitive edge: The value of cross-industry knowledge. *Handbook of Business Strategy* (Fall):142–147.

Pearl, Mona. 2006. Dangerous task. *Construction Today* (February):10–11.

Pearl, Mona. 2006. A new order. *US Business Review* (January):10–11.

Pearl, Mona. 2005. Actionable market research: Reducing business uncertainties. *Marketing Times* (December):8–9.

Pearl, Mona. 2005. Much ado about nothing. *US Business Review:*14–17.

Pearl, Mona. 2005. Up in smoke. *Construction Today* (December):12–15.

Pedersen, Paul B., and Mark Pope. 2010. Inclusive cultural empathy for successful global leadership. *American Psychologist* 65 (8)(November):841–854.

Petković, Todor, and Marko Rakić. 2010. Transnational companies—a global empire. *Megatrend Review* 7 (2):291–311.

Pooley, Richard. 2005. When cultures collide. *Management Services* 49 (1) (Spring):28–31.

Puck, Jonas F., Markus G. Kittler, and Christopher Wright. 2008. Does it really work? Re-assessing the impact of pre-departure cross-cultural training on expatriate adjustment. *International Journal of Human Resource Management* 19 (12)(December):2182–2197.

Riesenbeck, Hajo, and Anthony Freeling. 1991. How global are global brands? *McKinsey Quarterly* 4:3–18.

Ruderman, Marian N. 2008. Great expectations: Resolving conflicts of leadership style preferences. *Leadership in Action* 28 (4)(September/October):8–12.

Shan, Weijian, and William Hamilton. 1991. Country-specific advantage and international cooperation. *Strategic Management Journal* 12 (6)(September): 419–432.

Sonderegger, Petra, and Florian Taube. 2010. Cluster life cycle and diaspora effects: Evidence from the Indian IT cluster in Bangalore. *Journal of International Management* 16 (4)(December):383–397.

Taras, Vas, Piers Steel, and Bradley J. Kirkman. 2010. Examining the impact of culture's consequences: A three-decade, multilevel, meta-analytic review of Hofstede's cultural value dimensions. *Journal of Applied Psychology* 95 (3)(May):405–439.

Thinking global, acting global. 2006. *Business Africa* 15 (15)(August 1):4–5.

Tong Yang, and Meilin He. 2011. Study on the features of textile industry cluster in Guangzhong. *International Journal of Business & Management* 6 (1) (January):243–246.

Trompenaars, Fons. 1996. Resolving international conflict: Culture and business strategy. *Business Strategy Review* 7 (3)(Autumn):51.

Trompenaars, Fons, and Peter Wooliams. 2003. A new framework for managing change across cultures. *Journal of Change Management* 3 (4)(May):361.

Venaik, Sunil, and Paul Brewer. 2010. Avoiding uncertainty in Hofstede and GLOBE. *Journal of International Business Studies* 41 (8)(November):1294–1315.

Waite, Phillip, and Paul Williams. 2009. Collaboration or opportunism? The role of social capital in developing successful export clusters. *Journal of Strategic Marketing* 17(6)(December):499–512.

Wei-Wen Chang. 2009. Cross-cultural adjustment in the multinational training programme. *Human Resource Development International* 12 (5)(November): 561–569.

Ying Liu, Yizhou Zhang Zhang, and Cong Xu. 2010. Analysis of the international competitiveness of Chinese medicine industry based on the diamond model. *International Business Research* 3 (3)(July):165–170.

Zhang, Chun, Zuohao Hu, and Flora F. Gu. 2008. Intra- and interfirm coordination of export manufacturers: A cluster analysis of indigenous Chinese exporters. *Journal of International Marketing* 16 (3):108–135.

Zhanwen Ahu, and Haifeng Huang. 2007. The cultural integration in the process of cross-border mergers and acquisitions. *International Management Review* 3 (2)(June):40–44.

About the Author

Mona Pearl is an accomplished global expansion expert. She combines her long-established business skills with a unique global perspective to help clients navigate through the global expansion process. From actionable due diligence to the integration process, she helps companies increase global market share, enhance leadership, and engage stakeholders along the value chain. Her experience in international strategic development and global entrepreneurship has proven vital in helping companies from around the world design and execute global strategies that leverage their global competitiveness while addressing operational and strategic growth trends in international markets.

Ms. Pearl is known for her out-of-the-box thinking and ability to develop innovative solutions to tough challenges that produce positive bottom line results. Ms. Pearl's business expertise was developed as she founded and operated three successful businesses. Her ability to cross industries and cross borders is evident through a diverse list of clients, including distinguished firms such as Deutsche Telekom, Marriott, IMF, Fermilab, The Export Institute, SES GmbH, A.B. Dick, Navistar, Accenture, Michelin, Philip Morris, Bacardi, United Airlines, American Airlines, Virgin Atlantic, Delta, Continental, and many more which the reader may be less familiar with, and much smaller in scale. A full list can be found at www.BeyondAStrategy.com.

Ms. Pearl has lived on three continents and is proficient in six languages. She has been quoted by CNBC, NPR/WBEZ, Microsoft, Bloomberg, Crain's Chicago, and Entrepreneur.com. She is frequently interviewed by other media on global issues and strategies. Ms. Pearl is a renowned speaker at global-related conferences and has previously co-authored two books. Currently, in addition to circling the globe on project work assignments, she is serving in interim COO positions in globally oriented companies and sits on the board of several organizations. She is an adjunct Professor at DePaul University teaching International Business and guest lecturer in executive MBA programs around the world.

Ms. Pearl authors a column on current global competitiveness issues in *Management Today* magazine and is regularly published in other business-related magazines. Her LinkedIn profile can be found here: http://www.linkedin.com/in/monapearl.

Index